CAMBRIDGE
UNIVERSITY PRESS

Decoding Theory of Knowledge

for the IB Diploma

SKILLS BOOK

Wendy Heydorn & Susan Jesudason

CAMBRIDGE
UNIVERSITY PRESS

University Printing House, Cambridge CB2 8BS, United Kingdom

One Liberty Plaza, 20th Floor, New York, NY 10006, USA

477 Williamstown Road, Port Melbourne, VIC 3207, Australia

314–321, 3rd Floor, Plot 3, Splendor Forum, Jasola District Centre, New Delhi – 110025, India

79 Anson Road, #06–04/06, Singapore 079906

Cambridge University Press is part of the University of Cambridge.

It furthers the University's mission by disseminating knowledge in the pursuit
of education, learning and research at the highest international levels of excellence.

www.cambridge.org
Information on this title: www.cambridge.org/9781108933827

First published 2013
Second edition 2021

20 19 18 17 16 15 14 13 12 11 10 9 8 7 6 5 4 3 2 1

Printed in Poland by Opolgraf

A catalogue record for this publication is available from the British Library

ISBN 978-1-108-93382-7 Paperback with Digital Access

Additional resources for this publication at www.cambridge.org/go

› Contents

> Introduction

Theory of knowledge (TOK) lies at the very heart of the International Baccalaureate (IB) Diploma Programme, and helps to give the academic rigour that students, teachers, universities and employers value. It encourages learners to put several of the IB Diploma Programme learner profile principles into practice: to be reflective, knowledgeable, open-minded, communicative, balanced, thinkers, inquirers and risk-takers.

Decoding Theory of Knowledge is a student-friendly resource that is tailored to the new IB Diploma Programme subject guide for TOK. Presented in a clear, concise and highly accessible format, this versatile book can be used in the classroom, for self-study or alongside other TOK texts. It is designed as a practical guide that will enable you to navigate your way through the course by helping to understand both the content and the spirit of the subject. It also helps to decode the assessment requirements of the course, therefore helping to raise achievement in TOK assessment tasks.

This book is aimed at developing critical thinking and analytical skills, and shows you how to use the knowledge framework as a tool for your analysis. These skills will not only help you to perform well in TOK assessment, but will also deepen understanding of your other IB Diploma Programme subjects, and will be invaluable throughout life.

The book addresses central questions including:

- What is knowledge?

- What is a knowledge question?

- What is the knowledge framework?

- How can I compare different areas of knowledge?

- What skills do I need, and how can I further develop these?

- How will I be assessed?

Part One challenges ideas about knowledge, and investigates some of the ways in which knowledge can be classified. It raises questions about the nature of knowledge, and the certainty of knowledge claims and various TOK concepts, including truth. It introduces knowledge questions and the knowledge framework – a tool for analysis with four elements.

The knowledge framework is used to explore and analyse both the five optional themes in **Part Two** and the five areas of knowledge in **Part Three**. Both of these parts support your development of the nature of knowledge and knowing in each, and a richer understanding of the connections between both optional themes and areas of knowledge. You are required to study all five areas of knowledge, and two out of the five optional themes.

Part Four offers practical advice on the TOK assessment tasks and how to complete them successfully. The assessment criteria for the essay and exhibition are fully explained. As you progress through the course, you will see that the division between the various areas of knowledge, optional themes and IB Diploma Programme groups is somewhat arbitrary. Although, for example, psychology is listed as a human science, a great deal of psychology also falls under biological science, which is a natural science. Some of what is studied in geography can also be categorised under the natural sciences, while other aspects are strongly related to the human sciences, world religions and indigenous knowledge. In a similar way, language could be considered an area of knowledge, and mathematics could be considered a language. It is important to understand that there are no clear or sharp divisions between different areas of knowledge; all disciplines interact with each other and are interdependent.

TOP TIP

It is helpful to create a bank of personal experiences related to the different AOKs, core themes and optional themes, which you can draw on to use in your TOK essay. Personal examples tend to be more highly regarded than examples taken from textbooks, because your personal examples are original and demonstrate your ability to critically reflect on your experiences.

> How to use this book

This book contains a number of features to help you in your study.

LEARNING INTENTIONS

Learning intentions briefly set out the points you should understand once you have completed the chapter.

BEFORE YOU START

Before you start activities are designed to activate the prior knowledge you need for each chapter.

KEY POINT

Key points emphasise important information to support your understanding.

KEY WORDS

Key terms are important terms for your learning. They are highlighted in orange bold and defined where they first appear in the text.

TOP TIP

Top tips provide hints and tips to decode concepts, skills and assessment.

TOK IN YOUR LIFE

TOK in your life boxes contain examples and prompts to help you find examples of real-life situations in your own life.

TASK:

Throughout the book there are Task: Think about and Task: Activity boxes. These will help you with analysis, research and discussion, providing tools for critical thinking and for putting TOK into practice.

TOK LINKS

TOK links highlight knowledge framework links between the core theme, areas of knowledge and optional themes.

REAL-LIFE SITUATION

Real-life situation boxes present real-life scenarios for further thinking and exploration.

SKILLS SELF-ASSESSMENT CHECKLIST

Skills self-assessment checklists to help reflection on what you have learned, and your confidence level at the end of each chapter.

Further reading

Further reading lists provide details of extra resources that will help you to gain a wider perspective of the topic.

At the end of each chapter in Parts 1-3 you will find the following:

Knowledge questions

That provide thought-provoking questions to help develop your thinking skills.

Extended writing tasks

to help you enrich the quality of your written work.

Exhibition tasks

That offer clear guidance on how you can plan and deliver a successful exhibition

SUMMARY

In Part 4 there are checklists to help you with essay and exhibition planning.

Part 1
Knowledge and the knower

> Chapter 1
Who is the knower?

LEARNING INTENTIONS

In this chapter, you will explore how you, as a knower, bring your own unique perspective to everything that you know.

You will:

* analyse the relationship between personal identity, knowledge and experience

* become aware of some of the communities who contribute to your personal identity as a knower

* understand the difference between subjectivity and objectivity

* develop skills and a method for evaluating information

* build your analytical skills to help you evaluate ideas and arguments

* foster reflective skills that will help you to appreciate the importance of ethical knowledge, and develop your understanding of ethics.

1.1 Introduction

It may seem strange to start a book on knowledge with the question, '*Who is the knower?*'. However, knowledge cannot exist without some **sentient being** doing the knowing. A sentient being who *knows* anything, knows it within their own particular environmental, social, cultural and intellectual framework.

The act of knowing might be thought of as a relationship between the knower and what is known. Every time you learn, absorb or produce new knowledge, you are changed by it, and you flavour everything you know with your unique perspective on it.

One of the tasks of TOK is to encourage you to reflect on yourself as a knower and the knowledge communities you belong to, so that you are aware of what you add to the process of knowing, and the responsibilities and dangers that come with the knowledge relationship.

KEY TERM

sentient being: a creature with the faculty of sensation, with the ability to suffer and feel pain, as well as the power to perceive and possibly reason. The term is usually used for complex animals including humans

1.2 Personal identity

Your personal identity is the idea you have about yourself which develops throughout your life. Your identity may feature elements such as your nationality, ethnicity, religion, education or political views; it can also include your interests, hobbies and whatever matters most to you. You might see these features as the things that make you who you are.

Personal identity in this sense is **contingent** and **transient**. Some of the ways you identify yourself now might be different from the ways in which you have identified yourself in the past, and will probably be different from the ways in which you will identify yourself in the future. You might currently identify as an IB Diploma Programme student, but in years to come, you may identify yourself in multiple different ways, for example, as a parent and/or a professional person and/or an artist. Other ways in which you identify yourself may be more consistent. For example, you may be passionate about issues of social justice now and in the future, and your nationality may figure strongly in your personal identity throughout your life.

While we have focused on personal identity as the changing ways in which you identify yourself, it is also possible that others may identify changes in us that we are not even aware of ourselves.

KEY TERMS

contingent: subject to chance; dependent on circumstances

transient: temporary, not long-lasting

personal knowledge: the knowledge we have through our own experiences and personal involvement

Personal knowledge, identity and experience

Personal knowledge sometimes acts as a bridge between our personal experiences and our personal identity. As your experiences broaden, so your knowledge grows and your personal identity develops. This sets up a dynamic personal identity knowledge cycle because just as your knowledge and experiences shape your personal identity, so your personal identity will help to shape the experiences you have and the knowledge you acquire and develop. As your personal identity is involved in judgements you make about how to evaluate and use knowledge, and even whether to regard some things as knowledge at all, all knowing could therefore be construed as personal.

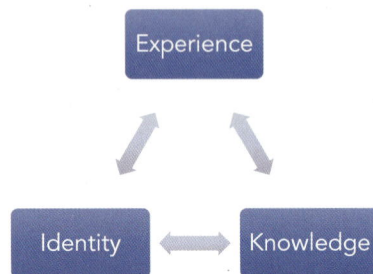

Figure 1.1: Identity, experience and knowledge all directly influence each other

From the time we are born, and arguably even before we are born, much of what we learn is gained through personal experience as we explore our environment. Basic knowledge such as what is food and what is not, who our care-givers are and how we can manipulate objects with our hands, are all learned through our early experiences of the world. It is only when we master language through listening and speaking and later, in particular, when we learn to read, that we are able to learn more extensively from the experiences of others. The experiences of the books that we read and the people we listen to help to shape the people we become.

TASK: THINK ABOUT 1.1

Can you identify a person, book or experience in your life that has helped to shape your identity in some way? How might you be different if you had never met that person, read that book or had that experience?

Personal experience can give us a depth of knowledge that is not always attainable through the experiences of others. No amount of reading about hunger will enable you to fully know what hunger feels like; you can only truly know what it feels like if you have experienced the gnawing sensation yourself. Similarly, if you say you know Ariana Grande's *No tears left to cry*, you mean that you are familiar with the music, the lyrics or both. If you have merely heard of the song, you may say you *know of* it, but you would not be able to say that you *know* it in any **experiential** sense. However, having personal experience of something does not necessarily mean you have a deep understanding of it. It is possible, for example, that you may visit another country on a holiday, but having visited does not mean that you really know the country, its people and institutions, nor its cultural and religious practices in any deep sense. The same can be true of books we read and music we hear.

> **KEY TERM**
>
> **experiental:** based on or related to experience

TASK: THINK ABOUT 1.2

What does it mean to *know* a person or place?

Tribalism and knowledge communities

Knowledge communities are groups of people with common interests and shared knowledge. They can include your school, your TOK class and any clubs or associations you may belong to, but they do not need to be formal organisations. For example, your family could be considered a knowledge community in that only members of your family know what it is to be a member of that family.

As a knower, you will belong to many different groups. The groups that you identify with most strongly are often known as your *tribes*. Your tribes need not be cultural groups; they can be a football team, a fan club or even a small clique of friends. What is significant is that your loyalty to and dependence on your tribes often has a strong influence on your perspectives and the ways in which you think. For example, if you identify strongly with a football team, and a member of the team you support commits a foul against the opposing team, your response to that foul is likely to be very different to your response if a member of the opposing team commits a foul against your team. You may even be *blind* to foul play by your team, but very angry about foul play against your team. This inherent bias towards the groups we identify with is a feature of **tribalism**.

Knowledge communities and tribes often overlap. For example, if you are participating in interschool sports or competitions, you might identify strongly with your school, and adopt a *tribal* attitude. You may similarly support members of your family to an extent that others may find unreasonable, such as by taking the side of a family member in a dispute even when you know that family member is in the wrong.

KEY TERM

tribalism: the behaviours and attitudes that arise out of membership of or loyalty to a particular group

TASK: ACTIVITY 1.1

In pairs or small groups, try to come up with an example of when you might take a tribal position and defend a member of your tribe who is in the wrong. Each group should role play the situation to the rest of the class. What do you notice about the nature of the arguments?

Discuss: Is loyalty to your tribe a valid justification for taking the side of a friend in a dispute when you *know* that friend is in the wrong? Or is bias unethical?

TASK: ACTIVITY 1.2

Create a mind-map that shows some of the tribes and knowledge communities you belong to. Try to identify (i) those that play the strongest roles in shaping your identity and perspectives and (ii) those that have the greatest effect on your emotions. Is there a correlation between the two groups?

CROSS REFERENCE

You can read more about the relationship between knowledge, personal identity and knowledge communities in Chapter 1 of the Course Guide.

When you are a member of a tribe or knowledge community, social pressure will often encourage you to conform to the attitudes, values and behaviours of the group you belong to. It is sometimes very difficult to think differently from others in the group, or to speak out in disagreement with them. TOK can help you to develop analytical skills that will enable you to think more independently and cultivate a clearer perspective on complex issues.

REAL-LIFE SITUATION 1.1

In 1951, Solomon Asch (1907–1996) ran some psychology experiments in which participants had to compare line lengths. In each group of eight participants, seven had been instructed which answer to give. Only one participant was a real participant. The seven pretend-participants had been instructed to give wrong answers in 12 of the 18 trials. Over the 12 critical trials, only 25% of the real participants always gave the correct answer. Instead, most of the real participants conformed with the majority in their group, even though they knew the majority were wrong. They preferred to conform with the group rather than give what they could see to be the correct answers.

1   Why might the participants have chosen to conform rather than give the correct answer?

2   In further trials, if the pretend-participants did not unanimously give a wrong answer, the participant was less likely to conform. Why might that be?

3   To what extent do our thoughts and ideas reflect the thoughts and ideas of those around us? How do we decide when we need to 'swim against the tide'?

One of the things we can learn from the Solomon Asch study is that just because a majority agrees, it does not necessarily guarantee that their view is true or objective. The truth of knowledge claims cannot be decided purely on the basis of the consensus of a majority. Therefore, the role of individuals in challenging prevailing views is potentially very important.

TOK IN YOUR LIFE

Can you think of times when you have held back giving your own opinion or viewpoint because you knew that your friends did not agree? Or perhaps a time when you did not even try to come up with your own point of view and simply accepted the view of others? Similarly, can you think of times when you have spoken up against the consensus of others? Reflect on why you might or might not have chosen to conform or let others think for you.

REAL-LIFE SITUATION 1.2

The world champion American boxer, Muhammad Ali (1942–2016), refused to join the US army to fight in the Vietnam War when he was called up for military service in 1966, because, as a devout Muslim, he believed war was against the teachings of the Qur'an. As a result, in 1967 Ali was convicted of evading the draft (compulsory military service) and fined $10,000, as well as sentenced to five years in prison. He was also stripped of his boxing titles by the professional boxing commission. The US Supreme Court eventually over-turned his conviction in 1971, but he had lost nearly four years while at his peak as an athlete. In the face of growing opposition, the USA ended the draft in 1973.

CONTINUED

Standing up against the state to be a **conscientious objector** can take a huge amount of courage, and in the past, many conscientious objectors around the world have been subjected to social **ostracism**, abuse, jail and even the death penalty.

Think about how confident you would need to be about your beliefs to be willing to stand up to the state. Would you feel more confident if you were one of many making a stand than if you were standing as an individual?

TASK: ACTIVITY 1.3

Try to find some examples of initially unpopular or rejected ideas that subsequently changed the world in some way.

1.3 Subjective and objective perspectives

When we consider **knowledge claims** as individual knowers, our perspective is **subjective**, which means that it is **susceptible to** personal bias. If I were to claim that my dog is the most beautiful dog in the world, I am expressing a subjective opinion. He may be the most beautiful dog in the world *through my eyes*, but most other people might think differently.

Figure 1.2: Could it be objective to say that Zachary is the most beautiful dog in the world?

KEY TERMS

conscientious objector: a person who refuses to serve in the armed forces or perform military service on the grounds of philosophical or religious beliefs

ostracism: exclusion, isolation

TOP TIP

It is useful to create a bank of examples that come from your own experience. When building an argument, using examples from your own experience will demonstrate your understanding and original thought far more than if you resort to using famous examples that have become cliché.

KEY TERMS

knowledge claim: a statement in which we claim to *know* something (knowledge claims will be dealt with in more detail in Chapter 2)

subjective: a personal view influenced by the knower's feelings, opinions or emotions

susceptible to: likely to be affected by

Generally speaking, people like to believe that knowledge is **objective**. In other words, its truth can be agreed by a wide range of people who do not have a clear emotional attachment to the **veracity** of the knowledge. For example, the claim *'Avocados and bananas are rich sources of potassium'* is held to be objectively true whether or not you like avocados and/or bananas, whether you profit from them in any way, or even whether you agree.

However, in 1958, Michael Polanyi (1891–1976), a medical doctor, distinguished physical chemist and social scientist, published his book *Personal Knowledge* in which he showed that all knowledge claims rely on personal judgements to some extent. As knowers, we cannot take an entirely objective view of the world in which we live, and we are dependent upon the beliefs and **assumptions** of the culture and era in which we live. For example, it used to be assumed that women would react to medications in the same way that men do, and as a result, nearly 80% of scientific subjects involved in studies carried out on humans and animals have been males. It is only in recent years that scientists have begun to question this assumption and discover that females react differently to males in numerous ways.

If we return to our earlier example of a knowledge claim, *'Avocados and bananas are rich sources of potassium'*, this may be true for most humans. However there may be some people who, for one reason or another, are not able to digest bananas and/or avocados, and for whom this knowledge claim would not be true. Avocados and bananas would still contain potassium, but they would not be a *source* of potassium for such people. The knowledge claim is only true from the perspective of those who are able to eat and digest avocados and bananas. Therefore, in a sense, it is subjective.

Knowledge depends on perspective and assumptions, therefore some people have attempted to eliminate these influences in order to 'purify' knowledge and produce knowledge absolutely free from all assumptions, including tribal, cultural and linguistic traditions. These attempts are sometimes called the search for a *view from nowhere*.

KEY TERMS

objective: referring to a detached view that focuses on facts in a way largely independent of the knower's personal perspective, and that expects to be corroborated (validated or shown) by a knowledge community

veracity: truth, accuracy, authenticity

assumption: supposition, something taken for granted

TASK: THINK ABOUT 1.3

1   Why can there never be a *view from nowhere* devoid of *all* assumptions and specific perspectives?

2   To what extent might we be able to get closer to such a view?

3   Why might it be desirable to have this view?

KEY POINT

There is no such thing as a *view from nowhere*. All knowledge is contextual, and dependent upon knowers who have certain assumptions and perspectives.

TOK LINK: LANGUAGE

There was a time when students were taught to write in the third-person and eliminate the first-person, so as to appear objective. For example, you would be told to write, *A bird was seen* rather than, *I saw a bird*. Nowadays, there is a growing trend towards writing in the first-person in some academic disciplines to explicitly acknowledge, and hopefully be more aware of, the role of the knower.

TASK: THINK ABOUT 1.4

1   To what extent is *appearing* more objective the same as *being* more objective?

2   If knowledge depends on tribes and communities, should we write in terms of *we* rather than *I*?

1.4 Methods and tools for acquiring knowledge

We have already seen that knowledge is acquired through experience, whether through our own personal experience or through the experiences of others that we can access in multiple ways. But when we listen to others, read books, blogs and journals, watch videos and so forth, we need to consider how we might judge the reliability of the information and knowledge we are given access to.

In the 21st century, we are bombarded with information on social media as well as mainstream media. There are few checks and balances on published material except when it comes from reputable publishing companies such as Cambridge University Press. Any person or organisation can set up a blog or YouTube™ channel, or distribute posts that can potentially fill your world with information, **propaganda**, **misinformation** and **disinformation**, which is sometimes called '**fake news**'.

It has long been known that people tend to search for and believe information that confirms what they already think is true – this is known as confirmation bias. Studies have shown that people are less sceptical about information they find on social media because this information usually comes from friends and family members (members of their *tribes*), as well as pages they have *liked* to reflect their interests and identity.

An important aspect of TOK is to equip you, as a knower, with skills, methods and tools that will help you to discern useful information which will contribute to your wealth of knowledge, and enable you to recognise and dismiss misinformation and disinformation without being fooled.

Evaluating information

If you were to accept every piece of information that you came across as knowledge, you would soon find yourself struggling in a sea of contradictory material. If, instead, you were to only accept information that supported what you already believe or know, you would be in danger of finding yourself deeply entrenched in very limited or false ideas. If you are to try to make sense of the world in an honest and truthful way, you need to be willing to engage with ideas and information that challenge your beliefs and current knowledge, and be prepared to change your beliefs and knowledge if those ideas and information are sufficiently compelling. This means that you have to be prepared to be open to, and evaluate, new ideas and information.

When evaluating new information, it is important to ask a series of questions:

1   Who wrote or produced the information? Is the author or producer sufficiently qualified and unprejudiced?

KEY TERMS

propaganda: advertising that promotes specific ideas and perspectives that are usually political

misinformation: information that is distorted or only partly true

disinformation: false information deliberately designed to mislead or confuse

fake news: fabricated stories that are presented as genuine news items

2 What kind of information is it? The evidence you will need to consider to determine the truth of any new information will depend on the type of information you are looking at. For example, if you are shown experimental results or polls, are you told in detail how the experiment or poll was set up and conducted? Is a political article clear about who is funding it? Does an academic report have references that enable you to access the source material?

3 Where did you find the information? Did it pop up in your news feed or did you go looking for it? Does it come from a reputable publisher or a legitimate and reputable website?

4 When was the information produced? Is it up-to-date or out-dated? Is it old but relevant and/or authoritative?

5 Why was the information published? Is it aimed at a particular audience? Does it offer an argument that tries to persuade you of anything? Is it balanced?

TOP TIP

Snopes is an excellent website for checking disinformation and urban legends that come up on social media. The Big Project is a very good website for finding media outlets from around the world if you would like to compare different accounts of a news event.

KEY POINT

Before using any new information that you find in any of your academic work, particularly your extended essay, you should try to verify it by cross-checking with an independent source, and always cite your sources.

Evaluating ideas and arguments

As well as evaluating information, it is perhaps even more important for knowledge that you evaluate new ideas and arguments. This involves making a judgement about the suitability of an idea for a particular purpose and in a particular context.

When you are evaluating ideas and arguments, it is important first to be clear about what the ideas and arguments you are evaluating are actually saying. It is sometimes too easy to misinterpret a position and then argue against it. You should also give other viewpoints for comparison, and weigh up the different alternatives.

Questions you could ask to evaluate any idea or argument include:

1 Does the author make any explicit or hidden assumptions? Are those assumptions reasonable?

2 Does the author display any **bias**?

3 Is the author knowledgeable about the issue that the idea or argument addresses?

4 Does the author give enough **corroborated** evidence to support any arguments, and is that evidence reliable?

5 Has the author considered alternative viewpoints in a fair and balanced way?

6 Has the author considered possible outcomes and consequences of the ideas presented?

7 What are the ethical dimensions of any assumptions, actions and/or consequences related to the idea or argument?

KEY TERMS

bias: prejudice, one-sided preference

corroborated: verified, confirmed or supported

TASK: THINK ABOUT 1.5

For the questions above, how would you decide whether the author is sufficiently qualified and/or knowledgeable about the issue being addressed?

TASK: ACTIVITY 1.4

Read an editorial about an issue in your region, and try to summarise the argument. Can you identify any assumptions or biases that the author has? Is the argument supported by relevant and accurate evidence? Does the argument consider other perspectives in a fair and honest way? Write a short paragraph to say whether or not, on balance, you agree with the editorial, and why.

KEY POINT

The ability to weigh alternatives, evaluate evidence and make good decisions is essential for success in all aspects of life. It is this essential role of individual involvement that makes knowledge personal.

It is important when looking for ideas and information for any academic work including your TOK essay, extended essay or any of your IB Diploma Programme subjects that you do not just look for ideas and information that support any beliefs or positions you hold. You must also look for information and ideas that challenge and counter your position, so that you can provide balanced arguments before coming to a final conclusion.

1.5 Ethical considerations

As well as being responsible for evaluating knowledge, knowers have a responsibility to consider the ethical dimensions of any knowledge they create, access or share. As a knower, you will have your own beliefs, opinions, attitudes and values that will all contribute to the ethical positions you take when exploring different areas of knowledge including the TOK optional themes. In some cases, you may have very strong personal views; in others, you might be willing to conform to a standard advised by your friends, the school, your tribes and/or the law. Your ethical beliefs might influence both the types of knowledge you pursue and the methods and tools that you are willing to use in your pursuit of knowledge. For example, if you believe the ethical principle of doing the least harm applies to all animals, you might not be willing to use animal testing for scientific studies.

Each chapter in this book will address some of the ethical issues specific to the core theme, area of knowledge or optional theme under discussion. As a knower, you will need to think about these issues from your own perspective. But it is also important that you question your own ethical beliefs and values. As with any knowledge, we can only be confident of our ethical knowledge by continually questioning and evaluating it.

TASK: THINK ABOUT 1.6

1   Where do your beliefs, opinions, attitudes and values come from?

2   Which of your ethical beliefs, if any, would you regard as ethical *knowledge*?

3   What would cause you to question your ethical perspectives?

KEY TERM

ethics: the branch of knowledge to do with right and wrong, and the study of the moral principles that govern our beliefs and behaviour

Ethical knowledge comes from understanding our own emotions and empathising with the emotions of others. However, our ethical knowledge is largely contextual and conditional. While we might agree that certain actions are good or bad, they are so in a particular context and under certain conditions. Often, in **ethics**, there are no *right* or *wrong* answers completely independent of perspective (as if *seen from nowhere*); instead, an ethical analysis might lead us to believe that some actions are *better* or *worse* than other alternatives, or that their rightness or wrongness depends upon a particular tribal or cultural perspective.

Ethical knowledge is necessary to be able to engage with different perspectives in a constructive way to bring about **resolution**.

KEY TERM

resolution: harmonious convergent progress, solution

REAL-LIFE SITUATION 1.3

In cities around the world, young professional people who cannot afford housing in the areas they grew up in are moving to cheaper areas. Once young professionals are established in those cheaper areas, restaurants, cafes and other service businesses tend to open up, *revitalising* the areas and making them more desirable places to live in. The impact of this is that housing prices rise and the revitalised areas soon become unaffordable for people who lived in the areas before they became desirable. This process is known as *gentrification*.

Think about the process of gentrification from the perspective of the young professionals who have moved to a poor area, from the perspective of poorer people who can no longer afford to rent in the area, and then from the perspective of business owners and landlords in the area. How does thinking about the issue from different perspectives help you to understand the complexity of the issue?

Figure 1.3: Are cities areas revitalised or gentrified? How do you decide?

1.6 Knowledge questions

1   How can you be sure that your beliefs and values are really your own, and not simply adopted from the tribes and knowledge communities you belong to?

2   What counts as an assumption? What are the roles of conscious and unconscious assumptions in the production of knowledge?

3   How can you decide whether indirect knowledge based upon the experiences of others is reliable, trustworthy and true?

4   What ethical responsibilities do you have as a knower?

1.7 Exhibition task

Consider how you might use a personal journal as an item for your TOK exhibition. Which internal assessment (IA) prompt question would you choose, and which theme would you choose to focus on? Write 250–300 words on the real-world context of the journal, and how it links to your chosen IA prompt.

1.8 Extended writing task

Write 400–600 words on one or more of the following questions:

1   What role does personal experience play in the formation of knowledge claims?

2   How do you decide which knowledge claims to trust when your personal knowledge or judgement differs from knowledge shared by the wider community?

3   To what extent can you have knowledge without faith?

SKILLS SELF-ASSESSMENT CHECKLIST

Reflect on what you have learned in this chapter and indicate your confidence level between 1 and 5 (where 5 is the highest score and 1 is the lowest). If you score below 3, revisit that section. Come back to this list later in your course. Has your confidence grown?

	Confidence level	Revisited?
Can I analyse the relationship between my personal identity and my knowledge and experience?		
Am I aware of some of the communities that contribute to my personal identity as a knower?		
Can I explain the difference between subjectivity and objectivity?		
Have I developed skills and a method that will help me to evaluate information?		
Do my analytical skills help me evaluate ideas and arguments?		
Do my reflective skills enable me to appreciate and articulate the importance of ethical knowledge?		
Do my reflective skills enhance my understanding of ethics and enable me to raise ethical questions?		

1.9 Further reading

To explore how to combine the perspective of a person with an objective view of the world, read: Thomas Nagel, *The View from Nowhere*, Oxford University Press, 1986

For an extended discussion of issues concerning objectivity, read: Michael Polanyi, *Personal Knowledge*, Routledge, 1958

To explore the foundations of meaning in creative imagination, read: Michael Polanyi and Harry Prosch, *Meaning*, University of Chicago Press, 1975

To learn about how the human mind works, read: Robert Winston, *The Human Mind*, Random House, 2004

To find out more the human propensity to conform, read: Saul McLeod, 'Solomon Asch – Conformity Experiment', in *Simply Psychology,* 28/12/2018

> Chapter 2

The problem of knowledge

LEARNING INTENTIONS

In this chapter, you will explore what we mean by knowledge and knowledge claims, and why the concept of knowledge is not as straightforward as we might sometimes assume.

You will:

- identify and analyse knowledge claims and knowledge questions
- understand some of the difficulties in justifying knowledge claims
- become better equipped to discuss and evaluate the justification for different types of knowledge
- become aware of some ethical issues that may arise when producing knowledge and making knowledge claims.

2.1 Introduction

The concept of knowledge is difficult. On the one hand we, commonly speak of knowledge and what we know, and we take it for granted that everyone who understands our language understands what we mean when we say we know something. On the other hand, when we try to say exactly what knowledge is and what makes it reliable, we find ourselves struggling. Yet it is an exciting struggle that takes us on an intellectual journey during which we will develop our skills as reflective thinkers and gain a much richer understanding of the world.

2.2 What is knowledge?

Perhaps the most famous definition of knowledge ever given – and one still widely used – comes from the ancient Greek philosopher Plato (c 427–348 BCE), who once defined knowledge as **justified true belief** (JTB), although he later refuted this definition in his book *Theaetetus*. According to JTB, we may call certain propositions *knowledge* because we have good reasons to believe them to be true, and they are indeed true; but this does not overcome the difficulty of how we *know* them to be true. JTB seems to assume that truth is somehow independent of our knowledge, but as we cannot access it other than through knowledge, the definition is somewhat circular.

For example, I may believe that I hear my dog barking in the garden. I may be justified in believing this because I have a dog with a bark just like the bark I can hear. But I can only say that it is *true* that my dog is barking if I *know* that it is indeed my dog barking, and not another dog close by, and I must know it to be *true* before I can claim to *know* it. This makes truth dependent on knowing and knowing dependent on truth, so the circularity becomes apparent.

In criminal courts of law, a justified belief needs to be held to be *beyond reasonable doubt* before it can be accepted as true. Perhaps we need a similar criterion for determining if knowledge is true. However, in criminal courts some people who were found guilty of a crime can later be shown to be innocent, so some of the beliefs that we once thought were true can later be shown to be false. *Beyond reasonable doubt* is not the same as *true*.

Knowledge claims

We frequently make **knowledge claims** about the past. We might, for example, say we *know* that Neil Armstrong was the first person to walk on the Moon. In saying this, we are claiming knowledge that is based on what our parents and teachers may have told us, or perhaps what we have read in books or (if we are old enough) what we saw live

KEY TERMS

justified: shown to be fair or reasonable

true: logically consistent, honest, correct and accurate

belief: a feeling that what you think is true

KEY TERM

knowledge claim: a statement in which we claim to know something, or a claim made about knowledge and knowing

on the television in 1969. It is a knowledge claim that is widely accepted around the world. Yet we cannot say that all people accept it as knowledge because there may be some people who have never heard of the 1969 Moon landing. Neither can we say that everyone who is aware of the knowledge claim accepts it as true, because there are a number of people who claim that the Moon landing was a hoax. Unless we were party to the Apollo 11 mission, we may not be able to say with *certainty* that Neil Armstrong was the first person to walk on the Moon. However, we can say that it is a claim accepted as true by most people because the world largely has faith in the truthfulness of NASA, the astronauts who went on the voyage and the media who reported the event. If we were asked in a quiz, '*Who was the first person to walk on the Moon?*' the expected answer would be Neil Armstrong. If we gave that answer, we might claim to *know* it.

However, in Chapter 1 we saw that knowledge is dependent on our tribes and our knowledge communities, so it is at least *possible* that any answer we give is only regarded as true within our knowledge community.

TASK: THINK ABOUT 2.1

Does *true* just mean *true for me and my knowledge community* or does it mean in some sense *true for all sentient beings*, or *true for all human beings*?

We also make knowledge claims about the present. We may say that we know Paris is the capital of France, or that the country that was once known as Burma is now known as Myanmar. We recognise a difference between somebody saying, '*I know Burma is now called Myanmar*' and saying, '*I believe Burma is now called Myanmar*'. The first is a claim of personal certainty: it is true that the country once known as Burma is now called Myanmar, and I am certain of this. The second claim recognises a personal uncertainty: I think it is true that the country once known as Burma is now called Myanmar, but it is possible I may be mistaken. Therefore, we can say the claim to *know* is linked with a subjective certainty: when I say I know something, I am claiming to be certain about it, but even though I *claim* to be certain, I may still be wrong.

TASK: ACTIVITY 2.1

1   Identify one or two examples of knowledge claims from each of your IB Diploma Programme subjects. Do they have anything in common?

2   Do some areas of knowledge make more certain knowledge claims than others?

Sometimes we might make a knowledge claim about a future event. For example, I might claim to know that the 2028 Olympic Games will be held in Los Angeles, USA. My belief is justified by the media reports declaring Los Angeles was selected to host these games by the International Olympic Committee. If Los Angeles hosts the games in 2028, my knowledge claim will be validated. Does that mean I can claim to *know* the venue for the 2028 Olympic Games now? If, due to unforeseen circumstances, the Olympic Games cannot be held in Los Angeles in 2028, my claim will not be validated. What would that mean for my knowledge claim now?

REAL-LIFE SITUATION 2.1

A meteorologist, having studied the weather patterns carefully, made a claim that it would rain the next day. It would seem reasonable to call the forecaster's belief that it would rain a justified belief because they possessed appropriate expertise and considered all the available relevant data.

The next day, despite the presence of heavy rain clouds in the sky, no rain actually fell, so the forecaster had a justified false belief; the meteorologist did not *know* it was going to rain when they made their forecast.

1   If it had rained the following day as the meteorologist had said, their justified belief would have been a true justified belief. But could we really say that the forecaster *knew* it would rain?

2   Is a prediction based on strong evidence the same as knowledge?

TOK LINK: LANGUAGE

Think about the role of language when making knowledge claims.

*   What do we understand by key concepts such as *opinion, belief, fact, certainty* and *knowledge*?

*   What roles do social, tribal or cultural conventions play in our use of these terms?

We may be able to decide on the truth of a predictive knowledge claim retrospectively because either it happens or it does not. But this is not very helpful. If we ask someone whether the next train will take us to Mumbai, we want to be sure that person knows the answer *before* we board the train. Some people question whether we can know the future in any useful sense of the word *know*.

CROSS REFERENCE

You can find out more about the problems of defining knowledge in Chapter 2 of the Course Guide.

TASK: THINK ABOUT 2.2

What if the prediction is almost certain? For example, can I say that I *know* if I hit a crystal vase forcefully with a hammer, it will break?

TASK: ACTIVITY 2.2

One definition of knowledge is *justified true belief*. Try to express the strengths and weaknesses of this definition in your own words, using your own examples.

2.3 Types of knowledge

The scope of knowledge could be said to be all-encompassing because it includes everything that we claim to know. It is therefore helpful to divide knowledge into different types. There are many different ways in which knowledge can be divided. For example, we might want to divide knowledge into *a priori* (before experience) and *a posteriori* (after experience); or we might prefer to divide it into first-hand knowledge and second-hand knowledge. In this chapter, we will divide knowledge into three types: practical knowledge, knowledge by acquaintance and factual knowledge.

Practical knowledge

Practical knowledge is knowing how to do something. We evaluate whether someone has practical knowledge according to how well they can do the task or practise the skill. For example, we might say a gymnast knows how to do a triple somersault if they can perform a triple somersault, even though they may find it difficult to explain how they do it. Practical knowledge is necessarily personal; each of us will bring something unique and personal to our skills.

> **KEY TERM**
>
> **practical knowledge:** knowledge we have about how to do things, like how to swim, play a violin or read Mandarin

---

TASK: THINK ABOUT 2.3

1   We could spend a lifetime improving upon and learning more about our skills. At what point can we say that we know how to perform a practical skill? For example, how fluent must we be before we can say we know how to speak Swahili?

2   Can we say that we know how to swim if we can only swim one metre? What about if we can swim half a length of a swimming pool?

3   How proficient do we have to be on the violin before we can say we know how to play it?

Knowledge by acquaintance

Knowledge by acquaintance is the knowledge we have first-hand. It can include knowing ourselves, people we have met, places we have been to or the taste of things we have eaten. It can also include knowledge that we acquire through reasoning. Of course, knowledge by acquaintance can be flawed. We can be mistaken about ourselves, as well as about places we have been to and people we have met. Our senses can also deceive us; for example, we may believe that we have enjoyed chicken fajitas and then discover they were turkey fajitas.

As with practical knowledge, we do not have to be able to explain knowledge by acquaintance. I might say that I know what chocolate tastes like even if I am unable to describe the flavour, or I know the city of Hyderabad even if I cannot give you detailed information about it. However, you might evaluate the extent of my knowledge by my attempts to give you information about it.

> **KEY TERM**
>
> **knowledge by acquaintance:** personal, first-hand knowledge

---

TASK: THINK ABOUT 2.4

1 What do we mean when we say we know a person or a place?

2 To what extent can others know us better than we know ourselves?

3 I may have eaten lots of chocolate, but who can say whether I *know* what it tastes like?

Factual knowledge

Factual knowledge is the collection of knowledge claims about the world that we believe to be true. Some factual knowledge claims are true by definition. For example, '*My parents are my mother and father*'. The definition of the word *parent* is a mother or father, so the claim is a *fact* of the English language. However, there is no guarantee that a truth by definition entails existence. For example, we can *know* that '*a unicorn is a horse-like creature with a horn rising from its forehead*', but this does not mean that unicorns exist.

Relatively few of our knowledge claims are based on definitions. Far more are made on the basis of our sense perceptions, emotions, faith, reason, learning and memories. Of course, only you can know what you can see, hear, taste, smell, touch, feel, learn or remember, and there is always a possibility that you might be mistaken.

The problem is compounded when we consider that most knowledge claims are made on the basis of somebody else's sense perceptions, emotions, reason and memories. Think about what you learn at school. Some of it will be through your own discoveries – perhaps in the science laboratories – but most will come from other people: your teachers, friends, media, and so on. This is all second-hand knowledge. How can you *know* that the claims of others are true, even if you accept that their claims are justified and have no reason to think that they are deliberately deceiving you?

KEY TERM

factual knowledge: knowledge about things that exist, events that have actually occurred or things that have been verified as true

---

KEY POINT

Our claim to know ultimately comes down to *whom or what do we trust?*.

Figure 2.1: In what sense, if any, do you think unicorns exist?

TASK: THINK ABOUT 2.5

Do unicorns *exist*?

How you answer depends on your understanding of language and the way that you use the word *exist*. You can extend this to other concepts. For example, do ideas exist? What about minds? Or souls? In what sense do colours *exist*? Can you really *know* about things that do not exist such as fairies or hobbits?

TASK: ACTIVITY 2.3

1   Consider the following knowledge claims: I know …

   a   how to ride a bike

   b   the time is 2 p.m.

   c   my mother loves me

   d   how to read Hebrew

   e   my way home

   f   Barefoot Cafe serves good food

   g   Leonardo da Vinci painted the *Mona Lisa*

   h   William Shakespeare wrote *Hamlet*

   i   eggs are a healthy food

   j   gold is a naturally occurring, soft, shiny, yellow metal

   k   my brother has a scar on his right arm

   l   the Earth revolves around the Sun

   m   a square is a quadrilateral with four equal sides

   n   Madrid is the capital of Spain

   o   I have a toothache

   p   Lee Harvey Oswald shot John F. Kennedy

   q   water is made up of two atoms of hydrogen and one atom of oxygen

   Which of these are examples of practical knowledge? Which are examples of knowledge by acquaintance? Which are examples of factual knowledge? Which are true by definition? Colour code your answers to match the types of knowledge with the knowledge claims.

2   How many are first-hand knowledge claims and how many are second-hand?

3   Which can you say with certainty are true? How many could be mistaken?

4   Are there any claims here that you would say we cannot know? Are there some that you would say we know, even if we cannot be certain they are true? Are some ambiguous, or only true in some circumstances?

2.4 Perspectives on knowledge

Given all the problems with JTB, we need to think about knowledge differently. We may want to say that knowledge is the set of beliefs we rely on when living our lives. In this case, we may treat some of our beliefs as knowledge if we think they are reliable enough to be used to help us evaluate other beliefs. Knowledge, then, is the set of beliefs that we trust. We may not be absolutely *certain* they are true, but we treat them as if they are because they are the best we can do right now.

TASK: ACTIVITY 2.4

Discuss the role of convention in deciding what to accept as knowledge.

- How do our social and cultural conventions shape what we claim to know?

- Some people say that knowledge is what a society agrees is knowledge. Is this the same as saying that truth is what societies agree on?

- Is there a difference between saying I am certain and It is certain?

- Is there a difference between saying Everyone agrees that X is true and saying X is true?

Different societies have different sets of beliefs that they live by, and different ideas about what should be regarded as knowledge. One society may agree that their ancestors watch over them and influence – or even control – what happens in their daily lives. If this is regarded as true, it will shape the ways in which the members of that society live their lives, and the 'knowledge' they pass on to their children. Another society may believe that there is no such thing as a spirit world, and dismiss talk of supernatural things as superstitious nonsense. Again, this will shape the ways in which members of that society live their lives, and the *knowledge* they pass on to their children.

This brings us to the difficulties of **relativism**. People who hold a relativist position want to say that what is true for you is your knowledge, and what is true for me is my knowledge; both are of equal value and both have equal status as knowledge. It is a claim we often hear, but few *really* believe it. It reduces knowledge to little more than personal opinion.

KEY TERMS

relativism: the belief that there is no absolute truth, only the truths that particular individuals or cultures believe

valid: well-grounded, justified, legitimate

TASK: THINK ABOUT 2.6

1   If *Pigeonalians* are a nation of people who claim to *know* that males are superior to females in every way, and use this *knowledge* to treat the women among them as livestock, would we really believe their *knowledge* is as **valid** as the knowledge of societies that regard men and women as being of equal value?

2   If *Daisinians* are a group of people who claim to *know* that the only way to keep their gods happy is to sacrifice all first-born children, would we be prepared to say that this *knowledge* is true because it is true for them?

CONTINUED

3   Perhaps the *Factual Party* is a political group that *knows* it has the only *correct* political policies on the planet, and its members *know* that they have a duty to fight until every country in the world has adopted their political system. Would we be prepared to argue that their *knowledge* is to be respected as much as anyone else's?

TASK: ACTIVITY 2.5

Discuss with a partner what the 'Task: Think about 2.6' examples suggest about the nature of knowledge and knowing. Does your society or culture have *knowledge* that other cultures or societies might disagree with? Try to come up with some criteria by which you could try to evaluate different cultural and political knowledge claims.

Although the three examples in 'Task: Think about 2.6' may seem rather extreme, they make the point that nobody really adopts the relativist's position consistently. To say that all knowledge claims have equal value is a ploy to avoid the very difficult and sometimes sensitive task of evaluating knowledge claims individually. Moreover, relativists need to deny others the right to be **absolutists** if they are to protect their right to be relativists, therefore relativism is self-contradictory.

This is one reason why **knowledge questions** need to be asked.

Knowledge questions

Knowledge questions are open questions that we ask about what knowledge is, and how we know what we claim to know. One example of a knowledge question is: *Are some methods of producing knowledge more reliable than others?*

Knowledge questions often relate to the knowledge framework (which you will explore in Chapter 3), asking questions about the scope of knowledge, different perspectives, the methods and tools used to produce and evaluate knowledge and ethical considerations.

By asking about the bases on which we hold our beliefs and knowledge claims, we may not change our minds about their truth, but we will gain a better and deeper understanding of what it is we hold to be true, and why. By exploring knowledge questions, we will grow to have a better understanding of the world and ourselves. We will begin to open our eyes to different perspectives and develop a richer appreciation for the diversity of the world. We may lose some of our *certainties* along the way, but we will be rewarded by the discovery of greater possibilities, and we will emerge with a fuller grasp of the certainties that we continue to hold.

KEY TERMS

absolutists: in this context, people who believe there are absolute truths that are true for all people at all times

knowledge question: an open question that explores issues of knowing

KEY POINT

Knowledge questions are always open questions – they cannot be answered by a simple *yes* or *no*.

Knowledge questions form the basis for *what* and *how* we know. They examine concepts such as justification, evidence, assumptions, judgement, interpretation and coherence, and take account of different perspectives. They also explore different ways in which we produce and evaluate knowledge, including examining the methods and tools used in different areas of knowledge, the scope of application for those methods and tools and any ethical considerations that might arise.

The purpose of knowledge

How does saying that something is *knowledge* rather than *opinion* or *belief* alter its status, and why does it, or should it, matter to us? Our answers to these questions might depend on the purpose of the knowledge claims we are considering. It could be said that knowledge is what we use to help explain the world around us, to further our understanding and to enable us to make decisions. Some of those decisions might be relatively insignificant. For example, you might rely on your knowledge that brinjal pickle is usually spicier than mango chutney when deciding which to choose to have with your lunch. Unless you suffer from allergies, your decision is unlikely to be significant.

However, suppose you are walking with a friend and come to a rickety-looking bridge over a deep river. If you were to cross the bridge, it might collapse under you, and you could possibly drown. You cannot know with certainty that the bridge will hold your weight; either you must take a risk and cross the bridge, or you can decide to go a long way around.

Figure 2.2: Would you be prepared to trust this bridge?

Your friend says, *'I know this bridge will take my weight.'*

1   If you weigh more than your friend, would you trust the bridge?

2   Even if the bridge has carried the weight of your friend in the past, how certain can you be that it will carry the same weight again?

What generally matters is the *extent* to which something is accepted as known or true by society, rather than what knowledge or truth *is*. However, there are some cases, such as in the case of the rickety-looking bridge, when agreement is not enough. This demonstrates the importance of not accepting knowledge claims at face value, and the responsibility we have to make decisions.

It is unlikely that any society will ever be able to agree on anything non-trivial that is true for all people in all places at all times. Even a seemingly *true* statement such as '*The Sun rises and sets each day*' is only true from an earthly perspective. Whether the Sun appears to rise, and the extent of any rise, depends on where observers are located, and the time of the year.

What we can say is: *Our knowledge is the best we can do right now* given that we are a particular group among a particular species in a particular place and time. The reason for this practical approach is that we cannot suspend our judgement endlessly while we await an absolute certainty that comes through possessing perfect information: we have to act; we have to decide. If what we are deliberating about has no consequences for our actions, it is of little importance whether we construe it to be *knowledge* or not.

TASK: ACTIVITY 2.6

Read the following knowledge claims:

a   Sheep remember faces.

b   Genetic material is made up of DNA molecules.

c   Abraham Lincoln was assassinated on 14th April 1865.

d   Kashmir is a disputed territory.

e   The polar ice caps are melting.

These are claims that you may or may not accept as knowledge. How you regard the importance of the truth of each of these claims will probably depend on who you are, what you do, where your interests lie and which society you belong to.

Think of some knowledge claims that are important to you. Do you think they would still be important to you if you had been born into a different family or in another country?

Are there any knowledge claims that are important for everyone everywhere, at all times and places?

Knowledge is a very difficult concept to pin down. Theory of knowledge (TOK) helps us to appreciate what matters, so that we learn to deal with knowledge claims in a way that shows some awareness of the difficulties and dangers of treating things as knowledge without question and without good reason.

In every subject in the IB Diploma Programme curriculum you will encounter knowledge claims, and these claims usually come with powerful support from a complex mix of tradition, authority and practice. But you should remember that claims to knowledge always come with these attributes, and in the past, similar claims were made in the name of what we now regard as discredited scientific worldviews, religious prejudices, superstitions, vested interests and errors.

2.5 The knowledge matrix

So far, we have looked at knowledge claims largely in terms of individual statements, but very few important knowledge claims arise in isolation; most are part of a complex web of ideas and claims about the world which we constantly cross-reference using skills and resources to see whether they are consistent with each other. A **knowledge matrix** is a *matrix of concepts, facts and relations* that we rely upon when assessing any individual claim we come across. When faced with a knowledge claim, we need to ask questions such as:

- For whom is this true?

- Is it true in all areas of knowledge?

- On what grounds is it claimed to be true?

- Does this knowledge claim cohere with or contradict knowledge claims that I already believe to be true?

- To what extent does society rely on this claim being true?

- To what extent can I rely on this claim being true?

- Can I consider this claim from other perspectives?

- What are the implications of accepting this claim as true?

- What difference does it make whether I regard it as certain or not?

- What are the consequences that I might face if I do not accept the truth of this claim?

> **KEY TERM**
>
> **knowledge matrix:** a communal network of intersecting ideas, beliefs and facts, within which new knowledge arises and develops

---

REAL-LIFE SITUATION 2.2

Three friends in Florida, USA, claimed to have seen an alien around 11 p.m. on 21st March 2012. They claimed that the streetlights began to flicker strangely just before the alien came into view. The alien was said to have been over 2 metres tall with fluorescent eyes. One of the witnesses later sketched the alien.

1   You would probably accept the eyewitness accounts of three people who claimed to have witnessed a crime, but you may be reluctant to accept an eyewitness account of an encounter with an alien. Why?

2   To what extent and in what circumstances can we rely on eyewitness accounts?

CONTINUED

3   Would you be more willing to believe this story if the witnesses were people you know and trust?

4   How does your knowledge matrix affect your willingness to believe the story?

Figure 2.3: How does our knowledge matrix affect whether we accept new knowledge claims?

TOP TIP

When investigating any issue, always consider claims and counter-claims.

2.6 The ethics of knowledge

As you explore the different areas of knowledge and knowledge themes in this book, you will consider some of the ethical issues that arise in producing knowledge in each of those areas. There are also some ethical questions that relate to the acquisition, storage, use and sharing of knowledge, however it is produced.

You may have heard a lot of discussion about data protection and the right to privacy. While data protection originally referred to protecting data from loss by having back-up systems, now a significant requirement of data protection is to prevent data theft and the unethical use of data.

Some dangers associated with unauthorised people accessing your data are obvious. For example, if your bank details are stolen, money could be taken from your account without you knowing. Other misuses of personal data are less obvious, but you should be aware of them. For example, the social media platforms you are active on can potentially gather large amounts of information about you, and this information is valuable to people who want to sell you products or feed you with certain political ideas. By sharing your data, you may be targeted with propaganda campaigns, misinformation and disinformation.

KEY POINT

Possessing knowledge carries with it an ethical responsibility to carefully consider the ways in which we use and share that knowledge.

TASK: ACTIVITY 2.7

Consider the following situations and decide whether it would be ethical to share your knowledge, whether it would not be ethical to share your knowledge or whether the ethics would depend on the context in which you were asked to share your knowledge. Tick the appropriate box in the table.

Knowledge	Share	Do not share	It depends ...
how to administer first aid			
your head teacher's personal phone number			
your friend's a medical condition			
the answers to the homework quiz			
your friend has removed a reference book from the library without permission			
your baby brother's belief in the tooth fairy is misguided			

If you have ticked any boxes labelled *it depends* ..., come up with one circumstance in which it would be ethical to share your knowledge and one in which it would not be ethical.

2.7 Knowledge questions

1   Can knowledge change or grow without individuals challenging commonly-held beliefs about what is true?

2   To what extent does our willingness to rely on eyewitness accounts depend upon our beliefs?

3   How important is it that knowledge with life-shaping importance has social approval and acceptance?

2.8 Exhibition task

Consider how you might use the alien sketch by the eyewitness as an item for your TOK exhibition. Which IA prompt question would you choose? Write 250–300 words on the real-world context of the eyewitness's alien sketch, and how it links to your chosen IA prompt.

2.9 Extended writing task

Write 500 words on one or both of the following questions:

1   How important is it that we are certain about what we claim as knowledge?

2   To what extent might it be more important for knowledge to be useful rather than accurate?

SKILLS SELF-ASSESSMENT CHECKLIST

Reflect on what you have learned in this chapter and indicate your confidence level between 1 and 5 (where 5 is the highest score and 1 is the lowest). If you score below 3, revisit that section. Come back to this list later in your course. Has your confidence grown?

	Confidence level	Revisited?
Can I identify and analyse knowledge claims and knowledge questions?		
Can I explain some of the difficulties in justifying knowledge claims?		
Am I able to discuss and evaluate justifications for different types of knowledge?		
Am I aware of some of the ethical issues that may arise when producing knowledge and making knowledge claims?		

2.10 Further reading

For a discussion on how we can know anything, read: A. J. Ayer, *The Problem of Knowledge*, Penguin, 1961

To find out more on what knowledge is and how we arrive at it, read: Duncan Pritchard, *What is This Thing Called Knowledge?*, Routledge 2006

To learn more about the development and evolution of scientific knowledge, read: Karl Popper, *Objective Knowledge*, Oxford University Press, 1972

'For an excellent talk on the nature of knowledge and the problem of bias, watch Professor Alex Edmans' Gresham College lecture entitled 'Critical Thinking'

> # Chapter 3
> # Knowledge questions and framework

LEARNING INTENTIONS

In this chapter, you will further explore what a knowledge question is, and how to understand knowledge questions. You will be introduced to the knowledge framework and will think about the links and connections, and similarities and differences between different areas of knowledge. You will consider the basis for ethical judgements.

You will:

- investigate how knowledge questions relate to different areas of knowledge and the world around us

- understand how the knowledge framework can be used as a tool for TOK analysis

- advance your TOK analysis through exploring and analysing knowledge questions

- develop logical, reasoned and appropriate arguments in response to knowledge questions

- sharpen your skills of analysis through your use of examples, evaluation of arguments and consideration of implications

- refine your TOK analysis by identifying and exploring the similarities and differences between areas of knowledge via the knowledge framework.

3.1 Introduction

In Chapter 2, we introduced knowledge questions. We briefly outlined the nature of knowledge questions: they are **contestable**, open ended and explicitly about knowledge and knowing. One aim of TOK is to teach you to analyse and answer knowledge questions. The TOK assessment tasks (the prescribed essay titles and the IA exhibition knowledge prompts) are all knowledge questions. To assist you to analyse and respond to knowledge questions, we will introduce you to the IB's knowledge framework.

KEY TERM

contestable: referring to a knowledge claim or question that can be argued about, where there is more than one possible interpretation or answer

TASK: ACTIVITY 3.1

Working with a partner, list questions about knowledge and knowing that you would like to ask and answer. Using the following four features as a guide, develop some of your own examples of knowledge questions.

Use your examples to discuss what makes a good knowledge-specific question, and what makes a knowledge question distinct from a subject-specific question.

3.2 Knowledge questions

Let us examine what we mean by a knowledge question in more detail.

1   *Knowledge questions are about knowledge and knowing.*

Every knowledge question is explicitly about knowledge and knowing. They are not the same as subject-specific questions, which focus on specific subject content.

From the following examples, you can see that knowledge questions relate to both the world around you and a given area of knowledge. The following examples show the difference between a real-life situation in the world around you, a related question that is subject-specific and a related question that is knowledge-specific.

TOP TIP

When you answer a knowledge question, be sure to identify how it exactly relates to knowledge and knowing.

- **Real-life situation:** *Salvator Mundi* by Leonardo da Vinci became the world's most expensive painting when it was sold for $450 million.

- **Subject-specific question:** Who decides the cost of a piece of art, and can we know for certain that Leonardo da Vinci painted *Salvator Mundi*?

- **Knowledge-specific question:** How do we know how to judge the value of art?

- **Real-life situation:** CRISPR is a method scientists use to edit genes.

- **Subject-specific question:** How do we edit the genes of a living organism, and what are the risks?

- **Knowledge-specific question:** How do we know what ethical considerations should influence our pursuit of knowledge?

2 *Knowledge questions include TOK concepts.*

Most knowledge questions contain a TOK concept that relates to knowledge and knowing.

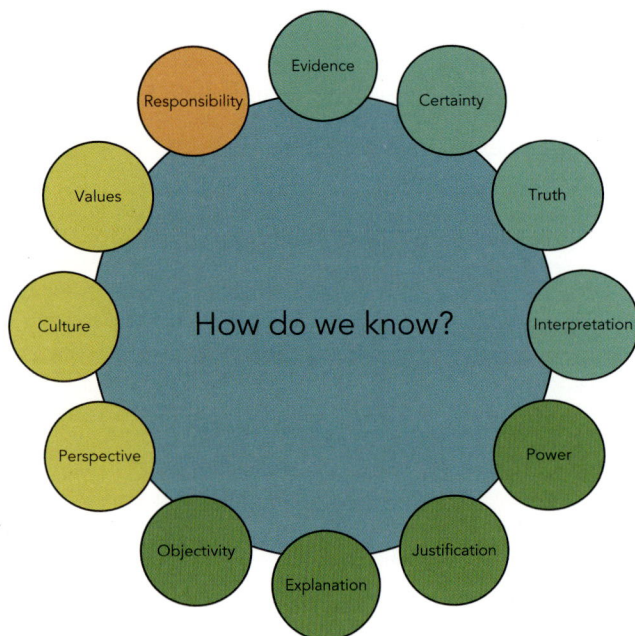

Figure 3.1: 12 TOK key concepts

3   *Knowledge questions include command words or instructions.*

Every knowledge question contains an instruction or a command. Command words can be explicit (e.g. *'Explain why …'*) or implicit. It is worth looking for implied commands, and be able to identify the instruction in a knowledge question.

For example, in the knowledge question, *Why do we pursue and share knowledge?* the instruction is explicit – to *explain why*. For the knowledge question, *In what ways should our values and ethical responsibilities influence how we produce and share knowledge?* the implicit instruction is that you should *explore* the various different ways in which ethical considerations might have an influence on knowledge.

4   *Knowledge questions are contestable.*

A contestable question is one that is open to different interpretations. Every knowledge question is contestable, open-ended and lends itself to various or multiple possible answers.

> **TOP TIP**
>
> When you answer a knowledge question, be sure to identify and explore the central concepts in the question. For example, in the following knowledge question, the key concepts are reliability and evidence: *'Can we know what counts as reliable evidence'?*

> **TOP TIP**
>
> When you answer a knowledge question, be sure to identify the command words in the question, so that you can be clear about what the question is asking you to do.

When you answer a knowledge question, be sure to identify and explore a range of possible answers to the question. Try and avoid oversimplified *right or wrong answers* such as *yes*, *no* or *maybe*. Instead, think about the question in terms of:

- What are some different possible answers to this question?

- What examples or evidence might support different answers to the question?

- How might the four strands of the knowledge framework help me to (avoid description and) analyse the question?

- Who might disagree with me and why?

- What are the different cultural and historical perspectives?

3.3 The knowledge framework

Every knowledge question can be answered using the four strands of the knowledge framework. The knowledge framework is a *tool for analysis and comparison* between different areas of knowledge. The purpose of the knowledge framework is to help you think *across* areas of knowledge. It is like a *map* to help you find your way and develop your sense of the connections between areas of knowledge. Like a map, knowledge is a representation of the world. Each area of knowledge can be considered in terms of at least four different strands. These four interacting strands are: (1) scope, (2) perspectives, (3) tools and methods and (4) ethics. Like a map, the knowledge framework can help you to find your way around different areas of knowledge, and make connections and links between them.

Throughout Parts 1–3 of this book, you will find a feature called 'TOK link' to help you make connections and links with different strands of the framework. These are intended only to support and guide you; they are no substitute for your own critical thought, ideas and analysis.

Part 1: Scope

The first strand of the framework invites you to explore what each area of knowledge is about, what defines our shared knowledge and what problems it addresses. *Scope* is to do with the subject matter, the extent and limit of the area of knowledge and how it fits in with the whole total of knowledge. For example, mathematics is about ideas such as shape, number and pattern. The topics studied as part of the history curriculum may be thought of as the subject content of history; however, *history* as an area of knowledge is very much broader than this. You might reflect critically on the factors that shape your impression of the subject matter: your personal experience of the subject, the IB Diploma Programme curriculum, your culture and your type of education.

The scope of subject matter within any area of knowledge is related to the scope of the problems and solutions that an area of knowledge addresses – from surreal numbers to understanding consciousness, to solving climate change or world poverty. There may be contexts where *knowing how* to solve a problem using creativity and imaginative thinking may be more important than *knowing about* a problem. In mathematics, we can address real-world problems such as the probability of a bridge collapsing in strong winds. Different areas of knowledge, and different fields within those areas of knowledge, may have many different **applications**.

> ### KEY TERM
>
> **applications:** how knowledge is used, for example to identify problems or find solutions

TASK: ACTIVITY 3.2

1   Can you think of any examples of the *scope* of two areas of knowledge, such as history and science? Compare the two areas of knowledge by making two lists, and outline examples of the different subject matter of each.

2   Can you think of any examples of the *practical problems and solutions* that two areas of knowledge, such as history and science, seek to answer? Compare the areas of knowledge by making two new lists with two headings, *The scope of history* and *The scope of science*, outlining examples of problems and solutions.

3   In what ways do you think your impression of the scope of an area of knowledge is influenced by your educational curriculum, your cultural context, your ethical values or any other factors?

4   Within a given particular area of knowledge, what questions remain contestable or unanswered, and why?

5   What is the limit to our knowledge? If we cannot know what we do not know, can we be sure of the limit to our knowledge?

Part 2: Perspective

What we know has a context. Our knowledge has a situation in place and time, and the concept of *perspective* invites you to explore this. Perspectives concern you directly, and give you opportunities to reflect on the things that influence and shape your perspective as a knower. What we know is personal to us, and our perspectives are influenced by multiple factors such as the communities we belong to. Furthermore, our knowledge occupies a place in time and history.

Your own personal knowledge is shaped by the knowledge you have been brought up with. For example, most people believe that the Earth is about 4.5 billion years old (unless of course they are **creation scientists** or their supporters, who hold a different viewpoint). This knowledge of our place in the world is influenced by the knowledge we receive from scientists who tell us about how relatively short our time on the planet has been.

> ### KEY TERM
>
> **creation scientists:** people who treat the theory that God created the universe as recorded in the Book of Genesis as a scientific theory

However, the subject knowledge we learn at school is grounded in a historical and cultural context. If you look back at an encyclopaedia from a century ago, you can appreciate that what we take for granted now as shared knowledge is radically different from what it was in the past.

The 'perspectives' strand of the framework therefore invites you to think about how an area of knowledge has developed over time. For example, consider the question, *How has the study of history developed over time?* Tracing the historical development of an area of knowledge can be a tool for analysis. If you ask the counterfactual question,

What if X had not happened?, you can speculate about how our knowledge might be partly the product of *accidents of history*. If the discovery of chemical elements had not been made in chemistry, we might not have the periodic table that we know today. Without the discovery of DNA, the study of biology would be very different. And our knowledge in physics would be radically different without the development of quantum mechanics.

In this strand of the knowledge framework, you might explore the history of reason and rational thought. For example, you could study the concept of *dharma* in Indian traditions from the Vedas to the present day, or the development of reason during the Islamic civilisation of the 10th century to the 12th century CE. You might also look at the intellectual movements of history, such as the Renaissance and the Enlightenment, which can help us appreciate how science and rationality have led to a modern understanding of our place in the universe. New concepts and ideas emerge and shape what we come to know.

There are other types of perspective to examine, such as cultural perspectives. By culture, we mean the way of life, traditions, customs and values that belong to a group of people. Culture is a complex phenomenon, and cultural perspectives can connect and interact with one another. For example, the culture of Bangladesh might connect with the rich Bengali culture that enjoyed a renaissance in the 19th and 20th centuries, characterised by developments in the arts and sciences.

Under perspective, you might also explore other factors that shape our viewpoint such as (but not limited to): age, social identity, gender, status, class, beliefs, religion, politics, education and nationality.

Figure 3.2: West Bengal chief minister Mamata Banerjee speaks to a crowd. How might your cultural identity influence your perspective as a knower?

TASK: ACTIVITY 3.3

Create a display or poster based on one of the following questions.

1   Given that our knowledge changes and develops over time, consider:

- How far is our knowledge a product of history?

- How far is our knowledge shaped by other factors such as our culture, social convention and authority?

- To what extent is your own knowledge one of many other possible perspectives?

2   What do you think is meant by an *accident of history*? Think of examples.

3   Choose an area of knowledge. What are the *key movements* and *key points* in the development of this area of knowledge over time?

4   How can we know if current knowledge or new knowledge is better than past knowledge?

TASK: ACTIVITY 3.4

There are various culture simulation activities online, including the BaFá BaFá simulation, which can be found online for *EU Intercultural Learning for Pupils and Teachers*. Choose one of these, and take part in a role play to explore the role of culture.

Part 3: Methods and tools used to produce knowledge

The third part of the knowledge framework invites you to think about the *methods and tools* used to gain knowledge in different areas. By *methods*, we mean the procedures and processes used to gain knowledge. **Quantitative** methods include statistical analysis, mathematical modelling and laboratory experiments. **Qualitative** methods include observation, interviews, questionnaires and case studies. The procedure, process and use of tools and methods for gaining knowledge vary according to each area of knowledge and optional theme, although some tools and methods may be relevant in different ways. For example, both science and history make use of hypotheses, and require data or evidence. The scientific method involves the formation of hypotheses which are tested by performing experiments. Historians use an empirical method based on interpretation of primary and secondary sources.

Different methods used will lead to different knowledge claims and explanations. A historical fact could include the date of an event, whereas an explanation of a historical event would involve an understanding of its causes.

By *tools*, we mean the abstract concepts and cognitive tools used to build knowledge in different subject areas, as well as practical and material tools. In this section, we explore various tools: rationality, sense perception, intuition and imagination.

KEY TERMS

quantitative: relating to, measuring or measured by the quantity of something, rather than its quality

qualitative: relating to, measuring or measured by the quality of something, rather than its quantity; qualitative studies use a method to give a detailed narrative about a human phenomenon that describes a culture or shares a story

CROSS REFERENCE

You can read more about the methods and tools used to produce knowledge, for example about different types of reasoning, in Chapter 3 of the Course Guide.

TASK: THINK ABOUT 3.1

1 When evaluating a knowledge claim, what tools and methods might you use?

2 How are methods and tools used to produce knowledge in different areas?

KEY POINT

Just as we need different tools for different practical tasks, we need to use different tools and methods to gain different types of knowledge. The main question in TOK is *How do I know?* or *How do we know?*. Tools and methods can give you help you to reach an answer to this question.

Reasoning

A vital tool for acquiring knowledge is reasoning. It is important to make distinctions between different kinds of reasoning.

Inductive reasoning begins with particular observations, and then moves to general conclusions. For example, my observation in a particular experiment that magnesium appears to increase its mass when it is burnt, could lead me to the general conclusion that all magnesium appears to increase its mass when burnt.

The reliability of inductive reasoning depends on the quantity and reliability of our observations, and the likelihood that a pattern can be generalised. For example, if I have observed many hundreds of ravens and all of them had been black, it might be reasonable (even if not infallibly true) to conclude that all ravens are black. However, if I were to drive through a village and see three people out walking their dogs, it would not be reasonable (even though it could conceivably be true) for me to conclude that all people living in that village have dogs.

Deductive reasoning draws upon general knowledge and constructs it in a way that a particular conclusion can be reached. This construction is called a **syllogism**. The following is an example of deductive reasoning:

Premise 1: Sri Jayawardenepura Kotte is in Sri Lanka.

Premise 2: Sri Lanka is in the Northern Hemisphere.

Conclusion: Therefore, Sri Jayawardenepura Kotte is in the Northern Hemisphere.

For deductive reasoning to be reliable, the knowledge used for the premises must be true, and the construction of the argument must be valid.

KEY TERMS

inductive reasoning: moves from particular observations, experiences or data to general conclusions

deductive reasoning: moves from the general to the particular

syllogism: a form of reasoning where a conclusion is drawn from two premises

KEY POINTS

Reason plays a key role in mathematics and science, but also extends to all areas of knowledge including how we judge art and how we arrive at ethical decisions.

Culture can influence the conclusions of reasoning because different cultures may generalise different observations when reasoning inductively, and might start from different knowledge bases when reasoning deductively.

Feelings and emotion

Another tool for acquiring knowledge is feelings and emotion. Our feelings can be regarded as either an obstacle to our knowledge (they may distort our interpretation) or a source of our knowledge (they help us to understand ourselves and make decisions). What we feel may be influenced by the culture we live in. However, it is believed that there is a physiological basis to our emotions, and that there are a number of universal emotions across all cultures including disgust, shock, fear and happiness. Emotion has a significant link with ethics, for example, feeling angry may be based on an ethical judgement that an injustice has occurred.

TOK LINK: THE ARTS

The arts have a strong connection with the emotions; we can feel moved when we read a novel or poem, look at a painting or listen to music. The arts can express emotions and also influence our feelings.

TASK: ACTIVITY 3.5

Prepare a short presentation based on one of the following questions, ready to share your ideas in class. Be sure to use your skills of analysis, and evaluate the question.

1   How do our feelings relate to different areas of knowledge such as mathematics, natural science or human science?

2   In what ways does our language express our feelings and attitudes?

3   Are our emotions a reliable source of knowledge?

4   In what ways can our feelings limit or inspire our curiosity, or motivate us to pursue certain types of knowledge?

TOP TIP

Make connections and links between areas of knowledge, and tools and methods. Think about how they interact to produce knowledge.

Sense perception

Another tool is sense perception. The sense data that our brain receives is determined by the biology of our senses: sight, sound, taste, touch and smell, our sense of heat, pain, movement and balance. Other animals perceive the world very differently from us. A dog has a superior sense of smell to ours, and a snake can see infrared light. Squids have eyes that are superior to ours – they are much better adapted to seeing in the dark. Sense data may be shaped and interpreted by other factors, including our expectations, our assumptions or prior concepts.

In all areas of knowledge we depend heavily on our sense perception, and on practical technological tools such as the microscope or the telescope which can enhance our sense perception. We cannot, however, make any judgements solely based on sense perception.

> **KEY POINT**
>
> It is important to make distinctions between sense perception (which refers to knowledge gained by our senses) and *perspective* or *viewpoint*, however you need to be aware that your perspectives will always affect your sense perceptions.

Intuition and imagination

Other tools include intuition and imagination. Intuition is our instinct or *gut feeling*. When we first meet someone, we might have an intuitive sense about their character – about what they are like as a person. We think we know, but intuitive feelings are not always reliable or correct. The character Elizabeth Bennett in Jane Austen's *Pride and Prejudice* (1813) has an intuition that Mr Darcy is a proud and rude man; an intuition that turns out to be wrong. We appear to have an intuition for art: we can instantly like or dislike it. Our intuition for art is shaped by other non-intuitive factors such as context, setting and expectation. In ethics, some people think that we have a moral sense or an intuition about right and wrong. Mathematical intuitions might offer a flash of inspiration or a moment of insight. Mathematician Andrew Wiles (1953–) had a deep intuition which, combined with many years of thinking and some collaboration with other mathematicians, led to his solution in 1994 of a famous and long-standing mathematics problem, *Fermat's Last Theorem*.

Imagination is often associated with creativity and *thinking outside the box*. Letting our imagination take over can lead to new knowledge. In many areas of knowledge, imagination is associated with empathy, creativity, problem-solving and originality.

You might imagine *what if* something had been different in the historical development of an area of knowledge. A number of subjects might require you to *imagine a scenario where X happens*. Imagination is needed for speculating about the past and the future. As well as being required in the arts, imagination can also be very important to mathematicians. You could consider how imagination links with memory; do we imagine the past?

> **TASK: ACTIVITY 3.6**
>
> 1 In what ways might rationality, imagination, evidence, observation and intuition lead to the justification of knowledge claims in different areas? Discuss this with a partner.
>
> 2 Choose a method or tool used to produce knowledge. What does this method or tool take for granted or assume?

Part 4: Ethics

The learner profile assumes that *acting in a principled way*, which involves honesty, fairness and responsibility, is what IB Diploma Programme students should do. You might question where your own personal values and standards of ethics come from. What is a good life? How should you live your life? What are the sources of your beliefs about right and wrong? Are there only personal standards of right and wrong, or are there broader shared standards or even universal standards across different cultures? If there are such standards, what is their justification? This strand of the knowledge framework is concerned with addressing how ethics influences areas of knowledge as well as our response to knowledge questions.

TASK: ACTIVITY 3.7

Discuss the following questions in a pair or small group:

1   Can you be sure where your values come from?

2   What responsibilities to do you have as a knower?

3   If people disagree about an ethical question, how can we decide between different ethical viewpoints?

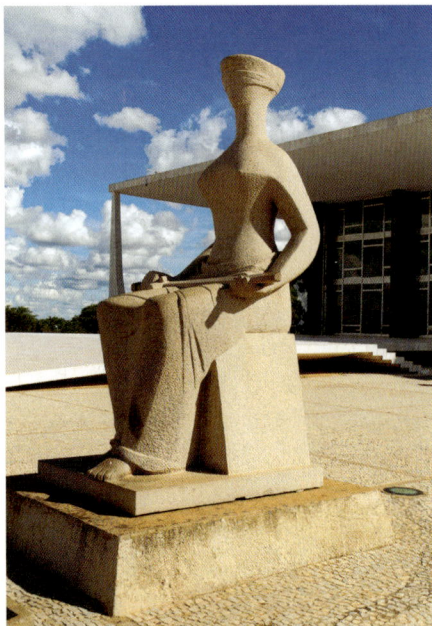

Figure 3.3: The statue *A Justiça* by Alfredo Ceschiatti, in front of the headquarters of the Supreme Court of Brazil. Can we observe right and wrong?

What is ethical knowledge?

What is considered right and wrong varies between countries and cultures. Kissing in public is acceptable in the UK, but public displays of affection should be avoided in Singapore, Turkey and some other countries. It is very easy to assume that this area of knowledge is simply a matter of personal preference. People might feel strongly about the ethics of a number of national and international issues, including world poverty, terrorism, climate change, oppressive political regimes, genetically modified crops or the violation of human rights. If there is limited agreement between people, or if we cannot make up our minds about ethical issues, it is sometimes assumed that ethics is all a matter of personal opinion.

You only need to break a rule in school or commit a crime to know that we are bound by rules and conventions everywhere. The IB Diploma Programme rule that *it is wrong to plagiarise someone else's work* carries with it an obligation not to do so. It follows that actions conform to or fail to conform to certain social or behavioural conventions. However, rules are not the same as morals. For example, some cultures regard it as *immoral* for girls to speak to boys without a chaperone present. Homosexual relationships were once widely regarded as *immoral and illegal*, however, today they are no longer illegal in most countries and most people no longer regard them as immoral. You might reflect critically on the relationship between ethics and rules. An action that breaks a rule might or might not be ethical. There may be scenarios when it is ethical to break a rule, for example if the rules are considered to be unjust or unfair.

As a knower, your source of right and wrong could include the standards you have been brought up with, and your individual **conscience**. Morality seems to be partly to do with social and cultural conventions. Children are taught right from wrong by their parents so that they conform with the standards that are considered normal in their society and culture. What we teach our children can become synonymous with what our society or culture agrees is right. Good behaviour is more than good manners. We mean something different from etiquette when we talk of right and wrong; we include every aspect of social behaviour from personal relationships through to the laws we enact to regulate society and our willingness or otherwise to comply with such laws.

REAL-LIFE SITUATION 3.1

In the early 1990s, controversial *performance* artist Rick Gibson (1951–) took *Sniffy the Rat* from a pet shop, where he might have been sold as live snake food. Gibson set up a device to crush the rat with a large weight and make an artwork with the remains. The rat was rescued by activists who felt that what Gibson had planned was wrong, but Gibson's point was to invite a discussion about the ethics of killing animals. If the rat had been sold as live snake food, it would have faced inevitable death.

1   When and how might art be used to make an ethical point?

2   Should the work of artists be influenced by ethical values and responsibilities? If so, what are they?

3   When, if ever, is it justified to make works of art that might shock or cause outrage?

KEY POINT

One branch of philosophy is the study of ethics. Ethics or moral philosophy explores human conduct and values. TOK ethics is concerned with whether or not we can have moral knowledge. It also concerns how we know what the best course of action is under within different ethical systems.

TASK: THINK ABOUT 3.2

As you work through the Task: Activity 3.7 that follows, reflect on the processes you use to arrive at ethical judgements.

1   When you answer the questions, to what extent do you use different tools and methods when you make your judgements?

2   When you answer the questions, in what ways does your own perspective affect your judgement?

TASK: ACTIVITY 3.8

Discuss with a partner:

1   Which do you think is worse?

   a   being rude and unkind to someone

   b   being rude and unkind to someone behind their back but being polite to their face

2   Which do you think is worse?

   a   killing one person deliberately

   b   killing two people by accident

   c   thinking about and planning how to kill someone, but missing the opportunity to do so by accident

3   Which student deserves the severest punishment?

   a   the student who deliberately steals someone else's mobile phone

   b   the student who has been cyber-bullying another student

   c   the student who is caught using the school photocopier for their own use without permission

What is the justification for ethical knowledge claims?

The transatlantic slave trade in the 18th century may now be thought of as appalling or repugnant, but some people considered it to be acceptable at that time. In the past, people watched Roman gladiators fight to the death for entertainment. **Ethical relativism** is the view that our sense of right and wrong depends on our cultural and historical context. However, within each historical setting or culture, the ethical view might be seen as absolute.

Considering the implications of ethical relativism, does it follow that anything is permitted? Arguably, it could follow that if female genital mutilation (FGM) is acceptable in one cultural context, there is no way that a **relativist** can challenge it, since there are no objective grounds on which an action can be judged right or wrong. However, there might be grounds based on cultural convention. A relativist may claim that it is acceptable to wear a face covering, but not in France. In 2010, the French government banned face coverings in most public places in France, making it an

KEY TERMS

ethical relativism: the view that there are no absolute standards of right and wrong; they vary and evolve differently across nations and cultures and over time

relativist: a person who thinks that there are no universal moral principles or absolutes, since what we claim to know about right and wrong depends on our culture, country and place in history

offence for women to wear a *burqa* (a full body garment that also covers the face and has a mesh screen over the eyes) or *niqab* (a veil that covers the nose and mouth). This led to different views on the ethics of the ban, with those supporting it claiming that face coverings can cause security risks, and those against the ban claiming that it limits individual rights. A relativist would argue that ethics are relative to the culture or the country you live in. This position might be argued for on the grounds that ethical judgements are **subjective** – that is, based on an individual's personal opinion.

KEY TERM

subjective: in this context, a subjective view of ethics is the idea that personal knowledge - our own thoughts, feelings, tastes and preferences - is the basis of our ethical judgements

Figure 3.4: What arguments might be used to support or oppose the right of women to wear the *burqa* or *niqab*? How might the requirement to wear facemasks because of Covid impact on arguments for and against the *burqa* and *niqab*?

TASK: THINK ABOUT 3.3

1   How far are we justified when making ethical judgements about our own society and culture?

2   How far are we justified when making ethical judgements about a society and culture that we do not belong to?

3   Consider your responses to questions 1 and 2, and explain whether or not they are similar or different answers.

4   Are there some ethical standards that you would expect everyone to agree with, regardless of their social and cultural differences?

There is an interesting relationship between ethics and **international-mindedness**. If we take a relativist position and promote tolerance of all practices in other cultures, what are the implications for ethics? Being internationally minded is not the same as being universally tolerant. It does not mean that we have to agree with practices in other cultures if we think they are unethical. Someone might be internationally minded

KEY TERM

international-mindedness: the mutual respect, understanding and interaction between different countries and cultures

and be a supporter of Amnesty International, a non-governmental organisation (NGO) that opposes the abuse of human rights and is against the death penalty. Being internationally minded might influence how someone thinks and acts; they may become committed to a set of ethical values which could lead to action.

An alternative approach is to appeal to moral standards that are *universal*. You could accept that standards vary between cultures, but still claim that we can object to practices that seem to infringe the human rights of others. Amnesty International campaigns to uphold universal standards of human rights and abolish the use of torture in all circumstances. The UN Declaration of Human Rights was published in 1948, and assumes shared moral standards regardless of national and cultural differences. This approach claims that there are universal rules, or **moral absolutes**. This position might be argued for on the grounds that ethical judgements are **objective**; there are moral rules and standards that are in some sense independent of our personal preferences, perhaps with a natural or a divine basis.

KEY TERM

moral absolutes: rules that apply universally, regardless of circumstances

objective view of ethics: the idea that there are moral truths which could be natural or divine; for example, statements such as *murder is wrong* are factual statements that are true or false in the same way that *I have three books on my bookshelf* is true or false

---

TASK: THINK ABOUT 3.4

1   Think of examples of people who you would describe as internationally minded. What attitudes and actions would you associate with someone who is internationally minded?

2   What is the distinction between an internationally-minded person and an ethically-minded person?

3   If you have helped others in need as part of CAS (creativity, action, service), reflect on the ways in which your involvement in CAS might have had an ethical dimension.

TASK: ACTIVITY 3.9

1   How do we defend our ethical values? In pairs, write a short speech that supports or opposes one of the following ethical issues: abortion, the death penalty, wearing the burqa or public displays of affection.

2   Write a critical analysis of your speech or someone else's speech.

   a   Which of the arguments do you think is strongest, and why?

   b   Which of the arguments do you think is weakest, and why?

   c   What values are you (or the speaker) assuming your listeners have?

   d   If everyone in the world were in agreement with what you say in your speech, how would the world be different?

3   How far do we have an ethical responsibility to pursue, acquire and communicate knowledge? Why?

4   How do values, responsibilities and ethics change over time?

CROSS REFERENCE

Chapter 3 of the Course Guide offers a more thorough exploration of ethics, including ethical theories.

3.4 Knowledge questions

1 To what extent do some tools and methods lead to more certain knowledge than others?

2 To what extent would you claim that any two areas of knowledge are different in terms of their scope, tools and methods?

3 How far should we judge the value of an area of knowledge according to its usefulness or practical applications?

3.5 Exhibition task

Consider these different categories: a recent news story in either the local, national or international news; an example of experts disagreeing; a community issue; a survey; an example of ambiguous evidence or a controversial situation.

- Choose one of these categories.

- Identify a specific object or objects that relate to the category.

- Link these objects to one of the IA prompts.

- Think about how the four strands of the knowledge framework might support your analysis of the IA prompt.

- Justify how and why your object/s relate to the IA prompt.

3.6 Extended writing task

Write 500 words on one of the following questions:

1 Outline the contribution of key thinkers to the historical development of an area of knowledge. Find out who the key thinkers are, and what their contribution to knowledge was. For example, what contributions to knowledge in the human sciences were made by either Foucault (1925–1984), Marx (1818–1883), Durkheim (1858–1917) or Habermas (1929–)? Or, what contributions to knowledge in ethics were made by Aristotle (384–322 BCE), Mill (1806–1873) or Kant (1724–1804)?

2   Choose one of the following aspects of the knowledge framework: scope, perspective, tools and methods, ethics. Explore how this aspect of the framework relates to what we know in two areas of knowledge. For example, you could explore tools and methods in human science and history, or alternatively, the scope of religious knowledge systems and science.

SKILLS SELF-ASSESSMENT CHECKLIST

Reflect on what you have learned in this chapter and indicate your confidence level between 1 and 5 (where 5 is the highest score and 1 is the lowest). If you score below 3, revisit that section. Come back to this list later in your course. Has your confidence grown?

	Confidence level	Revisited?
Do I understand what a knowledge question is, and can I identify the command words and key concepts in a knowledge question?		
Do I understand how to use the knowledge framework as a tool for TOK analysis?		
Am I developing the skills to evaluate a knowledge question and consider the implications?		
Can I identify and evaluate arguments and counter-arguments when I answer a knowledge question?		
When I answer a knowledge question, am I able to use specific examples to support an argument?		
Am I able to compare different areas of knowledge using the four strands of the knowledge framework – scope, perspectives, tools and methods, and ethics?		
When I answer a knowledge question, do I know how to judge when ethical considerations, values and responsibility might be relevant?		

3.7 Further reading

For an overview of the role of different types of thinking, read: Daniel Kahneman, *Thinking, Fast and Slow*, Allen Lane, the Penguin Group, 2011

For examples of practical problems to solve, read: Jeremy Stangroom, *Einstein's Riddle: Riddles, Paradoxes and Conundrums to Stretch Your Mind*, Bloomsbury USA, 2009

For an excellent overview of ethics, read: Simon Blackburn, *Being Good: A Short Introduction to Ethics*, Oxford University Press, 2001

For ethics and contemporary issues, read: Peter Vardy and Paul Grosch, *The Puzzle of Ethics*, Fount, 1994

For an exploration of why people make different ethical judgements read, Jonathan Haidt, *The Righteous Mind* first published in the USA by Pantheon Books 2012

> **Chapter 4**

Truth and wisdom

LEARNING INTENTIONS

In this chapter, you will explore the distinction between truth and objectivity, the nature of truth and how it connects with knowledge and knowing, and how truth relates to language. You will be introduced to truth and ethics.

You will:

- understand how the concept of truth relates to knowledge, knowing and the world around us

- develop your concept of knowledge further by examining the different meanings of truth, and consider different theories of truth, including correspondence, coherence, pragmatic, consensus, pluralist and redundancy theories

- investigate knowledge questions relating to truth

- sharpen your skills of analysis through your use of examples, evaluation of arguments and consideration on implications

- evaluate truth in relation to ethical knowledge claims.

BEFORE YOU START

1   What is true about the truth?

2   What does the word *truth* mean, and does it make any sense to talk about truth in different areas of knowledge?

3   Do I have a responsibility to pursue the truth and tell the truth?

4.1 Introduction

Truth can be understood as something *that is the case*. Truth could be a conviction about what you believe to be the case, such as the existence of your own free will or your belief in other minds. By truth, we might also mean something that you can observe, test or empirically verify. For example, the idea that *I can observe the green grass* is a truth that is believed by some to correspond to a fact about the observable world.

TOK IN YOUR LIFE

What counts as a true fact a) about yourself and b) about the world around you? Identify one or more specific real-life examples.

4.2 How does truth relate to knowledge and knowing?

The pursuit of knowledge and knowing assumes that there is some truth involved. Any enquiry in the natural and human sciences, arts, history, mathematics or your other IB Diploma Programme subjects, takes for granted the idea that you are endeavouring to get closer to the truth.

Truth underpins areas of knowledge in different ways, and might have varying meanings in particular contexts. For example, scientists try to describe the truth about what the world is like. However, modern science might also struggle to describe the **microcosmic** and **macrocosmic** levels of reality. For example, the truth about scientific claims about general relativity and quantum physics may be difficult to describe in non-scientific language. Historians work on the basis that there is some truth about the past which the historian can interpret and discern. In the human sciences, there might be an assumption that a robust qualitative or quantitative method might lead to the truth. The arts communicate a type of truth – a novel might articulate and share a truth about human experience, a truth about human relationships or a truth about love. In mathematics, you might think that there are objective mathematical truths waiting to be discovered.

In short, the pursuit of knowledge assumes we are searching for some degree or type of truth. Likewise, the methods and tools that we use to produce knowledge depend upon our assumptions that these are the appropriate methods and tools to help us find or get closer to some degree of truth. However, there is value in humility, and an important aspect of the pursuit of knowledge and TOK is knowing that you may not find the truth, or that you may think you know the truth and yet be wrong.

KEY TERMS

microcosmic: relating to the world in miniature, or a small-scale perspective which corresponds to what a larger-scale perspective is like

macrocosmic: relating to a big or whole organised system, or a large-scale perspective

The concept of truth is central to knowledge and knowing. The concept of truth is not the same as opinion, although it can come down to opinion about what the truth of any particular matter is.

REAL-LIFE SITUATION 4.1

For many years, scientists and medical doctors claimed as true the idea that peptic ulcers were caused by stress and aggravated by acidic diets. When Barry Marshall (1951–) and Robin Warren (1937–) refused to accept the idea, they were ridiculed until they were able to produce strong evidence that the ulcers were caused by a bacterial infection. They subsequently won the 2005 Nobel Prize for Medicine as a result of their evidence. What the medical profession had deemed to be an **objective truth** was in fact **subjective** in that it was *subject* to their limited knowledge and understanding at the time.

1   Under what circumstances is it reasonable to ignore the opinions of experts in various areas of knowledge?

2   When old knowledge is discarded and new knowledge is accepted, does this imply that progress is being made?

3   What are the implications of a broad consensus about knowledge within scientific disciplines?

KEY TERMS

objective truth: something that would be regarded as true by all knowers, regardless of their perspective

subjective truth: a perceived truth based on personal perspectives or individual feelings

---

KEY POINT

What we might like to think of as an objective truth may be overturned in the future. Most truths are necessarily subjective because we cannot step outside of ourselves.

Relativist truth

Relativist truth is particularly popular when talking about contentious issues such as politics and religion. It is often diplomatic to say that everyone has their own version of truth, so there is a truth for you and a different truth for me. This is the relativist view of truth.

A relativist concept of truth can also be valuable when discussing cultural differences. It may be true for some people that camels are the most reliable means of transport, whereas other people, llamas may be more reliable. These 'truths' are more than mere opinion; they may be true for a particular culture in a particular context, and given that both truths are equally valid, they are not necessarily contestable.

However, this type of truth can be problematic. In the case of peptic ulcers, for example, it would not be acceptable to say that *'peptic ulcers are caused by stress'* is true for you and *'peptic ulcers are caused by bacteria'* is true for me, and that both truths are equally valuable. The first claim is false and the second claim is true, according to current scientific evidence. We might even be bold enough to claim that the second is objectively true, but it is always possible that even this knowledge may be overturned in the future, so in that sense, truth is subject to what we know at this point in our history.

KEY TERM

relativist truth: something regarded as true in a particular context, according to a particular culture, society or place in history

---

TASK: ACTIVITY 4.1

Truth plays a significant role in the world around us. Investigate one of the following, and find out what the role of truth is in the example you have chosen. How is the truth decided?

1   In a sports match, a referee's decision is based on their view of the truth.

2   Big data might be able to tell us the truth about broad patterns of human behaviour. (You can read more about big data in Chapter 5.)

3   If you give evidence in a court of law, you are required to 'tell the truth, the whole truth and nothing but the truth'.

Using one of these examples as a starting point, explore the links between truth and the world around you.

REAL-LIFE SITUATION 4.2

An American journalist, Esther Honig (1990–), took an image of herself and asked for it to be edited to 'look beautiful' according to the cultural expectations of 25 different countries around the world. It showed how beliefs about what is beautiful are relative to different cultures.

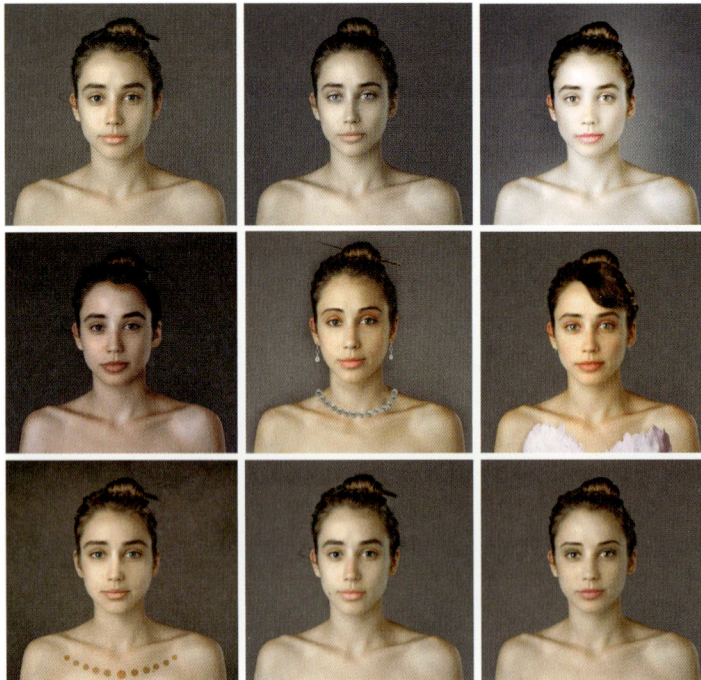

Figure 4.1: How might the concept of beauty vary within and across different cultures?

Some people assume that just as aesthetic tastes vary between people and cultures, so too is the concept of truth relative to our culture and society. Do you agree?

Theories of truth

There are six main theories of truth.

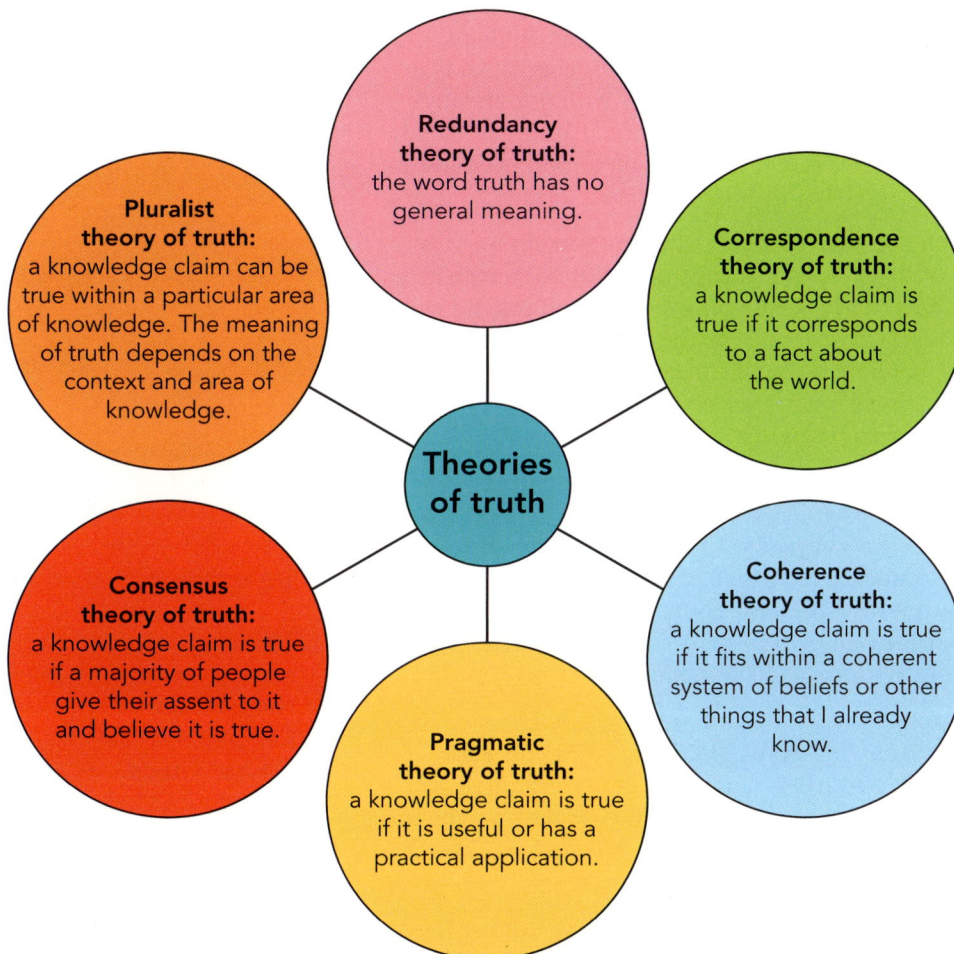

Figure 4.2: Theories of truth

The *correspondence theory of truth* says that whether a statement is true or false is determined by whether it accurately corresponds with the world. For example, you might claim that the statement, *'This piece of wood is a solid object'* corresponds with a fact about the world, because to you, the wood is solid. But if the wood were to be examined through powerful magnifying devices, you might discover that the piece of wood is highly porous, and at microscopic levels it is not solid at all. Which perception is seeing the wood as it really is?

In the *coherence theory of truth*, you can claim a statement to be true if it *coheres* or is logically consistent with other statements we hold to be true. Referring back to the case of peptic ulcers, one of the widely held medical truths at the time was that the acidity of stomach acids made it impossible for bacteria to live in the stomach. Because the claim – that peptic ulcers are caused by bacterial infections of the stomach – was incompatible with their contemporary *truth* – that bacteria cannot survive in the stomach, scientists and physicians at the time felt justified in dismissing the claim.

The key point with this theory is that what is accepted as truth depends on whether a claim fits into the *jigsaw* of what we already know is already believed to be true.

Generally speaking, the *pragmatic theory of truth* says that a claim is true if it is useful. There are several versions of the pragmatic theory, which might be considered a blend of the correspondence and coherence theories. The philosopher William James (1842–1910) believed that the truth of any knowledge claim is confirmed if it is effective when applied in practice – in other words, if it coheres with our already-held truths and works when applied in the world. In a rather extreme example, James argued that if the idea of God *works*, then it is *true*. This raises an important question about who decides what is useful.

The *consensus theory of truth* says that if people generally agree on something, it is true. It is not generally regarded as a reliable way of establishing truth; however, it is a method that is often used in practice. When we are unsure of something, we will often ask our friends. If our friends reach a consensus, we might often take it as truth. Similarly, if our culture agrees that something is true, we may accept it unquestioningly. It could be argued that the justice system partially relies on a consensus theory of truth to determine whether the accused is innocent or guilty.

According to the *pluralist theory of truth*, there are various meanings of truth depending on the context or area of knowledge. This assumes that subject-specific truth might vary in the context of historical knowledge or scientific knowledge. For example, in history there may be historical facts that are true, or historical interpretations that vary in their degree of truth. In the context of science, a scientific claim could be considered to have a truth value if it has not yet been falsified. The key point is that there is no single meaning of truth, and the meaning of truth depends on the context or area of knowledge.

According to the *redundancy theory of truth*, the word *truth* either makes no sense, or is unnecessary, given that it can be substituted for another word. For example, if I claim, *'It is true that Dhaka is the capital of Bangladesh'*, we do not need to use the word 'truth', and instead we can simply claim, *'Dhaka is the capital of Bangladesh'*. The key point is that truth has no general meaning or essential property, and is not needed.

> **CROSS REFERENCE**
>
> Theories of truth are explained in more detail in Chapter 4 of the Course Guide.

TASK: ACTIVITY 4.2

- Evaluate the following question as a pair or small group: *'Does truth have a single meaning, or do different areas of knowledge interpret the meaning of truth in different ways?'*

- Think of one or two specific concrete examples that you could use to support your points in relation to the question.

Can language describe the truth?

If we evaluate the correspondence theory of truth, a question arises about how far words can correspond to the world around us. Truth is difficult to describe, and some truths are not easily expressed in words.

If a map is a metaphor for knowledge, there is a difference between the actual territory in the real world, and the map which is a depiction of this territory. If the truth is the territory, then our knowledge – like the map – is a representation of that reality.

Objective truth is the idea that truth is in some sense independent of someone's own personal experience and knowledge.

The implication is that someone might not be able to know the truth about the world around them; instead, they can know how they perceive it to be. Some people might claim that it makes no sense to talk about a truth that cannot be known. On the other hand, if truth is reduced to a meaningless word, or to the same thing as someone's opinion, it might be said to have lost something of its essential meaning. When people speak about truth, they assume that they are making sense and referring to something beyond their own opinion. This is why the relationship between language and meaning is an important question to consider.

4.3 Is there truth in ethics?

If you know there is a cup of coffee on your desk, you can observe it. The knowledge claim appears to correspond to a fact about the world. However, if someone claims that it is wrong to cause animals to suffer, there is no such fact to which this claim corresponds. This raises a question about whether there are ethical facts, and what might justify an ethical truth claim. In short, are ethical claims based on some type of truth, or any degree of truth?

REAL-LIFE SITUATION 4.3

Examples of work being done by governments and non-governmental organisations (NGOs) to address ethical issues with a global or international perspective include:

- the work of Greenpeace to address the environmental issues, global warming and Greenland's melting ice sheet

- the work of UNICEF and its partners to run vaccination programmes and to save the lives of children.

Consider how these examples relate to the idea of ethical truth.

Truth and ethical theories

How we feel seems to influence our judgement of right and wrong – we may instantly feel repulsion to horrific acts. Our moral knowledge might be based on a gut feeling – an intuition that enables us to know the difference between right and wrong. For example, some people feel that the use of animal experiments in the development of pharmaceutical drugs is intuitively wrong. However, you may be able to put forward reasoned arguments to support or oppose the use of animal experiments independently of how you feel about the issue. Although we may have an intuitive sense of right and wrong, our intuition raises a number of questions. We might want to know the extent to which this "gut reaction" is the result of our up-bringing, our cultural values, or our life experiences. We might also question whether this intuition we have is due to a deeply held value system and belief framework, or whether it connects with a more universal 'truth'. And how can we know?

Although we often respond emotionally to ethical problems, there is usually a rational basis to our feelings of right and wrong. There are three main categories of ethical theory: deontological theories, consequentialist theories and virtue ethics. Deontological theories suggest actions are good or bad according to a clear set of rules. The philosopher, Immanuel Kant (1724-1804) is the main proponent of deontological ethics and believed that there is a universal moral law that all people are obliged to follow. He called this law the Categorical Imperative, and it is that we should always act in a way that we would be willing for it to be a general law that everyone else in similar circumstances should follow. For example, we should not steal if we would not want everyone else to be allowed to steal. Kant argued that it would be irrational not to obey this universal moral law. Some people regard the Categorical Imperative as a universal truth that all people have a duty to obey, regardless of their circumstances and their emotional state.

Consequentialist theories decide whether actions are good or bad based on the outcomes or consequences of those actions. According to these theories, the more 'good' an action produces, the better the action. Some people would regard it as true that a good action is one that produces the best outcomes for the largest number of people.

Virtue ethics is quite different in that rather than trying to distinguish between good and bad behaviours, it considers the moral character of the person carrying out the action. According to this theory, the same actions can be good or bad depending on the circumstances, and virtue is a moral characteristic that is developed by living virtuously. For example, a virtue ethicist might say that fighting can be good or bad depending on the circumstances, and a virtuous person would only fight if it were right and just to do so. Virtue ethics prompts people to ask, '*What sort of person do I want to be?*' and '*How can I become that sort of person?*' Some people would regard it as true that there are key virtues such as wisdom, justice, self-care and faithfulness.

Ethical theories are designed to help us know what is the morally right course of action, but they all fall short in some way. If we take the case of helping a terminally-ill person to die, a deontological approach might argue that human life is inherently valuable, and that our duty is always to preserve life, so euthanasia is wrong. However, an alternative deontological argument would be that we have a duty to reduce suffering, so if a terminally ill person is suffering in a way that cannot be relieved by anything other than death, we have a duty to help them die.

Similarly, a consequentialist might argue that death does not enhance the well-being of a terminally-ill person, and could have wider negative consequences for the person's family and the wider society, so it would be wrong to help them to die. Equally another consequentialist might argue that by helping a terminally-ill person to die, we are reducing that person's suffering, and this could have positive consequences for the person's family and the wider society.

TASK: THINK ABOUT 4.1

Consider how truth relates to any these key concepts: responsibility, values, ethical considerations.

A virtue ethicist might ask, '*Do I want to be the kind of person who helps to bring an end to a human life?*' or they might ask, '*Do I want to be the kind of person who will help to end a person's suffering?*'

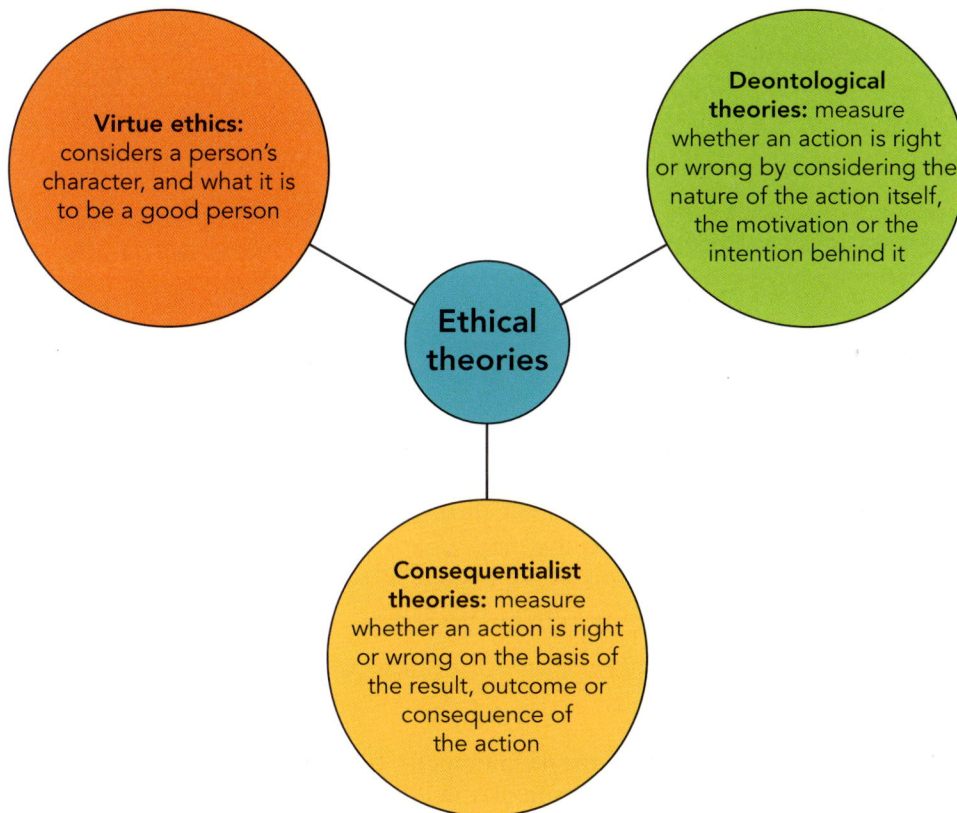

Figure 4.3: Ethical theories

As we can see, while ethical theories can provide us with a rational framework in which to discuss ethical problems, they do not absolve us from taking personal responsibility for our actions. There is no single answer that they unequivocally point us to.

People are unlikely to agree on all matters of ethical principle, but it is important that you support your position with reasoned arguments, and factual evidence where possible. For example, a disagreement about whether it is possible to regulate euthanasia might be resolved by looking at evidence from countries where euthanasia is legal. Similarly, you might investigate evidence behind the argument that legalising euthanasia could expose vulnerable people to feel pressured to end their lives.

The relationship between ethics and truth is complex, and there is no single answer, but ethical theories provide us with a moral map that can help us to clarify and navigate complex ethical issues.

CROSS REFERENCE

For further discussion of various ethical theories, see Chapter 3 of the Course Guide.

TASK: THINK ABOUT 4.2

'We know that an action is ethical because of the intentions behind the action, not the consequences it produces'. Evaluate this knowledge claim, exploring how we gain ethical knowledge.

Construct clear and coherent arguments to support both sides of the question, and for each one, think of at least three points to back up the case and three to argue against it:

1   we know that an action is ethical because of the intentions behind the action

2   we know that an action is ethical because of the consequences following from the action

3   we know that an action is ethical if it is performed by a virtuous person.

Evaluate each of these arguments, identify any assumptions and think through the implications of each argument. Decide which on balance is the most clear, coherent and compelling, and why.

4.4 Knowledge questions

1   Consider the definition of knowledge as 'justified true belief', the definition of knowledge proposed and later refuted by Plato. What role does truth play in the construction of knowledge in different areas?

2   How far are ethical knowledge claims a matter of personal preference or truth?

4.5 Exhibition task

Identify how truth relates to the world around us. Explore how truth relates to one or more of these categories:

- language in a local, national or international news story

- cultural norms and practices

- technology such as artificial intelligence (AI) or big data

- political propaganda such as fake news

- religious beliefs about what is sacred, or the practices of a world religion

- a disagreement between experts on a particular area of knowledge

- different textbook interpretations of the same historical event

- a scientific discovery that produces new knowledge or new ways of thinking.

For each category, think of a specific artefact or artefacts that links one of the items above with truth.

1   Choose three objects, and identity their specific real-world context.

2   Select one of the IA prompts that connect with your objects.

3   Justify how each object relates to your chosen IA prompt.

4.6 Extended writing task

Write 500 words on one of the following questions:

1   How far does knowledge depend on truth?

2   Is truth the same in two areas of knowledge?

3   Can we be sure about what counts as truth in the natural sciences and history?

4   How do we decide what is truth?

SKILLS SELF-ASSESSMENT CHECKLIST

Reflect on what you have learned in this chapter and indicate your confidence level between 1 and 5 (where 5 is the highest score and 1 is the lowest). If you score below 3, revisit that section. Come back to this list later in your course. Has your confidence grown?

	Confidence level	Revisited?
Can I identify and explore how the concept of truth relates to knowledge, knowing and the world around us?		
Am I able to evaluate a relativist view of truth and an objective view of truth?		
Can I explain how the concept of truth relates to knowledge and knowing?		
Am I aware of different theories of truth, and can I evaluate ethical knowledge claims?		

4.7 Further reading

For further discussion on the roles of truth and ethics today, read: H. Gardner, *Truth, Beauty and Goodness Reframed*, Basic Books New York, 2012

For a discussion of the concept of truth with Melvyn Bragg and guest philosophers, see the BBC podcast on Truth, *In Our Time*

For an exploration of different types of truth, read: Julian Baggini, *A Short History of Truth: Consultations for a Post-Truth World*, Quercus, 2017

> Part 2

Optional Themes

> Chapter 5

Knowledge and technology

LEARNING INTENTIONS

In this chapter, you will develop your skills to explore and analyse the impact of technology on knowledge and knowing. You will also develop your awareness of how technology has influenced knowledge throughout time. You will refine your skills to evaluate the benefits and risks that technology poses for the knower today – in particular, the ways in which technology is influencing how knowledge is produced, shared and used, and what it means to know something about the world around you today.

You will:

- evaluate knowledge questions that relate to technology

- discuss whether an expert has to be a human, and the implications of artificial intelligence for knowledge and knowing

- analyse how our perspective of the world around us might be changed by echo chambers created via social media and the existence of deepfake videos

- analyse the ways in which technology might extend our sense perception and cognition via augmented and virtual reality

CONTINUED

- evaluate the reliability of the technological methods and tools

- explore the concept of big data, who controls data, what is done with it and how far we can trust the systems that underpin the sharing of information

- identify and evaluate different ethical questions and issues associated with technology and knowledge

- hone your writing skills, in particular, your use of real-life examples to support an argument about the impact of knowledge on knowledge and knowing, and the implications that follow

- further develop your analysis of the relationship between technology and knowledge by exploring how technology connects with other areas of knowledge and the world around us.

BEFORE YOU START

1   How can we know the opportunities and risks posed by developments in technology such as big data and artificial intelligence?

2   Does a knower have to be a living being, or can a machine think and know?

3   Who decides what is an ethical use of technology, and how can we evaluate the impact of technology on the knower if and when experts disagree?

5.1 Introduction

Technology includes a vast array of *know-how* such as equipment and machinery, which have made astonishing achievements possible – from the building of the Taj Mahal in India and the invention of printing presses in China and Europe to the scientific research made possible by the International Space Station.

Digital technology such as **big data** is changing the way we create knowledge and share information, and changing what it means to know something. This chapter focuses on digital technology and the *information age*, in which rapid advances such as the internet, mobile devices and **social media** platforms present new opportunities and challenges for knowledge and knowing.

Technology is not only useful in its own right; it is a tool for extending our senses and our cognition. Developments in **artificial intelligence (AI)** also raise the question about whether machines can truly 'know', and the future of human knowledge; these developments even influence the way we might think about the nature of knowledge itself. Meanwhile, the increasing use of technology has led to many ethical questions. Artificial intelligence that is used for roles traditionally performed by humans raises questions about the future of work and what happens to ethical and empathetic decision making. In this chapter, you will develop the skills to navigate this territory and evaluate these questions.

KEY TERMS

big data: large data sets that can be combined in new ways to identify patterns and trends that may not be obvious to human knowers

social media: websites, platforms and apps that allow people to create networks as well as share digital content and information with one another

KEY TERMS

artificial intelligence (AI): the capacity for machines to perform the functions usually associated with human thinking, intelligence and cognition such as voice recognition; or the capability of a computer to teach itself or do 'deep learning'

TOK LINK: SCIENCE

CRISPA, the gene editing tool, is an example of how technology can be closely connected with science as an area of knowledge.

Do you think science causes changes in technology, or technological inventions cause changes in science? What implications does this have for the development of knowledge in science and technology?

TOK IN YOUR LIFE

Think about how your use of social media platforms, such as Instagram™, WhatsApp™, TikTok™ or Snapchat™ etc, might influence what you know.

5.2 The scope of technology

What is the relationship between technology and the knower?

Technology is very broad and all encompassing – from pen and paper to the technical instruments used for navigation, is not a single subject. If considered simply as the equipment, machinery and tools to perform a task, technology would have little impact on knowledge and knowing. However, developments in technology such as the internet, search engines and social media are changing the way we find and share information. For example, search engine algorithms determine which sites arise in our internet searches, and these strongly influence what we read. Further, technology is changing the nature of what it means to know something. Increasingly, machines and computers are having an impact on what and how we know.

TOK IN YOUR LIFE

In what ways does digital technology influence the way you search for information? Do you think that the information you find online counts as knowledge? Why? Why not? Identify two or more specific real-life examples to illustrate the distinction between information and knowledge.

TASK: ACTIVITY 5.1

Explore the following questions as a class. Write each question on a large sheet of paper. Then working in small groups, take it in turns to move around the classroom, adding your responses to each question. Continue until you have added as many responses as possible to each sheet. Then evaluate the responses to each question and discuss your evaluation of the questions as a class. Your responses could include:

- key analytical points in relation to the question

CONTINUED

- specific concrete examples to support the arguments for and the counter-arguments against

- an analysis using elements of the knowledge framework: scope, perspectives, tools and methods, and ethics

- the implications of the arguments and counter-arguments.

1 In what ways do you think digital technology influences the way you find information or gain knowledge?

2 What does the use of digital technology such as an internet search tell you about the distinction between information and knowledge?

3 In what ways does digital technology influence what it means to know something?

Does a knower or an expert have to be human?

Knowledge has been perceived as the domain of humans and other sentient beings. This perspective might include the know-how that animals possess in order to navigate and survive in their environment. However, if an expert is the *go-to* source on a given topic, a smart phone could be seen as more of an expert than a human: a smart phone's computing power enables it to be the *go-to* source of information – from apps that will find nearby restaurants to those that will help you navigate your way to an unknown destination.

This has significant implications for the nature of knowing. If we define were to knowledge as the capacity to process information, computers have this already. But do computers have the capacity to think and to be knowers? Computers can have weak artificial intelligence, which is the capacity of software to perform a specific reasoning or problem-solving task. Computers can also have strong artificial intelligence, which is the capacity to perform some of the same cognitive tasks that a human can but as yet they cannot do this with the same autonomy as a human.

Significantly, tasks that humans might consider to be ordinary, such as tying shoelaces, speaking or walking, are very difficult to replicate in machines. This is because these tasks are far from simple to programme, and involve multiple cognitive and physical processes (although recently, **androids** have been created that can perform gymnastics!). On the other hand, it is relatively straightforward to programme a computer to sift through huge amounts of information, such as multiple medical scans, to spot patterns that a human would find difficult or impossible to identify. This points to the fact that we mean slightly different things by human intelligence and machine intelligence. Human intelligence includes the cognitive ability to solve problems, emotional intelligence to empathise with feelings and social intelligence to know what appropriate behaviour and language is in a given context. By contrast, machine intelligence is capable of certain aspects of human intelligence, including: learning, playing and winning games such as AlphaGo™ against human world champions, and speech recognition and language learning via **chat bots** and visual recognition. However, it is not yet capable of compassion, empathy or humour. Nor is it able to understand what is considered appropriate human interaction in a social situation.

> **KEY TERMS**
>
> **android:** a robot that looks like a person
>
> **chat bot:** technology where a computer can simulate human conversation

Chat bots are a significant example of machine learning that has implications for knowledge and knowing. Chat bots are programmed to have conversations with humans that replicate ordinary conversation. However, unlike conversation in the context of human relationships, there is currently no meaning, emotion or intended purpose behind a computer's response. Instead, a computer is simply repeating learned words, and it comes no closer to *knowing* the human it is *talking* to than before the conversation occurred.

REAL-LIFE SITUATION 5.1

Google DeepMind™ is an example of machine learning, where **algorithms** can learn from raw data and are not pre-programmed by humans.

1   Can a machine acquire knowledge?

2   What implications does AI have for the future of human knowledge and knowing?

KEY TERMS

algorithm: a set of rules typically to be followed by a computer

TOK LINK: THE ARTS

Ian McEwan's novel *Machines Like Us* (2019) explores various ethical dilemmas including the capacity of a machine to understand the human heart. In what ways might the arts help us to explore the questions arising from technology such as AI?

TASK: ACTIVITY 5.2

Watch a clip online of Yuval Noah Harari's *Talks at Google* interview, where he discusses his book *21 Lessons for the 21st Century* and the role of AI and the future of technology.

Then analyse one of the following knowledge questions, with a particular focus on thinking through the implications.

1   In what ways is digital technology influencing what it means to know something?

2   Can a machine know something, or does a knower have to be a human?

3   Artificial intelligence can be used for roles traditionally performed by human knowers. Evaluate what this means for human empathy and decision making.

Consider and weigh up different perspectives, and reach a conclusion.

•   What are the implications of your conclusion?

•   How does your argument link to knowledge and knowing?

TOK LINK: OTHER AREAS OF KNOWLEDGE

What counts as a technological development in a particular area of knowledge such as maths, the natural and human sciences, history or the arts? What impact does technological development have on knowledge and knowing in one area of knowledge?

Figure 5.1: The app known as Shazam™ can 'listen to' and recognise a piece of music, and then display the song title and singer. Does it follow that a smart phone really knows this music? Why? Why not?

5.3 Technology and perspective

Technology influences the expression and transmission of knowledge over time – from the quill, the pen and the printing press to the keyboard. Technology gives us the potential to pursue knowledge, and yet with this opportunity comes a risk, therefore it is important to evaluate the balance. On the one hand, technology enables us to create networks and access information never seen before. It can facilitate global connections that allow people to form relationships, share information and create new networks. Whereas more traditional communities of knowers rely on a physical space to meet up, these *virtual communities* extend the range of our networks as the encounters take place in virtual cyber-space. The consequence of this new ability to communicate can impact on who we can get to know, how we can work in new ways and how we can interact with one another.

On the other hand, technology poses various risks to knowledge and knowing. **Deepfake videos** can show people speaking words that are not their own; this creates the appearance of reality, but is actually fake. Arguably, this could be used creatively and for neutral purposes. In China, this technology, via an app known as Zao™, allows ordinary people

KEY TERM

deepfake video: an edited video that shows a person speaking someone else's words, but making it appear as they are their own words

to swap faces with a TV or film star so that their own face appears in the film. The technology uses an uploaded selfie to make it look like you appear in the film.

Deepfake videos, however, could be used or misused with dangerous consequences. For example, a video of the Speaker of the US House of Representatives, Nancy Pelosi (1940–) was manipulated by editing it to show her stammer during a news conference, and this deepfake video was released by her political opponents. Many people who saw the video believed it was real. The technology to alter videos creates a problem for the knower, given that we cannot automatically trust the veracity of a video if, unbeknown to us, it is a deepfake. Moreover, some people have claimed that unfavourable videos of themselves are deepfakes, although they are in fact real: an attempt to blame technology for their misdeeds. Deepfake videos can therefore be used as a tool for propaganda, and have the potential to manipulate our perspective. However, an awareness of their existence and use might make us think more critically about video content that we might previously have accepted at face value. Deepfakes might make us less trusting of content we see online.

Social media can create **echo chambers** that reinforce narrow perspectives. The film *The Great Hack* (2019) explores the story of how a data company, Cambridge Analytica™, used private data to influence the opinions of undecided voters in multiple elections and political campaigns across the globe, including the 2017 US Presidential election and the 2016 UK Brexit referendum. This example illustrates the capacity of unknown organisations to use data and social media to influence perspectives.

Digital technology gives individuals the potential platform to create content, influence opinion and own private data. In this way, technology supports freedom of expression, but it also grants individuals an unaccountable degree of influence. For example, social media influencers and **Vloggers** can attract large followings. Felix Arvid Ulf Kjellberg (1989–), better known as PewDiePie, is a Swedish YouTuber with over 101 million subscribers. This means that technology makes it possible for one individual to have unprecedented power to comment and influence others, which raises questions about the freedom and responsibility of popular individuals on social media. Moreover Mark Zuckerberg (1984–), as the majority share-holder of Facebook™, owns vast amounts of personal data, raising questions about the responsibility of one individual in relation to **data privacy** of millions of users of the social media platform.

KEY TERMS

echo chamber: in the context of technology, the effect created by social media whereby people only encounter beliefs or opinions like their own, so they do not consider alternative ideas, and their own ideas are reinforced

vlogger: someone who posts videos online to a website

TASK: ACTIVITY 5.3

How does digital technology influence the formation of new tribes and community connections?

Look up the BBC Digital Human™ article 'What do modern tribes look like'? Listen to the embedded clips as you read the article, and evaluate the impact of technology on our identity, personal perspective and the groups we connect with. How do our beliefs influence the way we think about and use technology?

KEY POINT

Social media can be manipulated to function as an *echo chamber* to reinforce a person's existing prejudices. Companies have been known to use private data without consent to influence opinion, with the intention of shaping how people might vote in an election.

REAL-LIFE SITUATION 5.2

Bill Posters and Daniel Howe are famous for creating a deepfake video of Mark Zuckerberg in 2019. They have created an exhibition known as *Spectre*, using art to explore issues around how giant technology companies use personal data, AI, machine learning and deepfake videos.

Look up:

- Spectre exhibition launch – Bill Posters

- *'Spectre: A Detour Into Dataism'* (Short Film)

TASK: ACTIVITY 5.4

Find an example of a deepfake video, or try making your own. If you make your own please take ethical considerations into account such as consent and privacy.

5.4 Methods and tools

From magnifying glasses to microscopes and telescopes, technology offers a tool for extending our senses and our cognition. As technology develops, so too do our methods for gaining knowledge – for example, statistical analysis is made easier by the sorting of data in a spreadsheet.

However, technology does not just assist the processing and interpretation of data. It is also changing the scope of what it is possible to know. Wearable technology, such as a smartwatch, gathers biometric data which can monitor and track patterns in a person's health. This was impossible before the invention of these wearable devices.

Other technological developments, like big data, increase the possibility of finding new patterns and trends that would otherwise be unknown. Big data involves large volumes of data. For example, in China payments are mostly made via mobile digital payment apps, therefore there is a huge amount of information and data about the sale and purchases made by a vast population of people. Big data is more than large data; it combines data sets in new ways. For example, weather reports can be combined with health reports to establish the correlation between the two data sets. This combination makes it possible to establish connections between seemingly disparate sets of information.

Big data raises ethical issues, such as the responsibility of organisations that collect, store and interpret data, the right to data privacy of individuals, and the use of individuals' private data without their consent.

REAL-LIFE SITUATION 5.3

The city of Toronto in Canada is home to a diverse community, including the Inuit and Métis peoples. A project known as *Sidewalk* offers a technologically smart urban environment where people in Toronto can live in an affordable and sustainable community.

However, there is a community group that is concerned about the ethical issues of this project, including the right to privacy. Increasingly, **data rights** such as

---

KEY TERM

data rights: the laws that protect an individual's rights with respect to their personal data

CONTINUED

the right to access and the right to be forgotten are recognised as important by organisations and governments.

1   How do we know what is our right to privacy in a digital age?

2   What ethical considerations should influence the ways that digital data is gathered, stored and used?

Augmented reality and **virtual reality** offer new ways of extending what we as humans can perceive. A virtual reality headset such as an Oculus Rift™ is a device that uses a visual display, and sound and eye tracking sensors to generate a simulated world that appears real – an alternative reality. There are many uses of this type of technology – from learning to fly through flight simulation to the fantasy worlds of gaming.

People known as *transhumanists* upgrade their bodies with microchip implants and other technologies which can increase their sense perception. For example, Kevin Warwick (1954–) is an engineer who has had various operations to connect his body with machine technology. This raises ethical and scientific questions about whether transhumanists have the potential to know more than humans, and whether all humans in the future will need to become transhumanists to keep up with the evolution of knowledge and knowing.

KEY TERMS

augmented reality: technology that overlays a computer simulated digital world onto the world around us

virtual reality: technology that creates a simulated environment or world, such as in a computer game or a headset

TASK: ACTIVITY 5.5

Find out more about transhumanism by looking up *'BBC Transhumanism'*. Think about what this means for sense perception, knowledge and knowing.

Figure 5.2: In what ways might developments in technology influence our sense perception?

TASK: ACTIVITY 5.6

Discuss the following questions in pairs or small groups. In your discussion, develop your awareness of different perspectives and views, and evaluate the different perspectives or viewpoints in response to each:

1   In what ways might technology such as augmented and virtual reality extend our sense perception and knowledge?

2   Do you think humans will need to use technology, or merge with computers, in order to keep up with the evolution of knowledge?

3   How would humans be able to evaluate whether this will help or hinder the knower?

5.5 Ethics and technology

TOK IN YOUR LIFE

Have you ever clicked on something online that you regret? Are there some things that you think it is wrong to search for on the internet?

How can technology help you to create a better life for yourself and others? What are the ethical issues surrounding technology?

TASK: ACTIVITY 5.7

Read the online article, *'The rise of facial recognition technology'* published by the *Guardian* on 5th October 2019.

Evaluate the ethical and unethical uses of facial recognition technology. While it could be used for positive reasons such as to find missing persons, it could also be used to create a surveillance state. How far do you think it infringes on our right to privacy? How do we know?

Technology can be used to heal or to harm. Technologies such as the atom bomb, the guillotine and the electric chair raise serious ethical questions. On the other hand, the development of vaccinations, central heating and sewers have had obvious benefits for humanity. Developments in technology raise new questions relating to the ethical responsibilities of the inventors, producers and users of technology, and it is important for us to be able to consider and evaluate the ethics of technology from all perspectives. For example, driverless cars raise new questions about how cars should be programmed, and the responsibilities that go with the invention.

Digital technology theoretically allows us free and unlimited access to information for the first time. However, there are significant ethical issues surrounding big data, including who controls data and what is done with it. Cathy O'Neil (1972–) makes the point that we should not blindly trust the uses of big data, in her TED Talk™, *'The era of blind faith in big data'*. Further, we cannot assume that technology is neutral. O'Neil also argues that algorithms can make false or biased assumptions based on gender, race, and age. Algorithms are invented by humans, and are just as prone to bias as the humans who create them; therefore technology might contribute to unequal access or prejudice.

Hacktivism is the use or mis-use of technology for a political or social purpose. Some people would describe *hacktivists* as subversive misusers of computers or even cyber-terrorists, but others would describe their activities as justified in the name of free speech or freedom of information.

Our private data can also be misused to conduct mass surveillance by governments, as in the case of Edward Snowden (1983–).

REAL-LIFE SITUATION 5.4

Edward Snowden, is a US citizen who worked for the Central Intelligence Agency (CIA). In 2013, he leaked information from the National Security Agency (NSA) which showed the US government was accessing and using the private data of people. People disagree in their interpretation of Snowden's actions – for some he is a *traitor* to the US government for leaking the information, and to others he is a *hero* for championing the right to privacy. These contrasting descriptions show people can have very different interpretations of the same person or event, and also raise issues about language.

You could watch the film Snowden (2016), which explores his life and reflect on the questions arising relating to knowledge, authority, freedom and privacy.

Look up:

1   Can we be sure if technology increases or limits individual freedom and autonomy?

2   In what ways are governments responsible for the collection and use of data?

3   In what ways does technology raise political questions?

Figure 5.3: Edward Snowden speaking from Russia to an audience in Lisbon, Portugal in 2019. What ethical responsibilities relate to the uses of technology and the production and sharing of knowledge?

Social media also raises questions and provokes criticisms about the time we spend using it and how far it disconnects us from real physical interactions. One counter-argument to this is that social media allows groups to communicate in new and effective ways. However, the growth of internet use has not only had an impact on humans but also on the environment. A vast amount of power, space and electricity is needed to store and servers that make the internet function. Moreover, as the **internet of things** increases, and we rely on the web for more things like ordering our food shopping and switching on our house alarm, so too our dependency on digital technology for our lifestyles and survival.

Another ethical issue relates to the future of human knowledge. If AI develops to the point of singularity, where machine intelligence surpasses human intelligence, we cannot predict what will happen to human knowledge. So while technology is a tool invented by humans for our use, it may in fact jeopardise the future of human knowledge. We might therefore question what technology is for, and we might argue that technology should be used in a way to enhance our knowledge for ethical purposes, to create a fairer and better world.

> **KEY TERM**
>
> **internet of things:** the use of the internet to control devices and equipment in the world around you, such as an app that will switch a house alarm on and off

TASK: ACTIVITY 5.8

Discuss the following questions in pairs or small groups. Think of one or two specific concrete examples that you could use in response to these questions.

1   What are the responsibilities of the creators of technology? How do we decide what these responsibilities are?

2   How do we know what ethical considerations should influence the uses of digital technology?

TOK IN YOUR LIFE

How digitally dependent are you? How far do you depend on a smart phone or other mobile device, and what impact does this have? What do you think are the ethical issues relating to the creation and use of digital technology?

Take the online 'BBC digital dependency quiz' to find out how dependent you are, and evaluate the reliability of the method used by the questionnaire.

TOK LINK: SCIENCE AND THE ARTS

Are the ethical considerations that apply to technology the same as those that apply to the sciences and arts?

5.6 Knowledge questions

1   To what extent is technology changing the nature of knowledge and knowing?

2   What ethical considerations and responsibilities should influence how technology is used in the pursuit of knowledge?

3   Can we be sure if a computer can know something?

5.7 Exhibition task

Consider how you might use a technological example as an item for your TOK exhibition. Identify how technology relates to knowledge and knowing. Also explore how technology relates to one or more of these categories:

- a local, national or international news story that relates to technology

- technology in relation to cultural norms and practices

- developments in technology such as AI, big data or 'transhumans'

- effects of technology such as echo chambers, fake news or deepfake videos.

Think of a specific artefact or artefacts that links technology with one of the categories above.

1   Choose three objects, and identity their specific real-world context.

2   Select one of the IA prompt questions that connect with your objects.

3   Justify how each object relates to your chosen IA prompt.

4   Write 250–300 words on the real-world context of the technological artefact, and how it links to your chosen IA prompt.

> **TOP TIP**
>
> When you select an artefact for your exhibition, be sure to choose something with a real-world context. A technological object could include a 280-word tweet™ produced by a particular person at a particular time, or a specific article from a particular news website. Rather than general artefacts, select a specific artefact that relates to your chosen IA prompts, and which manifests TOK in the world around you.

5.8 Extended writing task

Write 400–600 words on one of the following questions:

1   How might technology extend the range of our sense perception?

2   Can we be sure if technology helps or hinders us as knowers?

3   How far does technology lead to reliable knowledge?

SKILLS SELF-ASSESSMENT CHECKLIST

Reflect on what you have learned in this chapter and indicate your confidence level between 1 and 5 (where 5 is the highest score and 1 is the lowest). If you score below 3, revisit that section. Come back to this list later in your course. Has your confidence grown?

	Confidence level	Revisited?
Can I evaluate knowledge questions that relate to technology?		
Am I able to discuss whether an expert has to be a human being?		
Can I consider the implications of artificial intelligence for knowledge and knowing?		
Can I analyse how our perspective might be changed by echo chambers created via social media and the existence of deepfake videos?		
Can I identify and evaluate different perspectives of technology?		
Am I able to analyse the ways in which technology might extend our sense perception and cognition via augmented and virtual reality?		
Am I able to explain and evaluate the reliability of the technological methods and tools, and how far we can trust the systems that underpin the sharing of information?		
Can I identify and evaluate different ethical questions and issues associated with technology and knowledge?		
Am I able to construct my own arguments, and offer examples to support my points?		
Am I able to identify knowledge claims and arguments that make assumptions that are taken for granted?		

5.9 Further reading

For an examination of the role of algorithms, read: Hannah Fry, *Hello World: How to be Human in the Age of the Machine*, W. W. Norton and Company, 2019

For a discussion of big data, read: Timandra Harkness, *Big Data: Does Size Matter?* Bloomsbury Sigma, 2016

For a discussion of the role of AI and the future of technology, read: Yuval Noah Harari, *21 Lessons for the 21st Century*, Vintage, 2018

> Chapter 6

Knowledge and language

LEARNING INTENTIONS

In this chapter, you will develop your skills to explore and analyse the relationship between language, knowledge and knowing. You will also develop your awareness of the richness and sophistication of language for sharing and communicating knowledge.

You will:

* identify and evaluate the nature and scope of language, what language is and what language is not and the importance of language for the knower
* analyse knowledge questions and develop the skills to construct an argument and a counter-argument, including the extent to which language influences what we know and the way we think about the world around us
* evaluate how language can express your own perspective and influence your viewpoint
* identify how specific examples or evidence can be used to make an analytical point about language and knowledge
* analyse knowledge claims by identifying assumptions behind them and the implications that follow

CONTINUED

- analyse language as a tool for description, communication, persuasion and expression of values
- analyse the ways in which language can be used to influence and persuade, in the context of power relationships
- identify and evaluate different ethical questions and issues associated with language and knowledge, and the responsibilities involved with language.

BEFORE YOU START

1   The world around you depends on language, but how much do you know and understand about the science of language and how it works, including the anatomical, cognitive and social aspects of language?

2   If every civilisation and culture that has ever existed has had spoken language, does it follow that the same concepts and ideas can be expressed in, or translated into, every language?

3   How far does your language express what you know, influence what you know or determine how you think?

6.1 Introduction

Language is universal. In its broadest sense, language is to do with our intended communication, words, sounds and gestures. It is a way to communicate our knowledge, and pass it between different cultures and onwards to the next generation.

In this chapter you will develop the skills to navigate this complex and fascinating territory, and evaluate the opportunities and challenges that language poses for the knower today – in particular, the ways in which language influences the way that knowledge is produced and shared.

6.2 The scope of language

Language can be thought of as the 6,500 or so spoken languages including French, Japanese, Russian, Spanish and English. You need language to describe the world, to share your thoughts and ideas and to express your experience of the world around you. The different vocabularies and grammatical constructions of each language means that the language you speak can have an enormous impact on your knowledge and knowing.

TASK: ACTIVITY 6.1

Working with a partner, sit back-to-back so you cannot see one another, with one of you holding a pen and paper. Think of a symbol and gives verbal instructions without saying what that symbol is, The person with the paper attempts to draw what they describe.

Reflect on what this shows you about the strengths and limits of language.

TOK LINK: SCIENCE

The development of speech and language in a human requires the Forkhead box protein P2, which is a protein encoded by the FOXP2 gene.

Think about the link between language and science. What can science tell us about the nature of language? What can language tell us about the nature of scientific knowledge?

What is the relationship between language and the knower?

The task of analysing language and its relationship with knowledge is particularly challenging given that we are constantly immersed in spoken language. Think about the number of words you have spoken today, or yesterday, or last week. Spoken language is a continual stream of sounds that we articulate to convey meaning, and when we listen to others speaking, we can make sense of words spoken by other people. This may seem like an obvious point, but it sheds light on the everyday *wonder* of language that we take for granted.

Every known human society has a spoken language. Language can be thought of as a technology that has evolved as a mechanism for producing and communicating thought and influencing beliefs. The science of language suggests that it is an extremely complex phenomenon which requires highly sophisticated biological and psychological processes, in addition to a rich social and cultural context.

Everyone has a mother tongue – the original language they were taught to speak as children. Some people are bilingual; others are multilingual, and the languages you speak relate to your social and cultural identity. There are some important distinctions to make between what is language and what is not language. These include:

1 *Distinctions between language, human communication and animal communication.* Not all communication is language. However, many animals, like humans, have a complex way of communicating, and this is a subject of study in its own right.

2 *A distinction between spoken language and written language.* Written language is specific to some (but not all) cultures and societies. Children need to be taught written language. Whereas children appear to pick up language and vocalise naturally, they need specific instruction to learn to write language.

3 *A distinction between spoken language and body language.* Body language is one way we communicate, often unconsciously. In contrast, sign languages are distinct languages that communicate through actions and gestures.

Learning a language and speaking (or signing) a language is the result of a complex process of knowing. But how does language relate to *what* we know? If you are bilingual or multilingual, you may be aware of problems with translating exact meanings from one language to another. Some people claim they think and feel differently when speaking different languages.

The 1958 novel *Things Fall Apart* by Nigerian author Chinua Achebe (1930–2013) is set in south-east Nigeria in the early-20th century. The author describes Igbo culture, and uses many Igbo words in the novel rather than translating them into English, as this would have inevitably watered down their meaning. For example, the word *obi* from the Igbo language means *hut*, but as soon as it is translated into English, we see our version of a hut and not Achebe's. This example suggests that words in a language have a meaning in their original cultural context which can become lost in translation.

TASK: ACTIVITY 6.2

In pairs, take it in turns to mime the following examples of everyday scenarios, and see if your partner can guess the scenario. Only use gestures and body language – do not use spoken words:

- eating a sandwich for lunch

- answering a phone call from a friend

- preparing to take your dog for a walk

- finishing a piece of IB Diploma Programme coursework on your computer.

Think about the outcome of this miming activity as you answer the following questions:

1 What is body language? How is it similar or different to spoken language?

2 What are the difficulties with trying to convey what we mean using only mime, body language and gesture?

3 What intended or unintended meanings might we communicate with our body language?

4 What does this activity suggest about the nature of communication and language? Identify specific examples you could use to support your analytical points.

How far does language influence what we know?

The Sapir-Whorf hypothesis – named after the American linguists Edward Sapir (1884–1939) and Benjamin Lee Whorf (1897–1941) – suggests that language does more than communicate our knowledge; it also determines or influences the way we think and what we can know. There are two versions of this theory:

1 the stronger version, known as **linguistic determinism**: language determines what we think and can know

2 the weaker version, known as **linguistic relativity**: language influences our thinking and shapes what we know.

These are debates to explore – can we know something without the words or language to express it? If we are articulate and fluent, are we regarded as knowledgeable?

The case for the Sapir-Whorf hypothesis

According to Edward Sapir, a language represents a unique social reality. For example, French speakers inhabit a particular language world that is distinct from that of Russian or Chinese speakers. Sapir claimed that we cannot inhabit an objective

KEY TERMS

linguistic determinism: the idea that language determines what we think and can know

linguistic relativity: the idea that language influences our thinking and shapes what we know

world, given that the language habits of the group we belong to limit and shape our interpretation of the world. This suggests that languages create different worlds and social realities, and that we think differently in different languages.

This naturally leads to the conclusion that translation from one language to another is highly problematic. And indeed, there may be words you can think of that are difficult to translate from one language to another. For example, in Japanese, the word 'wabi-sabi' is sometimes translated into English as *beauty*. However, the two concepts have distinct associations; the idea of *wabi-sabi* is based on the Buddhist idea of beauty found in imperfection, incompleteness and impermanence, in contrast to classical European ideas of beauty. The key point is that it is difficult to translate the exact meaning of the word *'beauty'* from one language to another. The implications of this are significant for knowledge and knowing.

> **CROSS REFERENCE**
>
> In Chapter 11 of the Course Guide, we further explore the concept of *wabi-sabi*, beauty and aesthetics.

Figure 6.1: A photo taken in November 2019 in Tokyo, Japan, which relates to the idea of imperfection and impermanence. The word *wabi* refers to the beauty found in the imperfect, the asymmetrical or the unbalanced. The word *sabi* relates to the beauty in things that are aged or impermanent. Do you think that the concept of *wabi-sabi* can be adequately translated?

KEY POINT

It is a fact of language that some people are incapable of thinking about things for which they have no conceptual framework. It could also be argued that all people are necessarily trapped in their own linguistic world.

TASK: THINK ABOUT 6.1

Discuss the following question with a partner or in a small group.

1   Is it possible to translate from one language to another with precision and accuracy? Think of specific examples from your own experience.

2   If you are bilingual or multilingual, do you think differently when you speak in different languages?

3   Do bilingual or multilingual people 'know more' than people who only speak one language?

Then consider the implications of these questions for translation, and the idea that language influences thoughts. What follows?

In what ways might our knowledge be influenced by our labels?

Benjamin Lee Whorf, a student of Edward Sapir, further developed Sapir's thinking during the 1930s. He claimed that language organises and classifies the world around us into concepts that have significance. How we classify the world around us then influences how we think about the world.

In the context of historical knowledge, when describing and explaining the past, language can highlight the bias of built-in **value judgements**. For example, you might consider whether it would be appropriate or not to use some of the following words to describe a person in history: hero, conqueror, pioneer, super-star, martyr, villain, coward, demon, tyrant, dictator, enemy. You might consider how far these words could count as descriptions of historical people based on their past actions, but also to what extent these words impose value judgements and bias. The historical question arising is how far neutral language can be used to describe and explain people and events.

Another example that shows why our classifications matter is in the everyday context of law, for example where a jury would need to decide whether a defendant is guilty of an action that would satisfy the definition of either murder or manslaughter.

KEY TERM

value judgement: a knowledge claim made about the worth, importance or value of something

TOK LINK: HISTORY

In the context of history, when describing and explaining the past, discuss whether the following language is justified and appropriate – and why or why not.

Words to describe and classify events in history: massacre, war, invasion, conquest, conflict, catastrophe, turning point, false dawn, golden age, backward, primitive, dangerous, ancient history, middle ages, Renaissance, enlightenment, modern history

Do these words offer descriptions or value judgements? How can we avoid bias in language when describing and explaining history?

TASK: ACTIVITY 6.3

Working with a partner or small group, discuss the following questions.

1   When we classify things into groups or categories, do the labels we attach matter? What implications might the labels have for the knower? Think of specific examples.

2   How does the organisation and classification in our language shape the way we think and the way we construct knowledge? Think of specific examples.

Evaluate your examples, and consider whether it follows that categories and labels influence how we think and what we know. What are the implications of this?

Edward Sapir's research supported the conclusion that there are cognitive differences in speakers of different languages – a claim that is contestable, and has since been challenged. Sapir used anthropological and linguistic studies of various peoples and cultures, with their unique languages as evidence to support the view that language relates to how people think.

The existence or non-existence of equivalent words has been used to promote the view that people who speak different languages actually think differently in the different languages they speak. For example, the native American Hopi, from Arizona USA, who, reportedly, had no word for *time*, were believed to think differently from people in cultures whose languages included the words *past*, *present* and *future*. However, linguist Ekkehart Malotki (1938–) challenged this idea and example, and suggested that it is a pseudo-example which does not support the conclusion that language influences thought.

Furthermore, some interesting studies have been carried out involving people who are fully fluent in more than one language. The authors of these studies claim that their subjects responded to questions very differently depending on the language in which the questions were asked. However, not everyone agrees that this would count as evidence that language determines or even influences thinking.

TASK: ACTIVITY 6.4

As a class, discuss the following questions:

*   What do the conflicting studies tell you about the reliability of evidence to support a theory?

*   What type of evidence – and how much evidence – is needed to justify a general conclusion?

TASK: THINK ABOUT 6.2

Consider the different fonts and words to describe text on a keyboard – from Comic Sans™ to Times New Roman™. Do you have a different emotional response to different fonts which might result in you thinking differently?

The case against the Sapir-Whorf hypothesis

The counter-argument to the Sapir-Whorf hypothesis is that thought does not depend on language. It is obvious that the same thought can be expressed in a variety of ways, implying that thinking is not constrained by language. For example, before young children begin to make sounds and learn to speak, there is clear evidence that they are thinking. As children learn language, they can use imagination to think of other worlds and other possible realities that they may have no words for. Furthermore, as a child, teenager or adult, you may have thoughts (for example, emotions or expressions of certain truths) that you cannot easily articulate in language. It does not follow that you do not know these things, just that language does not always seem adequate for conveying the intended meaning. Lastly, even languages that are very different from one another are nevertheless translatable to some degree, challenging the assumption that languages make us inhabit separate worlds that are entirely distinct from one another.

TOK IN YOUR LIFE

Can you express everything you know using language? Are there things you know that you cannot quite articulate with accuracy using words?

TOK LINK: TECHNOLOGY

Do you believe that language and/or technology can influence or even determine your thinking? What other factors might influence, shape or even determine thought?

TASK: ACTIVITY 6.5

Identify and evaluate the arguments for and against one of the versions of the Sapir-Whorf hypothesis.

1   Construct clear and coherent arguments in response to the hypothesis – think of at least three or more points to develop your argument and counter-argument.

2   Think of one or two specific concrete examples that you could use as evidence to support your argument and counter-argument.

3   Evaluate your arguments, identify any assumptions and think through the implications.

Reflect on how far your arguments are clear, coherent and compelling, and why.

TOK IN YOUR LIFE

Think of times when you have found it difficult to express what you mean, or when you have said something but failed to express what you really mean. Reflect on what this shows you about the ability of language to convey meaning with accuracy.

Can you have a non-verbal thought?

6.3 Language and perspective

In Chapter 1, we explored how our language is connected with our cultural heritage and identity as knowers. Linguist and philosopher Noam Chomsky (1928–) put forward the idea that regardless of the particular languages we happen to know as a result of our nationality and upbringing, we all share a natural capacity for language and grammatical structure. In other words, almost all humans will develop a language with rules of grammar such as nouns and verbs, regardless of their culture or experience. This suggests that language gives humans a common perspective which unites them. However, the words we use say something about our identity and the groups and language communities that we belong to. The words we choose allow us to share what we know and express our own perspective. Equally, language can influence our viewpoint.

REAL-LIFE SITUATION 6.1

An international language, known as Esperanto, was constructed by L. L. Zamenhof (1859–1917) in the 1880s, with the intention of promoting understanding and cooperation. Esperanto does not belong to any one country; it is one of the most spoken constructed languages in the world. The number of speakers is only around 2 million, and only a few thousand use it as a native language.

1   Would knowers be helped or hindered if they only had one common shared language?

2   What would be gained and lost if there was only one universal language?

3   What do you think would be the consequences and benefits of a universal language?

REAL-LIFE SITUATION 6.2

In 1990, an image of Earth was taken by the Voyager 1 spacecraft from a distance of 6 billion kilometres away. In this image, the Earth appeared as a pale blue dot.

Read the following text written by astronomer Carl Sagan (1934–1996), and respond to the questions on the following page.

'The Earth is a very small stage in a vast cosmic arena … Our posturing, our imagined self-importance, the delusion that we have some privileged position in the universe, are challenged by this point of pale light. Our planet is a lonely speck in the great enveloping cosmic dark … There is perhaps no better demonstration of the folly of human conceits than this distant image of our tiny world. To me, it underscores our responsibility to deal more kindly with one another, and to preserve and cherish the pale blue dot, the only home we've ever known.'

Carl Sagan, *Pale Blue Dot*, 1994

CONTINUED

1 Reflect on the language used by Carl Sagan to describe the place of our Earth in the vast expanse of the universe. Consider the meaning of the words: *'very small, point of pale light, lonely speck* and *home.'*

2 How far can language offer a new perspective?

3 Do you agree with Carl Sagan's perspective?

Figure 6.2: Astronomer Carl Sagan, who used the words *'pale blue dot'* to describe our planet within the perspective of cosmic space-time

How might language help or hinder the knower?

On the one hand, language might be said to help knowledge and knowing. One of the benefits of language is how it can enable us to share and communicate our ideas. When knowledge is communicated from one person to another, or from one generation to the next, language is an essential feature of that transmission. Without language, we cannot communicate what we know.

On the other hand, there are a number of ways in which language might be said to hinder knowledge and knowing; it can also be vague, ambiguous and misleading. Meaning is not fixed, and language is open to interpretation – this is the subjective nature of language. Nevertheless, the inherent ambiguity of language might also be thought of as one of its strengths.

Language and interpretation: denotation and connotation

The *denotation* of a word is what it literally describes, whereas the *connotations* are the associations of a word – both positive and negative. For example, single words whose literal meanings can be found in dictionaries carry subtle social and cultural associations connected to that word. The word *house* literally describes a building or the ability to shelter from the weather, but there are many associations connected with the word 'house' which are to do with safety and security, privacy, warmth or a place to invite friends. However, not everyone will share the same associations with the word *house* if they do not connect it with a positive experience. There are various associations to a single word, and it follows that language can have a rich meaning which is beyond plain factual description.

> **KEY TERM**
>
> **denotation:** the primary meaning of a word; the literal, direct, or explicit meaning
>
> **connotation:** the secondary meaning of a word; the feelings, associations and implicit meaning

> **TASK: THINK ABOUT 6.3**
>
> Discuss the denotation and connotation of these words: *knowledge, belief, opinion, observe, describe, explain, experiment, hypothesis, data, falsify, certainty, interpretation.*

6.4 Methods and tools

If language itself is a tool for self-expression, sharing ideas and describing the world around us, we can analyse the nature of it. In this section we consider how language relates to metaphors, models, labels and categories.

> **TOK LINK: SCIENCE**
>
> Find out more about the methods for studying the science of language.

Metaphors, models and language used to represent knowledge

> **TASK: THINK ABOUT 6.4**
>
> 1   Do you agree with the following quotation?
>
>   *'Whereof one cannot speak, thereof one must be silent.'*
>
>   **Wittgenstein** (1889–1951)
>
> 2   When have you found it difficult to put what you know into words?
>
> 3   Are there some areas of knowledge where this is a particular challenge?

Language plays a significant part in sharing and communicating what we know to others. Some types of knowledge are more open to interpretation than others. The use of **metaphors** in the construction of knowledge might make ideas easier to understand, and connect abstract ideas to the world around us. However, they might also lend themselves to various different interpretations.

Whereas a literal description of the world around us can be done using plain language, a metaphor or **simile** uses a comparison for understanding. For example, in Chapter 3 we introduced the idea that *knowledge is like a map*. This connects the abstract idea of knowledge with an everyday object – a map. Such **analogies** might assist understanding; however, a false analogy is one where the comparison is unjustified, and this is something to be avoided.

On the other hand, an original comparison between a concept and everyday life might lead to new perspectives or a solution to a problem. For example, in the context of climate change, the metaphor of a *footprint* might encourage us to reduce our carbon emissions and *carbon footprint*. The value of a metaphor is that it can make sense of a complex concept using the language of everyday experience. For example, the everyday experience of growing plants in a greenhouse lead Swedish scientist Svante Arrhenius (1859–1927) to describe the warming of our planet as the *greenhouse effect*.

KEY TERMS

metaphor: a non-literal comparison, for example, *'My love is a red rose'* or *'My knowledge is a map'*

simile: a comparison using the words *like* or *as*, for example, *'My love is like a red rose'* or *'Knowledge is like a map'*

analogy: a comparison between two things for the purpose of explanation or clarification, for example, *'Dr Jones drew an analogy between the President and her favourite historical figure'*

blank slate: the concept of a person in a 'pure' state with no experiences or influences

TASK: ACTIVITY 6.6

Here are some examples of comparisons used in various areas of knowledge. Draw a graph and plot the following statements – label the X axis so that one end represents *justified analogies* and the other end *false analogies*. Discuss where you think the statements should be placed along the axis.

In your discussion, be sure to identify the assumptions made and the implications that follow. You could also research other examples and add these to your line.

1   in natural sciences, the analogy of Robert Hooke (1635–1703), who observed cork under a microscope and compared what he saw to a *cell* or room inhabited by a monk or a nun in a monastery

2   in history, the interpretation of events as an 'arms-race'

3   in religious knowledge systems, the relationship between God and people, via the metaphor of *God as a parent* or people as *children of God*

4   In philosophy, the concept of human nature via the '**blank slate**' metaphor

5   In English literature, Shakespeare's metaphor for death: *'our little life is rounded with a sleep'* (*The Tempest*)

TOK LINK: SCIENCE

Given that it is difficult to perceive the macrocosmic (solar systems, galaxies, etc.) and the microcosmic (cells, atoms, sub-atomic particles, etc.), how far is the language of science metaphorical? In what ways might this support our knowledge and understanding?

Is there more of a responsibility for the way we use language in the sciences or in the arts?

Knowledge that is open to interpretation

The arts have been described as the *language of the emotions*, and there may be some truths that can only be articulated via the visual, literary or performing arts. For example, poetry attempts to articulate feelings and experiences that are difficult to articulate in prose form. Furthermore, religious experience is ineffable, meaning that the nature of the experience can be beyond straightforward description in language.

TOK IN YOUR LIFE

When you study poetry or prose, where do you look for the meaning – in the text itself or in the interpretation of that text which takes place in the social and cultural context of your class, or a combination of the two?

What implications does this have for language, meaning and the way we think about *knowing how* to interpret a literary text?

6.5 Ethics and language

The relationship between language and values is an important one. There is an ethical dimension to the words we choose to speak. We might believe that we have a responsibility to speak out in a just cause, or we might believe that it is wrong to use outrageous language that would deliberately cause offence.

The language we use communicates our values – one person's animal rights activist is another person's industrial saboteur. If you look closely at the language used to report news stories, you will be able to analyse the denotation and connotation. For example, the language to denote the same person could have very different connotations: crusader, campaigner, activist, champion, advocate or a promoter.

Figure 6.3: Members of the international organisation Animal Equality protest against industrial livestock farming in Madrid in December 2019. In what ways does language describe or express our opinion and values?

Language functions in a number of different ways – it relates to your identity, it describes, it connects with your experience, it expresses your values and it is influenced by your status and relationship with the person you are speaking to. Language relates to power and authority, and it can be used for persuasion, manipulation or even propaganda. Some languages today have so few speakers that they risk extinction, and various ethical and political questions arise from endangered languages. The capacity of machines to learn language and developments in technology, such as computer voice recognition and chat bots, raise questions about the relationship between speech and values.

REAL-LIFE SITUATION 6.3

Uighur is a language that uses an Arabic script, and is spoken by Uighur Muslims, a group of about 12 million people in north-west China. From 2012, Uighurs were able to communicate using their own language on the Chinese social media platform, WeChat™. However, the Chinese authorities did not understand their language and were unable to monitor their communication. Therefore, in 2016 the Chinese authorities began to collect biometric data and track the Uighurs' activities on WeChat. Today, Uighurs are required to present their smart phones to the police, along with their IDs, and have been discouraged from speaking their language and celebrating their culture.

CONTINUED

The knowledge questions that arise around language relate to the link between language and politics, and the ways that governments might seek to control languages and monitor and limit communication via social media. The knowledge questions also relate to the role that language plays in relation to our social and cultural identity.

1   How does language connect with our identity, culture and sense of belonging?

2   If a language is lost or destroyed, what else is lost or destroyed with it?

Language and technology

Language is one of the most original technologies available to us, and is the tool by which we can convey our meaning and ideas with others. Increasingly, machines and computers are capable of recognising speech and simulating conversations with us, which suggests that a computer can, in some sense, learn and 'know' a language. Technology makes instant communication possible. It can also blur the distinction between private and public communication, and influence the ways in which we might or might not select or censor what we say online. Technology raises questions about the value, meaning and responsibility of the language we use.

TASK: THINK ABOUT 6.5

Listen to Jon Ronson's 2015 TED Talk™, 'How one tweet can ruin your life'. What does this TED Talk™ suggest about the relationship between language, technology and ethics?

TASK: ACTIVITY 6.7

Look at some examples of tweets™ that are trending on Twitter™. Have a go at writing your own examples of tweets™, in fewer than 280 characters, about how language influences or is used to communicate knowledge in one area of knowledge.

How far can a tweet™ convey accurate meaning? What is a brief summary of fewer than 280 characters useful for? What is lost in a 280-character limit?

Reflect on this as an example of one way in which technology can influence our use of language. Discuss the question: What ethical considerations might influence our use of language on social media?

CROSS REFERENCE

For more information on the relationship between technology and knowledge, see Chapter 5 of this book, and Chapter 5 of the Course Guide.

TOK IN YOUR LIFE

'If we don't believe in freedom of expression for people we despise, we don't believe in it at all.'

Noam Chomsky

What are the assumptions behind and implications beyond this quotation?

6.6 Knowledge questions

1   To what extent can rely on language as a reliable tool in two areas of knowledge?

2   In what ways does language help or hinder the knower?

3   What role does language play in the way we construct knowledge?

6.7 Exhibition task

Consider how you might use language as an object for your TOK exhibition. Which IA prompt would you choose, and which theme would you focus on? Write 250–300 words on the real-world context of your chosen linguistic artefact, and how it links to your chosen IA prompt.

Identify how language relates to knowledge and knowing. Explore how language relates to one or more of these categories:

•   the use of language in a local, national or international news story

•   language in an IB Diploma Programme text you have studied in Group 1

•   language used in the context of social media such as Twitter™ or another platform.

For each category, think of a specific object or linguistic artefact that links language with one of the items above.

1   Choose three objects, and identity their specific real-world context.

2   Select one of the IA prompts that connect with your objects.

3   Justify how each object relates to your chosen IA prompt.

4   Write 250–300 words on the real-world context of the linguistic artefact, and how it links to your chosen IA prompts.

TOP TIP

When you select an object for your exhibition, be sure to choose something with a real-world context. Some examples of an object to do with language include the speech made by the climate activist Greta Thunberg (2003–) at the 2019 United Nations Climate Action Summit, or the speech made by female education activist Malala Yousafzai (1997–) at the United Nations in 2013.

Rather than general objects, select a specific artefact that relates to your chosen knowledge prompt, and that manifests TOK in the world around you.

6.8 Extended writing task

Write 400–600 words on one of the following questions:

1   What part does language play in the justification of knowledge claims in different areas of knowledge?

2   In what ways do our values affect the language we use and the knowledge that we seek?

3   Choose one or two areas of knowledge, such as the natural sciences and/or the human sciences. How far does language influence the development of knowledge in these areas?

SKILLS SELF-ASSESSMENT CHECKLIST

Reflect on what you have learned in this chapter and indicate your confidence level between 1 and 5 (where 5 is the highest score and 1 is the lowest). If you score below 3, revisit that section. Come back to this list later in your course. Has your confidence grown?

	Confidence level	Revisited?
Can I articulate the nature and scope of language, and its importance for the knower?		
Can I identify arguments and counter-arguments about the impact of language on knowledge and knowing?		
Can I construct an argument about the influence of language on knowledge?		
Am I able to identify and evaluate different perspectives of language?		
Can I offer examples or evidence to support or illustrate a point about knowledge?		
Am I able to identify knowledge claims and arguments that make assumptions that are taken for granted?		
Can I analyse language as a tool for description, communication, persuasion and expression of values?		
Can I evaluate the ways in which language can be used to influence and persuade, in the context of power relationships?		
Am I able to identify and evaluate different ethical questions and issues associated with language and knowledge and the responsibilities involved with language?		

6.9 Further reading

For a discussion of the nature of language, read: Stephen Pinker, *The Language Instinct*, William Morrow and Company, 1994

For discussion of the origins and evolution of language, read: Guy Deutscher, *The unfolding of language: The evolution of man's greatest invention*, Arrow Books, 2006

For an exploration of language, culture and the mind, read: Guy Deutscher, *Through the Language Glass: Why the world looks different in other languages*, Arrow Books, 2011

> # Chapter 7
Knowledge and politics

LEARNING INTENTIONS

In this chapter, you will explore some of the ways in which knowledge and politics are intertwined, and develop skills that will help you to identify the difference between knowledge and disinformation.

You will:

- understand the complex relationship between politics and knowledge

- consider and evaluate the impact of your own political perspectives

- compare the tools and methods of producing knowledge about politics with tools and methods used in other areas of knowledge

- develop a critical awareness of the ways in which media can be used to promote disinformation and fake news

- analyse the role of ethics in the development of political knowledge

- build awareness of your ethical responsibilities as a citizen to be politically well-informed and think critically about political issues.

7.1 Introduction

Knowledge is intrinsically political because what counts as knowledge and who decides are political questions. Issues surrounding how knowledge is produced, protected and shared are also largely political issues. In addition, there are knowledge issues that involve the discipline and practice of politics, and what we might call political knowledge. This includes knowledge in political science, political philosophy and the politics of daily life.

7.2 The scope of political knowledge

Political science compares and contrasts different political systems and different electoral systems, political **policies** and political administrations, endeavouring to critically evaluate each system. It also looks more broadly at **international relations**, and analyses the ways in which different political systems interact.

Political philosophy critically examines concepts such as freedom, human rights, property rights, law, authority, legitimacy and duty. It has strong ethical dimensions, and different political philosophies are often based on different assumptions about the nature of human beings, and what constitutes a good life. For example, Thomas Hobbes (1588–1679) was concerned with the problem of social and political order. His political philosophy is based on a bleak understanding of human nature, and he believed that without a strong government to maintain order, people's lives would be *'solitary, poor, nasty, brutish, and short'*.

Beyond political science and political philosophy are the daily politics of government, the work of politicians and the politics of daily life which you may experience in the power dynamics within and between your different friendship groups. You may also be familiar with politicians arguing about who is most trustworthy, who has better policies and who would bring the greatest good if in power. In some regimes, politics may be in the form of government representatives telling you why they should be trusted and not be challenged. In all of its forms, politics is intrinsically intertwined with responsibility, authority and power.

KEY TERMS

policies: principles, rules and guidelines to help an organisation reach its long-term goals

international relations: the way in which two or more nations regard and interact with each other

TASK: THINK ABOUT 7.1

1   Why is it important to be knowledgeable about contemporary issues in order to be politically responsible?

2   How much knowledge is enough knowledge to be politically responsible?

Many questions we face in our social, educational and economic lives are political. For example, *Which is more important: affordable housing or protecting wildlife?* and *How can we know what the medium- and long-term consequences will be of the proliferation of AI technology, climate change or changing demographics?* are questions that are largely political in nature, even though our responses may be informed by other areas of knowledge. It may be difficult to ascertain the facts and assess the consequences of such questions. However, it is only by answering such questions to our own satisfaction that we can confidently address more explicitly political questions such as: *How can we know which political party's policies will be best for our region, state or country?* It is also the case that our party-political views may affect our evaluation of and responses to those social, educational and economic questions.

TASK: THINK ABOUT 7.2

To what extent does every knowledge claim fall under the scope of political knowledge?

TASK: ACTIVITY 7.1

Choose two of the following social and economic issues. Plan an answer to the question: *To what extent does your knowledge of these issues influence your political views, and to what extent do your political views affect the way you think of these issues?*

- conservation
- social care
- renewable energy
- immigration
- intensive farming
- nationalised health service
- private education
- free tertiary education
- affordable housing
- minimum wage.

In small groups, discuss the roles of fact and opinion in politics.

Often, what we accept as knowledge reflects a political decision based on who we trust and our political leanings. The scope of political knowledge includes considering how factual evidence can be dismissed, ignored or even twisted to suit personal and party-political **propaganda**. This practice, known as **truth decay**, includes fake news, fake science, fake history and fake social media accounts.

KEY TERMS

propaganda: information, especially of a biased or misleading nature, used to promote a political cause or point of view

truth decay: the diminishing roles of truth and analysis in public life

7.3 Political perspectives

There are many different political **ideologies**, but broadly speaking, they can be grouped into five major categories: **anarchism**, **absolutism**, **conservatism**, **liberalism** and **socialism**.

Most people's political perspectives can be classified within one or more of these ideologies. However, it is not unusual for people to be conservative about some issues and liberal about others, or to advocate absolutism in some circumstances but promote liberal or even anarchic views in other circumstances. Similarly, most political parties will be situated somewhere in between these different ideologies, and some contain strong elements of more than one ideology; for example, the Liberal Party of Australia promotes economic liberalism but is considered socially more conservative than the Australian Labor Party. Similarly, Germany's Partei des Demokratischen Sozialismus (Party of Democratic Socialism) could be regarded as both socialist and liberal.

Figure 7.1: The Australian Prime Minister answering questions during Question Time in the Australian House of Representatives.

TOK IN YOUR LIFE

Think about the different ideologies listed here. Where would you align your own political views? How do they affect your attitude towards contemporary social and environmental issues?

TOK LINK: KNOWLEDGE AND THE KNOWER

How does your identity shape your political perspectives?

How do your political perspectives shape your identity?

KEY TERMS

ideology: a system of social beliefs

anarchism: the belief that society should be run on a voluntary, cooperative basis without any need for government

absolutism: in a political context, the believe that power to govern a society should be in the hands of a single ruler or very small group

conservatism: the belief that stability based upon traditional values is essential to an orderly society

liberalism: the belief that governments should interfere minimally in society, and the rights of individuals to act freely on the basis of their own wishes should be protected

socialism: the belief that the rights of the collective should have priority over the rights of individuals, that property should be publicly owned and wealth should be equitably distributed

---

TASK: ACTIVITY 7.2

Visit The Political Compass organisation website, and complete their online test to see where your political values lie based on your economic and social viewpoints.

Reflect on the Political Compass methodology. How accurate do you think their analysis is?

Relativism and political perspectives

The rise of **relativism** in the 20th century led to the emergence of more **egalitarian** societies in which, for example, the perspectives of women and minority groups were heard. While relativism has many merits, it is open to exploitation by those who want to revive ideas that have been shown to be false, such as Holocaust denial. It is increasingly difficult to be seen to respect different perspectives without giving moral equivalence to all opinions.

The idea that not all opinions or perspectives are equal may seem unthinkable at first because we are all encouraged to be open-minded and respectful of different points of view. However, conflicts arise if we tolerate the perspectives of the intolerant, or of those who would deny our right to political freedom. This raises important questions about freedom of speech, and whether all people should have the right to be listened to in a democracy.

TASK: ACTIVITY 7.3

Consider the following opinions coming from different perspectives.

1   We should all be concerned about climate change.

2   We do not have to be too concerned about climate change because scientists will find a solution.

3   We do not have to worry about climate change because current generations will have died before the planet becomes unfit for human life.

4   We can probably minimise climate change if we stop developing nations from developing.

5   Climate change is a curse brought on by redheads.

6   Climate change is due to God's judgement on human sin.

KEY TERMS

relativism: the belief that knowledge, truth, and morality are not absolute; rather they exist in relation to cultural and historical contexts, and all perspectives are of equal value

egalitarian: based on the principle that all people are of equal value, and deserve equal rights and opportunities

---

CONTINUED

Do you regard all of the opinions above as equal? What criteria did you use to decide? In small groups, discuss the following:

- In a world where there are nearly 8 billion individual human perspectives, how do we decide which perspectives to listen to? Are there any perspectives that should not be listened to? Who should decide?

- To what extent is freedom of speech essential to democracy?

American politician Daniel Patrick Moynihan (1927–2003) once claimed, *'Everyone is entitled to his own opinion, but not to his own facts'*. However, many people now have difficulty in knowing what the facts are, particularly in the age of social media, where the political tactic of repeating false knowledge claims over and over serves to leave many people in confusion. The philosopher Hannah Arendt (1906–1975) wrote in her book *The Origins of Totalitarianism* (1951), *'The ideal subject of totalitarian rule is not the convinced Nazi or the convinced communist, but people for whom the distinction between fact and fiction and the distinction between true and false no longer exist.'*

KEY POINT

One of the tasks of TOK is to help people discern genuine knowledge claims from false and misleading knowledge claims.

Faced with uncertainty about what to believe, many people uncritically adopt the political values and beliefs of their families and *tribes*. Others will vote according to their perceptions of different political party leaders, without always having a clear idea of what the leaders stand for.

TASK: THINK ABOUT 7.3

What types of knowledge contribute most to shaping your political opinions?

REAL-LIFE SITUATION 7.1

Edward Snowden is a US citizen who worked in the US Intelligence Community. Working as a consultant at the National Security Agency (NSA) in 2013, Snowden publicly revealed NSA's mass surveillance programs. The US government charged Snowden with putting the national security at risk. Snowden is now living in Russia, where he was granted **asylum**. Some people see Edward Snowden as an American hero; others see him as a traitor.

Watch Edward Snowden's 2014 TED Talk™, *How we take back the internet*. In small groups, discuss whether his release of NSA documents was reckless or heroic.

1   At what point do methods of acquiring knowledge become unethical?

2   To what extent does knowing something carry an ethical responsibility?

TOP TIP

When using political stories for TOK, it is preferable to use news items from your own country or local area, so that you are better able to connect with the stories.

KEY TERM

asylum: shelter and protection

People who do not have strong ties to any one party, and who place their votes according to their perspectives on issues and party policies at the time that they vote, are known as **swing voters**. It is often the swing voters that political campaigners try to appeal to most in the lead-up to elections.

TASK: ACTIVITY 7.4

Is there an ethical conflict between loyalty to a political party or ideology and a responsibility to vote according to election issues?

Consider arguments on both sides, and try to provide evidence from contemporary issues in your own country.

7.4 Methods and tools for developing political knowledge

Political knowledge is so broad, therefore the methods and tools that are employed to produce political knowledge are drawn from all areas of knowledge.

Inference

Perhaps one of the most common ways of developing political knowledge is through the use of **inference**. Political scientists and other social scientists conduct research using small samples of a **population**, and use the results to make inferences about the population as a whole.

For inference to be reliable, the samples need to represent the population as a whole, as far as possible. There are various ways in which samples can be drawn.

One of the most familiar samples is the *random sample*. This is when (in the case of people) everyone has an equal chance of being sampled. In theory, this may be the simplest form of sampling, but it can be very difficult in practice, particularly if the whole population is large and complex.

To overcome the difficulties of finding random samples that accurately represent the population, many researchers use a *stratified random sample*. This is similar to a random sample, but it sets out to draw random representatives from specified subpopulations in ratios that match the proportions of the subpopulations in the whole population. For example, if you wanted to survey your school based on age and gender, if there were an equal number of students in each year group, and at each level there were the same number of boys and girls, you would randomly choose an equal number of boys and girls from every year group for your sample. If your school had twice as many boys as girls, you would randomly select twice as many boys in your sample, or you could draw equal numbers and weight your results differently.

TASK: ACTIVITY 7.5

Stratified random samples need to be context specific. For example, if you want to know about different religious perspectives on a political issue, your sample will need to reflect the different religious perspectives in the population. Working with a partner, plan to draw a stratified random sample based on a school with 1,000 students of which 40% are Christian, 40% are Buddhist, 10% are Muslim and 10% are Hindu. Compare your sampling strategy with another pair's plan.

Another method of sampling is known as *cluster sampling*. This is when sampling happens in clusters, often based on geographic areas. Samples are then taken within those clusters. The sampling may be simple in this method, but the mathematical weighting of probabilities is much more complex.

Polls and surveys

Polls and **surveys** are important tools in politics. Mainstream media often reports the results of political polls to indicate changes in public opinion, and to try to make predictions about the way people will vote. But polls are notoriously uncertain – even if the sampling methods are sound, not everybody will turn out to vote, thereby upsetting the prediction. One way of countering this effect is for pollsters to discount the demographic groups that tend not to vote. This assumes that people who have not voted in the past are unlikely to vote in the future, but such assumptions are also unreliable.

KEY TERMS

poll: participants are asked a single multiple-choice question

survey: participants are asked multiple questions which may be of different types (e.g. multiple choice, short answer)

Figure 7.2: Staff in a telephone centre in Germany conducting a representative opinion poll

TOK LINK: LANGUAGE

How questions are worded in a poll or survey can significantly affect the result. Wording questions and answers fairly is essential in the framing of polls and surveys.

One of the concerns regarding polls is that they do not just measure political opinions; they can actually shape political opinions. In a study in 1947, political researchers canvassed American public opinion about a fictitious *Metallic Metals Act*. There was no such act, but 70% of respondents took a firm view for or against the act when they were polled. This suggested that respondents can feel pressured to take a view on something, even if they know nothing about it.

TASK: THINK ABOUT 7.4

How might the publishing of polls prior to an election affect the outcome of that election?

> **CROSS REFERENCE**
>
> You can read more about the issue of leading and loaded questions in the course book, Chapter 12.

Technology

Political science uses technology to help produce political knowledge. Big data, machine learning and computerised text analysis together allow millions of texts to be analysed in very short periods of time, allowing political scientists to know, for example, the ways in which political preferences are changing, and how political language is evolving.

This use of technology also allows political scientists to use scientific experimental methods to investigate issues such as voters' behaviour and decision-making processes.

As well as changing the ways in which political knowledge is produced, technology is changing the ways in which political knowledge is shared. The rise of social media has led to widespread sharing of political information, and has also opened the doors to widespread sharing of political disinformation. There is concern that foreign powers are able to spread disinformation through social media to influence public opinion and political outcomes.

TASK: THINK ABOUT 7.5

1   How has technology changed the nature of political research?

2   To what extent has technology changed the ways in which our political perspectives are formed?

Mathematical modelling

The field of quantitative political methodology addresses political questions such as *How can we detect voting irregularities?* and *How does trade facilitate international cooperation?*. It does this by developing statistical methods that combine data analysis with political science.

However data is gathered, a variety of mathematical methods are needed to interpret the data and make inferences from the patterns that are found. Statistical modelling uses mathematical analysis to formalise the relationship between two or more variables and look for **correlations**. The model can also be used to make predictions. Political researchers make use of a wide range of sophisticated mathematical techniques specially designed to suit political data.

> **KEY TERM**
>
> **correlation:** a relationship or statistical connection between two or more variables which shows how strongly the variables are related

> **KEY POINT**
>
> Correlation does not imply causation. Just because two independent factors appear to be correlated, we cannot assume that one factor is the cause of the other.

> **TASK: ACTIVITY 7.6**
>
> In pairs, consider the following correlation: *People with higher incomes are more likely to vote.*
>
> With your partner, try to come up with possible explanations for this correlation. Can you think how you might plan a way to test one of your possible explanations?

7.5 Methods and tools for sharing political knowledge

Political scientists and others working in different fields within the human sciences, technology and mathematics produce a great deal of political knowledge, but most of us receive our political knowledge in other ways.

Political rallies

A political rally is a large public meeting held to show support for a political party or a political candidate. Such events usually involve political speeches, and in some countries, they may include live music by top artists and guest appearances by celebrities to help create a festival atmosphere and attract large crowds. Creating a large festival event also increases the chances of good media coverage for the political speeches.

People might attend political rallies for a variety of reasons including:

- to support their preferred party or candidate
- to find out what a candidate stands for
- to protest against the political party or candidate holding the rally
- to take part in a festival activity.

However, research indicates that those attending often get caught up in the excitement of the rally, regardless of their original motivation to attend, and this often leads them to vote for the candidate promoted in the rally.

TOK LINK: LANGUAGE

How might emotive language be used in political campaigns to persuade and manipulate the electorate?

Mainstream and social media

Mainstream media are important tools for politicians to communicate their ideas, values, actions and knowledge, and for the public who want to stay politically informed.

As well as communication, mainstream media provide the public with an interpretative framework for understanding past, present and future events. This inevitably opens the way for media bias: how a political event is framed can greatly impact the way it is received by media consumers.

Some people believe that the media facilitate democracy by allowing a wide variety of views to be expressed. However, others believe the media are undemocratic because they are able to manipulate the way that people perceive different politicians and political views.

TASK: ACTIVITY 7.7

Investigate a political story from your state or country in more than one media outlet, and compare how the story is presented in those different media. If possible, try to compare media that are known in your country for having different political perspectives.

How do the different versions of the story compare? If you find differences, are they reasonable reflections of different journalistic styles, or do you think they are deliberately trying to shape your opinion of the event they are writing about?

How could you try to reach a balanced perspective on a political story?

Fake news

News information used to be distributed through traditional media such as newspapers, television and radio. These were bound by legal and professional standards to report facts, and journalists would check all information carefully for accuracy. However, in the 21st century, many people get news from social media where fact and fiction are often indistinguishable.

Complicating the picture is when fake news stories lead to real news events, and when community leaders question the credibility of legitimate journalism if they do not like the real stories being told. The public often no longer know who or what to believe. If citizens are unable to make informed decisions, democracy is put at risk.

TASK: ACTIVITY 7.8

When you see news stories on social media, how do you decide whether to believe them?

Consider the following, and say whether you are more or less likely to believe them:

- stories that confirm what you already believe

- stories that challenge or even contradict your beliefs

- stories that are reported in mainstream media

- stories that come from partisan sources

- stories that are verified by an expert from a reputable organisation.

Try to come up with one or two specific examples for each category.

People used to check news stories by looking at two independent media outlets, but with an ever-increasing number of social media sources opening up, most people do not know which are independent and which are not, or where the stories come from. There is a tendency to believe that if we see different versions of the same story in more than one place, it must be true; but those who spread disinformation and fake news flood social media with several versions of a fake story through multiple outlets, so now we must rely on reputable fact-checking sites.

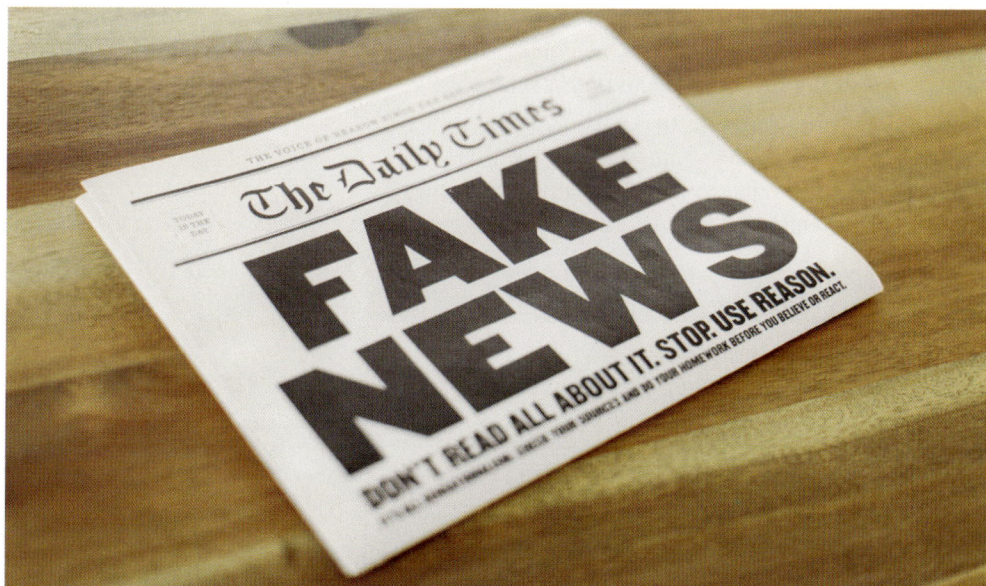

Figure 7.3: How can you decide what to believe?

> **REAL-LIFE SITUATION 7.2**
>
> In the lead up to the 2019 elections in India, fake news stories and the spread of disinformation were rife.
>
> The Indian government claimed that their air strikes against Pakistan on 26th February 2019 had resulted in the deaths of many Pakistani militants. The Pakistani government, on the other hand, claimed that there had been no casualties. In March 2019, social media was flooded with photographs claiming to prove the success of the Indian air strikes. The photographs purported to show dead militants and a destroyed training camp, but were later discovered by a fact-checking team to have been old photographs from a 2005 earthquake and a 2014 suicide bombing.
>
> 1   How does propaganda influence our perception of events?
>
> 2   Under what circumstances, if any, might propaganda be justified?

Social media **algorithms** are set up so that people tend to see more posts from like-minded people and more posts on viewpoints and topics they *like*, creating **echo chambers**, which tend to make people more confident in their beliefs and opinions. Social media companies are under increasing pressure to identify and remove fake news stories before they have a chance to spread. Many people believe that social media companies also need to change their algorithms to promote the possibility of people encountering information and opinions that they disagree with. Encountering diverse opinions can help shake people out of complacency and encourage them to think more critically about their beliefs.

Advertising campaigns

Political advertising is an important aspect of any political campaign. Marketing and advertising expertise are used to influence voters leading up to elections and referenda, and to influence political debates. Many countries restrict the use of broadcast advertising to try to prevent wealthy political parties or lobby groups having an unfair influence.

In recent years, social media has become an important tool for the sharing of political knowledge and political messaging because it can reach a large number of people at a very low cost. Social media tends to spread news that is popular or *trending*, rather than news that is accurate or important, making it an ideal vehicle for the spreading of disinformation.

> **REAL-LIFE SITUATION 7.3**
>
> In October 2019, Twitter™ announced that it would ban all political advertising. Facebook™, however, decided to exempt ads by politicians from third-party fact-checking, and from a policy that bans false statements in paid advertisements. Twitter's CEO argues that advances in digital advertising technology, including deepfakes – fake or manipulated videos that appear real – combined with disinformation, create new challenges to public conversations, and money should not be the arbiter of truth. Facebook's CEO argues that political advertising is about free speech, and tech companies should not be the ones to decide which messages are acceptable.

KEY TERMS

algorithm: a set of rules typically to be followed by a computer

echo chamber: an environment in which people only encounter beliefs or opinions like their own, so they do not consider alternative ideas, and their own ideas are reinforced

CONTINUED

In small groups, discuss:

1   To what extent should politicians and political parties be expected to be truthful?

2   Should all political advertising be banned? Consider reasons on both sides of the debate.

7.6 Ethics and political knowledge

Politics and ethics are closely bound in numerous ways. As well as the ethics surrounding the methods and tools by which political knowledge is produced and shared, ethical issues are also political in nature. How you approach ethics may also be political. For example, if a political party has a **consequentialist** approach to ethics, the outcome of its political campaign might be more important than the methods it adopts. If it believes that its policies would create the best future for the state or country, it might feel justified in misleading the public to win an election, and believe that it acted ethically in doing so.

If a party has a **deontological** approach to ethics, its campaign might be conducted in a more honest way, but at the risk of losing.

TASK: THINK ABOUT 7.6

1   Politicians often talk about being ethical, but they rarely say what their ethical approach is. Why might it matter?

2   How can we decide which politicians to trust?

Creating political policies involves making ethical judgements. All governments have limited budgets and endless demands on those limited funds. When a government decides how public money should be spent, there are multiple considerations to weigh up, and they must sometimes make choices that are unpopular with the electorate. They are then faced with questions of whether to do what is ethically right and risk losing votes, or whether to do the wrong thing but appease the people.

Sometimes political leaders need to make decisions that they know will harm innocent people, for example ordering military action. In democracies, politicians act on behalf of the people. As politicians, they also have rights and obligations that most of us do not have. Their duties may at times require them to use force, lie, keep secrets and break promises in ways that would be regarded as wrong by most people in private life.

KEY TERMS

consequentialist: consequentialist theories judge whether an action is ethically right by the consequences of that action

deontological: related to the study of duty

CROSS REFERENCE

You can find out more about different approaches to ethics in Chapter 3 of the Course Guide.

TASK: ACTIVITY 7.9

Imagine that you are stranded on a desert island with 50 of your schoolmates and have no prospect of rescue. How would you organise yourselves? Would you select leaders, and if so, how? What rules would you create? How would you enforce these rules?

Share your ideas with a classmate and try to reach agreement. Then join up with another pair. Try to reach consensus across the whole class.

Another ethical issue facing politicians is how policies can be adopted, enacted and enforced when citizens disagree about what is best for their community, state or nation. This is a particularly difficult issue when the government has to weigh up short-term benefits over longer-term benefits, especially when shorter-term benefits tend to influence the ways that people vote more directly. Other difficult decisions must be made when one community might clearly benefit from a policy, but the country or even the world might be disadvantaged.

REAL-LIFE SITUATION 7.4

Approximately 90% of Suriname is covered in rainforest. In 1994, the Suriname government made an agreement in which 25% of the country's land area (3 million hectares) would be made available to international loggers with no provision for environmental protections or reforestation. Logging companies argued that this would have economic benefits for local employees, as well as for businesses that provide goods and services to the loggers. However, it was estimated that logging companies would earn US$28 million from Suriname's agreement, while Suriname would only receive US$2 million.

In some countries, an income of US$2 million plus the promise of employment may seem an attractive proposition; however, in this case, a public outcry caused the contract to be cancelled. Nevertheless, around the world many communities and countries face similar dilemmas.

1   How might different ethical approaches help politicians to decide between short-term economic benefits and potentially broader benefits over a longer period?

2   How can politicians decide between competing interests when making political decisions?

Figure 7.4: How do you make decisions about political issues when there are many competing interests?

Another ethical issue associated with political knowledge is that of civil disobedience. If a government makes unjust laws or unfairly treats some groups within its society, some would say that citizens should have a right, a responsibility and perhaps even a duty, to protest.

TASK: ACTIVITY 7.10

In pairs or small groups, consider the quotation below and answer the following questions:

'Under a government which imprisons any unjustly, the true place for a just man is also a prison.'

Henry David Thoreau

1   What do you think Thoreau means by this? Do you agree with him?

2   How would you decide whether a government is acting justly or unjustly?

3   What criteria would you use to decide whether civil disobedience is justifiable?

7.7 Knowledge questions

1   How is political knowledge different from political opinion?

2   What criteria can we use to judge the fairness of different political systems?

3   How might the use of big data and data analysis in politics create new ethical challenges?

7.8 Exhibition task

Consider how you might use a political opinion poll as an item for your TOK exhibition. Which IA prompt question would you choose? Write 250–300 words on the real-world context of the opinion poll, and how it links to your chosen IA prompt.

7.9 Extended writing task

Write 450–550 words on one or more of the following questions:

1   On what basis might a politician or political party claim to know what is right for others?

2   To what extent does the end (the result) justify the means (the way the result is achieved) in politics?

SKILLS SELF-ASSESSMENT CHECKLIST

Reflect on what you have learned in this chapter and indicate your confidence level between 1 and 5 (where 5 is the highest score and 1 is the lowest). If you score below 3, revisit that section. Come back to this list later in your course. Has your confidence grown?

	Confidence level	Revisited?
Do I understand the complex relationship between politics and knowledge?		
Am I able to evaluate the impact of my own political perspectives when I address contemporary social and environmental issues?		
Can I compare the tools and methods of producing political knowledge with tools and methods used in other areas of knowledge?		
Do I have a critical awareness of the ways in which media can be used as a tool to promote disinformation and fake news?		
Am I able to analyse the role of ethics in the development of political knowledge?		
Am I aware of my ethical responsibilities as a citizen to be politically informed?		
Can I think critically about political issues?		

7.10 Further reading

For more about the relationship between science, knowledge and political policies, read: Kat Smith and Richard Freeman, 'A New Politics of Knowledge? Exploring the contested boundaries between science, knowledge and policy' *LSE Impact Blog,* 24th May 2014

For more about the issues surrounding truth decay, read: Michiko Kakutani, *The Death of Truth*, William Collins, London, 2018

Chapter 8

Knowledge and religion

In this chapter, you will look at the nature of religious knowledge and the ways in which people arrive at it, and develop the skills to evaluate some of the knowledge claims and the knowledge questions that arise.

You will:

* learn to identify different types of knowledge claims about religion systems

* consider and evaluate the impact of religious and non-religious perspectives

* develop a critical awareness of some of the sources of religious knowledge

* consider how the tools and methods of producing religious knowledge compare with tools and methods used in other areas of knowledge

* compare and contrast religious ethical knowledge with philosophical ethical knowledge.

8.1 Introduction

Religious knowledge is perhaps the most contentious of all areas of knowledge. There are some people who would claim that there is no such thing as religious knowledge, while there are others who regard their religious knowledge as the most certain of the truths that they hold.

Religious traditions embody an array of knowledge. Some of this knowledge will be about the origins of the religion; its traditions and artefacts; and its history of interpretation, ethical beliefs or rites, rituals and festivals. This type of knowledge is similar to knowledge in history and the human sciences – a great deal of it will be historical in nature, and its justification may be subject to the same criteria as any historical knowledge or knowledge in the human sciences.

Such knowledge is usually widely accepted outside the religious tradition, as well as by believers. For example, many people accept the **historicity** of Siddhartha Gautama and Muhammad without being Buddhists or Muslims. Many people of different religions, including people with no religion, accept that these leaders were real men who lived in particular places and times, just as they accept that Cleopatra and Genghis Khan were real people who lived in the past.

KEY TERM

historicity: historical authenticity

TOK IN YOUR LIFE

To what extent do you think that religion is about believing, belonging, or both?

8.2 The scope of religious knowledge

The scope of religious knowledge includes more than knowledge about the origins and practices of religions. It also includes claims about the significance of a religion, and it is here that most of the contention arises. Even though non-believers may accept the historicity of say, Guru Nanak and Jesus of Nazareth, it is usually only members of Sikh and Christian religious communities respectively who treat their religious claims as knowledge. Moreover, even within a single religious tradition, believers will differ in which claims they accept and how they interpret and understand the knowledge claims they assent to.

Examples of religious claims include:

- The Noble Eightfold Path is the way to the cessation of suffering. (Buddhism)
- Jesus Christ is the Son of God. (Christianity)
- Observing the five pillars of Islam is necessary to secure a place in heaven. (Islam)
- God is one. (Judaism)
- The Jade Emperor governs the realm of the mortals. (Taoism)

Believers may claim such statements from their own religion as things that they know, but it is unlikely that many non-believers would regard these statements as true. These are knowledge claims based on faith. Believers may regard them as true, and feel justified in their belief, but non-believers may dismiss them as both unjustified and untrue.

Religious language

Religion is a difficult area of knowledge to discuss, not least because the ways that words are used when discussing religious ideas are often different from the ways in which the same words are used in other contexts. For example, when people claim *polar bears exist*, they base the claim on quite different criteria from those used to claim *God exists*. Before we can decide whether the claim *God exists* is justified, we have to know what we mean by the words *God* and *exists*.

The different use of words can have some very strange consequences. Take, for example, four people – two who claim *God exists*, and two who claim *God does not exist*. If Mark and Sameera both claim *God exists*, we may think that they agree with each other. But Mark might believe God to be the entire universe (**pantheism**) and Sameera might believe God to be something other than the universe (**theism**). Therefore although they say the same words, what they mean by these words is very different.

Similarly, Olga and Carlos might both claim *God does not exist*, and we might also think they agree with each other. But Olga may believe there is no God (**atheism**), and Carlos might believe in a God who has no *physical* existence. If this were the case, Carlos would be much more in agreement with Sameera than Olga, despite making an apparently contradictory claim.

Theism and pantheism are only two of many ways of thinking about who or what God is. There are others, such as **panentheism** and **deism**, which you might like to research.

> ## KEY POINT
>
> Often when people argue about religion, they argue at cross-purposes because they have different understandings of key religious concepts. Similarly, people can appear to agree because they use the same words, but they may mean quite different things.

> ## TASK: THINK ABOUT 8.1
>
> How important is it that we know what a word refers to, before we can be said to know anything about it?

There are multiple ways that people can understand the words *God* and *exist*, and so a lot of religious discourse is about attempting to clarify meanings and reach common understandings, often using **metaphorical** language. But metaphorical language can itself create misunderstandings, with some people interpreting as literal what is meant as metaphorical, and vice versa, because it is not always obvious how a religious text is to be understood.

TOP TIP

Do not write about religion as if all religions are the same. Not all religions have identifiable founding figures, not all have holy scriptures, not all have a god or gods, not all have creeds and not all have beliefs about an afterlife or reincarnation. Even within a religion, there can be many different sets of beliefs and interpretations.

KEY TERMS

pantheism: the belief that God is everything

theism: the belief that there are one or more gods who interact with the world

atheism: the belief that there are no gods

panentheism: the belief that God contains everything in the world, but would also continue to exist if the world ceased to exist

deism: the belief in a creator God who does not interact with the world

metaphorical: representing one thing by referring to something else with similar characteristics

TASK: ACTIVITY 8.1

Explore ways in which you might answer the following knowledge question, being sure to consider both sides:

To what extent can people outside a religious tradition understand the tradition's key ideas when those within the tradition do not have a common understanding of them?

How might your response apply to traditions within other areas of knowledge?

KEY POINT

How we interpret language is important for all areas of knowledge, but particularly so in religion because ordinary words can be used differently in religious discourse.

In his book *Systematic Theology I*, philosopher Paul Tillich (1886–1965) argued: '*God does not exist. He is being itself beyond essence and existence. Therefore, to argue that God exists is to deny him*'. In other words, if we believe in God, we should say that God *does not* exist. Do you agree with this statement?

Finally, atheists and believers reach a consensus.

God is incredible!

in-cred-i-ble
adj.
1.
not credible, so implausible as to elicit disbelief

in-cred-i-ble
adj.
2.
extraordinary, astonishing

Figure 8.1: Even when we speak a common language, our words may be misunderstood or misinterpreted

8.3 Religious perspectives

One of the reasons religion tends to be a contentious area of knowledge is that people often have very fixed views, whether in favour of a particular religion, against particular religions or even against *all* religions.

Some people who have firm beliefs about one religion will sometimes uncritically accept all religious claims from their own religion as true, and dismiss religious knowledge claims from all other religions as false. Others may dismiss all knowledge claims that they perceive to conflict with their religious beliefs as false, such as when a scientific knowledge claim conflicts with their understanding of a religious knowledge claim. This uncritical allegiance to particular religious interpretations helps to give rise to accusations of **blind faith**.

TASK: THINK ABOUT 8.2

1   Blind faith is often associated with religion. Can you think of instances in which it might be applied in other areas of knowledge, such as history or the natural sciences?

2   Why might blind faith be undesirable and even dangerous in any area of knowledge?

It is not only religious people who may be subject to blind faith and uncritical thought. You may have heard claims along the lines of, *'Religion is the cause of all wars'*, or *'All religious leaders are charlatans'*. As a TOK student, you will recognise that these statements are sweeping generalisations which uncritically dismiss the crucial role that different religions have played in bettering the lives of people, including in the struggle for universal human rights.

While most religions – like most nations – have been involved in violence, repression and prejudice throughout their histories, it can be argued that the concepts of dignity and responsibility, shame and respect, restraint and regret, restitution and reconciliation so necessary to human rights, are largely religious ideas. Some scholars have even questioned whether it is possible to justify human rights apart from religious beliefs.

Whether you are religious, an **atheist** or an **agnostic**, it is possible – and perhaps even probable – that your perspectives on religion will influence your perspectives on issues within all areas of knowledge.

TASK: ACTIVITY 8.2

Find examples to show how different religious perspectives have influenced approaches to history, politics, technology, the arts and the natural sciences. What about mathematics?

TASK: ACTIVITY 8.3

There are some religious claims that may ring true for many believers of different religions and non-believers alike. One example might be *All human life is valuable*.

- With a partner, try to think of some others.
- Explain whether or not you would regard such claims as knowledge.

KEY TERMS

blind faith: faith that is not open to evaluation or critical thought

atheist: someone who believes there is no God or gods

agnostic: someone who does not know if there is a God or gods; someone who does not think the existence of a God or gods is provable

8.4 Sources of religious knowledge

If we set aside the issue of language, and assume for now that we can all agree on what is meant when someone makes a claim to have religious knowledge, we are still left with the question of where the religious knowledge comes from. Most religions have one or more authoritative sources, such as religious leaders, religious texts and religious traditions.

Direct revelation including mystical experiences

Direct revelation (or special revelation) is a type of **spiritual experience** that is said to occur when God reveals Godself to a person. Examples of this include the revelation of the Torah to Moses and the revelation of the Qur'an to Muhammad. Direct revelation can also include **mystical experiences**.

Many people of different theistic religious traditions believe that God can communicate with them directly, for example through dreams, visions or an inner voice during prayer and meditation. Most of the world's religions have mystical traditions in which believers feel oneness with the divine or a profound and powerful loss of self. By their nature, mystical experiences cannot be shared; they have to be experienced. However, poetry, metaphors, *koans* and paradoxes are some of the ways in which mystics try to communicate their experiences to others.

Many Hindus believe that God may be revealed through *darshan* (the Sanskrit word for seeing) in which God sees and is seen by the worshipper. As in English, the word carries the double meaning of visually seeing and understanding; therefore a pious Hindu may experience a revelatory sense of understanding by looking at a *murti* (the representation of a god).

Figure 8.2: This Hindu statue of Lord Ganesha is rich with symbolism

KEY TERMS

spiritual experiences: feelings of awe or oneness with the universe that a person might experience when doing things such as looking at a breath-taking landscape, serving others or practising yoga

mystical experiences: a type of spiritual experience that gives the feeling of oneness with God or the Absolute, and a sense of religious knowledge that can only be reached by losing one's sense of self

koan: a paradoxical story or riddle without a solution, used in Zen Buddhism to help practitioners see 'beyond reason'

A person who has a revelatory experience often claims to recognise the revelation by the experience of accompanying emotional changes such as a sense of awe, love, peace or inner calm. The strong emotional connections that people have with their religious beliefs are one of the reasons why religion is such a sensitive area.

TASK: ACTIVITY 8.4

With a partner, brainstorm specific examples that you might use to respond to the following question:

Many religious scholars assume that some specific knowledge from the past is reliable, and that direct revelation is possible. How might assumptions behind religious knowledge systems compare with assumptions made in other areas of knowledge?

TASK: THINK ABOUT 8.3

1   Sound is how our brains interpret particular vibrations. Therefore, what is the difference between hearing a voice and hearing *a voice in your head*?

2   How can we know if someone has had a direct revelation; what evidence might we want?

3   Why might it be easier to believe in direct revelations that were claimed to have happened long ago?

Indirect revelation

Indirect revelation is when people claim to experience a revelation through reading or listening to records of special revelations received by others. Religious scriptures are said to record memories of revelatory experiences and miracles, as well as the activities and beliefs of early followers, thereby providing current believers with knowledge about early teachings and practices.

Although scriptures may be regarded by believers as *directly revealed*, when a believer is inspired by the texts, this inspiration is called *indirect revelation.* For example, the Adi Granth, the Qur'an and the Vedas are believed to be directly revealed or inspired, and therefore regarded as authoritative by Sikhs, Muslims and Hindus respectively. A person who reads or listens to a reading from one of these texts may feel inspired by it in such a way that the person feels that God is communicating through the text. This is indirect revelation.

TASK: ACTIVITY 8.5

Choose one of more of the following questions to discuss with a partner. Then share your ideas with another pair.

1   Even if we accept that direct revelations have occurred, how can we be certain that the surviving compilations of texts accurately represent what was revealed?

2   In many ancient religions, the teachings have been passed from one generation to the next orally. It is often many years – and sometimes centuries – after the revelatory events that the teachings have been written down. What may have been lost or added along the way, by whom and why? How can we know?

3   Even the most careful translations from one language to another create changes to meaning. Reading a text in its original language may give some advantage, but language is a dynamic system, and the use of words changes over time. When reading ancient texts, how can we be sure that what they meant when they were written is what we think they mean now?

Miracles

Miracles are a feature of many religions, and are often used to justify belief in God, gods or other supernatural entities. How miracles are understood varies widely. Some people regard miracles as seemingly impossible events that interrupt the laws of nature; others argue that miracles are evidence of a supernatural being working within the laws of nature (even if they involve natural laws not yet discovered).

For many people, an unlikely event such as recovery from a life-threatening illness may be considered a miracle; others may regard even relatively common-place natural events as miraculous; for example, people often refer to *the miracle of birth*.

TOK IN YOUR LIFE

Can you think of an occurrence in your ordinary or everyday experience that you might want to describe as a *miracle*? What might justify this description?

TOK LINK: LANGUAGE

How might the way we define *miracle* affect our willingness to see miracles in the world around us?

REAL-LIFE SITUATION 8.1

In January 2006, the name *Allah* written in Arabic was recognised in the pattern of spots along one side of a two-year-old Oscar (a species of fish). On the other side of the fish was the name *Muhammad*. Within hours of the discovery, the fish was at the centre of a media frenzy. Many people declared the markings on the fish to be a miracle, and believed the fish was a sign from Allah.

1   Assuming the markings are legible, why might people regard it as a miracle?

2   On what grounds might their beliefs be justified?

Figure 8.3: Can you discern Arabic writing on the side of this fish?

Religious authorities

Most established religions have religious authorities: priests, imams, mufti, ayatollahs, lamas, shamans, Brahmin, rabbis, monks, theologians and others. One of the functions of authorities is to interpret the teachings and traditions of their religion for **lay people**, and to determine which variations of interpretation are permissible. Religious authorities also have some responsibility for discerning and deciding which accounts of direct revelation and miracles are authentic. In other words, they often decide what counts as religious knowledge and what does not.

> **KEY TERM**
>
> **lay people:** in this context, people without professional or specialised knowledge in their religion

TASK: THINK ABOUT 8.4

1   On what basis is the authority of a religious leader established?

2   Why might some religious leaders have extensive political powers?

TASK: ACTIVITY 8.6

In a small group, choose an intellectual movement (e.g. enlightenment, modernism, post-modernism, empiricism). Research answers to the following questions and prepare a short (10–15 minute) presentation to your class which answers the following:

- What is the intellectual movement you have chosen, and what did it promote?

- How did your chosen intellectual movement shape our knowledge and understanding of one religious knowledge system and one other area of knowledge? (For example, how did modernism affect our knowledge and understanding of Christianity and European history?)

Tradition

Religious tradition might be regarded as a faith community's memory. It is the beliefs, practices and interpretations of the community of believers as they are passed down from one generation to the next. Traditions are not static; they evolve from and draw upon the full interpretative and ritualistic history of a religion.

Typically, religious traditions vary from one culture to another despite common origins. For example, the forms of Buddhism practised in Sri Lanka tend to be markedly different from those practised in China or Japan. Within most of the world's major religions, there are numerous traditions. These may sometimes differ quite significantly from each other in their religious practices, as well as in their acceptance and interpretations of religious teachings.

TASK: THINK ABOUT 8.5

1   How do traditions change and grow?

2   Is this the same as saying they progress?

8.5 Methods and tools for developing religious knowledge

Many of the methods and tools used to develop religious knowledge are similar to those used in other areas of knowledge. We have already considered the importance of language, which might be considered a knowledge tool as well as a distinct knowledge theme.

Reason and logic

You may be surprised to discover that reason and logic are regarded as important methods for developing theological knowledge for many of the world's theistic (god-based) religions, as well as nontheistic religions (such as Jainism, Buddhism and Confucianism) which are often philosophical in nature. Theologians depend on reason to develop their understanding of the nature of God or the metaphysical world, and sometimes make logical arguments from religious axioms.

KEY POINT

The terms *reason* and *logic* are often used interchangeably, and the two concepts are very closely related. The difference is that logic is a science that uses defined rules which produce consistent answers, whereas reason is more of an art that encompasses all forms of critical thinking.

KEY TERMS

ontological: related to the nature of being and existence

a priori: based on deduction from self-evident premises, rather than empirical observation

One example of the use of logic in religion is known as Anselm's **ontological** argument. St Anselm (1033–1109) was an Italian Benedictine monk and Roman Catholic theologian. His argument was an attempt to prove the existence of God *a priori*. It was as follows:

Premise 1: God is the greatest being we can imagine.

Premise 2: The idea of God exists in the mind.

Premise 3: It is greater to exist in reality than to exist only in the mind.

Premise 4: If God exists only in the mind, then we can conceive of a greater being – that which exists in reality.

Premise 5: We cannot conceive of a being greater than God.

Conclusion: Therefore, God must exist in reality.

As you discovered in Chapter 4, no matter how logical the argument, the validity of any conclusion reached is only as reliable as the validity of the axioms or premises on which it is based.

> ### TASK: ACTIVITY 8.7
>
> With a partner, decide whether you think Anselm's ontological argument is convincing. Which premises might you challenge? How else might you challenge the argument?

Pascal's wager

Blaise Pascal (1623–1662) was a French mathematician and theologian. Pascal's wager is a reasoned argument for living as if God exists, based on probability. The argument can be summed up as follows: If we bet that God exists (and live accordingly) and we are right, we will get the rewards of heaven. If we are wrong, we do not lose anything. However, if we bet that God does not exist and we are right, we do not gain anything. But if we are wrong, we could end up in hell. Therefore, Pascal regarded it as sensible for us to assume that God does exist and live accordingly, because that way we can only win. We cannot lose.

> ### TASK: THINK ABOUT 8.6
>
> 1   What assumptions does Pascal make that are necessary for his conclusion to be reasonable and sensible?
>
> 2   Do you think reason alone could lead to religious conviction?

Imagination, myths and narratives

Some people are reluctant to consider imagination as a method for developing, discovering or transmitting knowledge, particularly in the area of religious knowledge. They may be concerned with the historicity of religious narratives, and believe that unless narratives are historically accurate, they are fictional and therefore *untrue*. Others would argue that narratives can convey profound religious truths whether the narratives are historically true or not.

> ### TOP TIP
>
> Do not make generalisations about any religion or religious group. Statements like *Christians believe the world was created in seven days* are inaccurate, and will weaken your arguments.

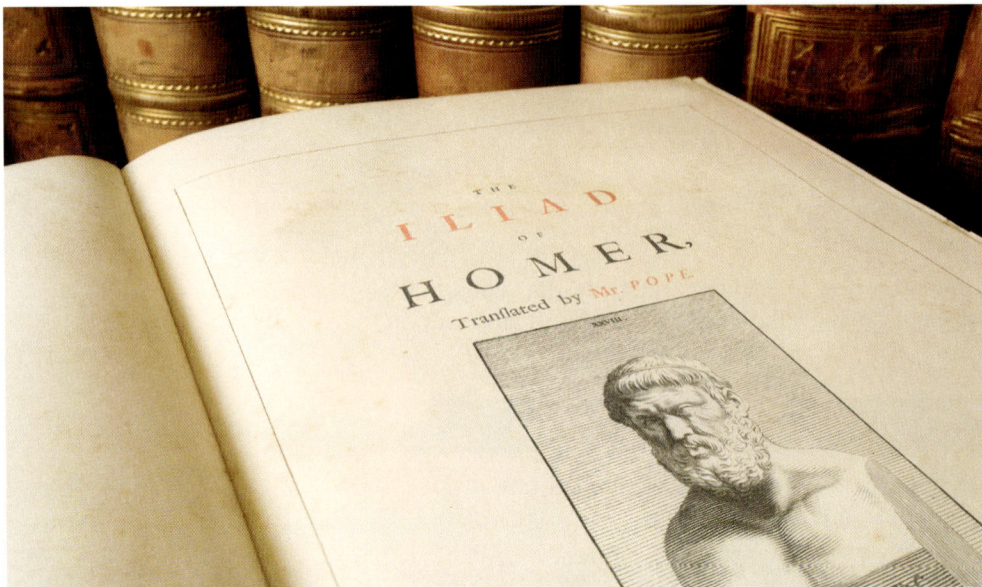

Figure 8.4: The *Iliad* is an account of the psychology of individual heroes and Greek gods. Modern scholars do not believe the events described in the *Iliad* are historically factual but they do believe the stories contain memories from Mycenaean times

TASK: ACTIVITY 8.8

In pairs or small groups, consider some of the literature you have studied in school. What are some of the messages or *truths* that may be conveyed through great novels? What is it about novels that can make them such powerful messengers?

What difference does it make whether a wonderfully inspiring narrative describes something that really happened or not? Can we be as inspired by fiction as by fact?

In many religious traditions, imagination has played a significant role in discovering, articulating and transmitting religious knowledge. **Parables** and fables are simple short stories that illustrate moral teachings, and can be found in a number of religious traditions. Imaginative **myths** have also been used to explain the world, relationships and rituals, and to teach different ideologies, morals and behavioural models.

TASK: ACTIVITY 8.9

1   Compare creation stories from two different religions. How are they similar and how are they different?

2   What truths might they contain? How would you decide what, if any, knowledge they convey?

KEY TERMS

parable: a short story that conveys a truth or moral ideal

myth: a traditional story about gods, heroes or groups of people

Faith

The word *faith* comes from the Latin *fidere*, which means to trust, and a great deal of religious knowledge is accepted on trust. But it is not necessarily a trust without evidence, or a trust that flies in the face of evidence; it is a trust and confidence in something for which we may have enough evidence to justify our belief, although not enough for incontrovertible proof.

Although the words *religion* and *faith* are often used interchangeably, faith is not limited to religion. In many areas of life, we develop theories and conclusions based on our experiences. This is inductive reasoning, which you will have read a little about in Chapter 4.

A simple example of faith built on inductive reasoning might be when I set my alarm clock. If I set my alarm clock for 6 a.m., I take it on trust that it will work, based on my experience that it has always worked in the past. I cannot prove in advance that it will work tomorrow. It is always possible, and indeed probable, that there will come a morning when it will not work.

A great deal of the knowledge we rely on in our day-to-day lives is necessarily grounded in faith. That faith is based on the evidence of our experiences, and is not diminished by the lack of concrete proof.

> **TOP TIP**
>
> Avoid making generalisations about religion. Statements like *'Religious knowledge is based on faith while the natural sciences are based on reason'* are inaccurate and misleading. You need to demonstrate that you can discuss religion in a fair and balanced way.

> **TASK: THINK ABOUT 8.7**
>
> 1   To what extent do the natural sciences rely on faith? What about history?
>
> 2   How does faith differ from belief?

8.6 Ethics and religious knowledge

It is often assumed that religion and ethics are closely related because, to some extent, both religion and ethics try to determine what are right or wrong actions in different situations.

Religions develop their ethical teachings by reasoning largely from the principles of the special revelations of their founders, and authoritative interpretations of those revelations. Ethics, on the other hand, reasons from more **humanistic principles** than the different philosophical approaches such as deontological ethics, consequentialist ethics or virtue ethics (see Chapter 4 for more on ethical theories).

Although religious and secular ethics do not derive their authority from the same sources, there is often a great deal of common ground between them. For example, all religions and ethical systems would regard murder as wrong, but there are various

> **KEY TERMS**
>
> **humanistic principles:** principles that support the value and agency of human beings

opinions in all religious and philosophical ethical systems regarding the rights and wrongs of killing during warfare or as a state-endorsed punishment in a penal system.

There are times when philosophical ethical systems and religious ethics appear to clash, but the dividing lines in such clashes are often more to do with cultural norms than religious versus philosophical ethics. In most, if not all, controversial issues there are disputes within the different philosophical and religious ethical systems. To take one controversial topic, the issue of same-sex marriage is often put forward as an example of *conservative* religious ethics versus *progressive* philosophical ethical systems. However, there is no such divide. Arguments for and against same-sex marriage occur in all ethical systems including religious ethical systems. In Islam, for example, many Muslims believe that homosexual relationships go against the teachings of the Qur'an, but a growing number of Islamic scholars are re-examining Islamic teachings and suggesting that some of the antipathy towards homosexuality is due to misinterpretation. Same-sex Muslim weddings are now performed by a few individual imams, and inclusive mosque communities that welcome LGBTQ Muslims are increasing in number. Similarly, in Judaism, while most Orthodox regard same-sex relationships as forbidden by the Torah, other Jewish denominations now support same-sex marriage. Even within the Orthodox tradition, there are a growing number of Orthodox Rabbis and observant Jews who are actively engaged in fighting for LGBTQ rights.

TASK: ACTIVITY 8.10

In pairs or small groups, choose an ethical issue such as abortion, euthanasia, animal experimentation, pacifism, or capital punishment, and research attitudes towards that issue in two religions and two philosophical ethical systems. Can you find arguments *for* and *against* your chosen issue in each of the systems you examine?

Discuss: If there can be different perspectives and opinions on any issue in all ethical systems, including religious ethics, how can we decide what is right or wrong?

TASK: THINK ABOUT 8.8

1   Religious ethical positions are often labelled as *conservative*. Is there a value judgement embedded in such labels?

2   To what extent do you think this labelling is fair?

8.7 Knowledge questions

1   How can we know whether spiritual experiences are a connection with the divine (however that might be conceived) or simply strong emotional responses?

2   What might we mean by *progress* in religious knowledge?

3   Can religious knowledge systems provide us with knowledge that cannot be found in other areas of knowledge?

8.8 Exhibition task

Consider how you might use an image or statue of Lord Ganesha as an item for your TOK exhibition. Which IA prompt question would you choose? Write 250–300 words on the real-world context of the *murti*, and how it links to your chosen IA prompt.

8.9 Extended writing task

Write 450–550 words on one or more of the following questions:

1   How might the number of people making a knowledge claim affect our willingness to accept the truth of the claim in religion and one other area of knowledge?

2   To what extent can we rely on the opinion of authorities when assessing a knowledge claim?

SKILLS SELF-ASSESSMENT CHECKLIST

Reflect on what you have learned in this chapter and indicate your confidence level between 1 and 5 (where 5 is the highest score and 1 is the lowest). If you score below 3, revisit that section. Come back to this list later in your course. Has your confidence grown?

	Confidence level	Revisited?
Can I identify different types of knowledge claims about religion systems?		
Am I able to evaluate the impact of religious and non-religious perspectives on different areas of knowledge?		
Do I have a critical awareness of some of the sources of religious knowledge?		
Can I discuss some of the tools and methods for producing religious knowledge?		
Can I compare these tools and methods with those used in other areas of knowledge?		
Am I able to compare and contrast religious ethical knowledge with philosophical ethical knowledge?		

8.10 Further reading

For an articulate and well-informed argument for God, read: Karen Armstrong, *The Case for God*, Alfred A. Knopf, 2009

For more about the relationship between religions and human rights, read: John Witte and M. Christian Green, *Religion and Human Rights: An Introduction*, Oxford University Press, 2011

For a good introduction to many of the world's major religions, read: Ninian Smart, *The Religious Experience*, Macmillan, 1991

> Chapter 9

Knowledge and indigenous societies

9.1 Introduction

Indigenous peoples are distinct communities whose identities and customs are inextricably linked to a land they have inhabited for many generations. Depending on the definitions adopted, there are estimated to be 270–370 million indigenous people in the world, living in 70 countries.

Indigenous peoples usually self-identify as indigenous, and they claim continuity with **pre-colonial communities**, as well as strong links to the lands in which they live. Typically, they have their own distinct languages, as well as distinct political and social systems; they may also have their own religions. Embodied in the lifestyles, beliefs and traditions of indigenous peoples is a body of indigenous knowledge that has accumulated over centuries of living in a particular environment. As indigenous peoples have been **assimilated** into mainstream societies, much of their indigenous knowledge has been lost. In recent years, people around the world have started to appreciate the value of indigenous knowledge, and are now taking steps to preserve it.

> **KEY TERMS**
>
> **pre-colonial communities:** communities that existed before modern colonialisation which began in the 15th century
>
> **assimilate:** absorb, integrate

9.2 Defining indigenous peoples

When we think of indigenous peoples, we often think of hunter-gatherers and nomadic herders who have maintained their traditional ways of life across the centuries, and who often live in isolation from the modern world. Over generations, however, many indigenous peoples have intermarried with non-indigenous inhabitants of their land, recent immigrants and neighbouring peoples. This has led to significant debates about who the indigenous peoples are. Different countries have resolved the problem in different ways.

The New Zealand government, for example, defines a Maori as *'a person of the Maori race of New Zealand; and includes any descendant of such a person'*. In this case, any person with just one Maori ancestor, however remote, may claim indigenous rights as a Maori. In Australia, however, the Australian High Court defined an Aboriginal or Torres Strait Islander as *'a person of Aboriginal or Torres Strait Islander descent who identifies as an Aboriginal or Torres Strait Islander and is accepted as such by the community in which he or she lives'*. Other countries such as Canada have adopted more legalistic definitions, which may depend upon factors relating to parentage and marriage.

The different approaches and different ways of categorising indigenous peoples raise significant social and political questions.

Figure 9.1: Under New Zealand law, anyone with a Maori ancestor can declare themselves to be Maori

In many countries, it is often people who live rurally who continue to identify with their indigenous roots. Indigenous people who live in cities tend to be assimilated into a broader culture, particularly if they intermarry. Many of their indigenous skills and knowledge are no longer necessary in urban living, and are often lost. But this is not always the case; there are some city dwellers who continue to strongly identify with their indigenous origins.

TASK: THINK ABOUT 9.1

1   Where does an indigenous culture stop and more general society begins? Why does it matter, and who should decide?

2   If paleoanthropologists are right and all people originated in the Horn of Africa where Eritrea, Ethiopia, Somalia, and Djibouti are today, to what extent are any of us indigenous to other places?

TOK IN YOUR LIFE

Do you know where your ancestors came from? If you were to discover that your great-great-great grandparents came from another continent, to what extent do you think it would affect your sense of identity?

9.3 The scope of indigenous knowledge

Indigenous knowledge is knowledge that is predominantly related to community survival in a particular environment. It often involves a deep understanding of local ecology, and includes beliefs, practices and languages that are embedded in the community's culture. This knowledge can sometimes be used to maintain social, economic and ecological sustainability for indigenous communities.

Indigenous knowledge can include philosophical views and concepts. For example, the concept of *abundancia*, which is found in many South American indigenous communities, is the idea that the environment will provide for all needs. This concept encourages people to think more in terms of communal custodianship than individual property rights, and long-term planning can seem meaningless.

TASK: THINK ABOUT 9.2

1   In a finite world with a burgeoning human population, how sustainable is the concept of *abundancia* from a global perspective?

2   To what extent can we expect the Earth to continue to provide for all human needs?

In recent years, there has been a growing appreciation of the valuable contributions that indigenous knowledge can make to the rest of the world in fields as diverse as conservation, agriculture and medical science. For example, the rosy periwinkle is a plant native to Madagascar, and natives use it as a medicinal plant. Researchers were able to derive a drug called vinblastine from it, and this drug is now used to treat cancers such as Hodgkin's lymphoma. Indigenous peoples are sometimes believed to have a deep or even **innate understanding** of how much can be harvested from the land, how many animals can be killed and how to balance hunger and need with husbandry and stewardship if they are to have anything to eat next year or in future generations.

As well as offering unique philosophical viewpoints and a deep understanding of local ecology, indigenous knowledge encompasses language, systems of classification, social interactions, rituals and spirituality.

KEY TERM

innate understanding: understanding that we are born with

TOP TIP

If you are writing about indigenous knowledge, use specific examples because each community is unique, with its own beliefs and customs. Take care not to romanticise indigenous cultures; they can be just as unjust, destructive and imperfect as any other culture.

9.4 Perspectives on indigenous knowledge

Over the centuries, many people have regarded indigenous peoples as *primitive*, superstitious and ignorant. However, uncritically dismissing indigenous knowledge in this way has left humankind much the poorer. In recent years, people have started to develop a new understanding of, and appreciation for, the cultural, linguistic, ecological and scientific insights to be found in indigenous peoples and their knowledge.

While there is a growing movement to preserve indigenous knowledge and use it to complement mainstream scientific knowledge, perspectives differ over whether it is helpful to distinguish between indigenous knowledge and knowledge from other sources. Some people argue that keeping indigenous knowledge distinct from other knowledge enables indigenous peoples to be properly recognised and accredited. Others argue that focusing on a distinction commits some researchers into maintaining a distinction to preserve their own academic niche.

Another perspective on indigenous knowledge argues that in the current trend to integrate indigenous and scientific knowledge, indigenous knowledge has had very little impact on **development practice**. Proponents of this view suggest that indigenous knowledge should be thought of more as a method of knowing, with less emphasis on content and more emphasis on how indigenous peoples discover and develop their knowledge. This might imply, for example, that we should respect the reasons for and methods of indigenous peoples in developing indigenous knowledge, but not be committed to accepting the truth of the content.

Some would argue that while modern science and technology have been important for human development, there is no reason why science should be standardised. They argue that because indigenous knowledge includes knowledge that has been accumulated over centuries, it has been vetted by communities over time, and should therefore be granted equal status with knowledge attained through scientific methods, even if it fails to satisfy the kinds of rigorous tests to which the natural sciences submit.

Whichever perspective you take in this debate, it is important to remember that not all indigenous knowledge would be regarded as knowledge in a more rigorous knowledge system. Also, much of the indigenous knowledge that is preserved and utilised outside of the indigenous society that it arises in, is preserved and evaluated using scientific methods and modern technology. This makes it difficult to distinguish indigenous knowledge from other knowledge sources in many cases, and again raises political questions about who decides which knowledge is to be preserved, and how.

> **KEY TERM**
>
> **development practice:** the tools, management techniques and strategic approaches used by international development practitioners

> **CROSS REFERENCE**
>
> Details of scientific methods are discussed in Chapter 13 of this book and Chapter 13 of the Course Guide.

> **TASK: ACTIVITY 9.1**
>
> In 2013, the Indian scientist, Suman Sahai asserted, *'A scientific system's validity lies not in its being credible everywhere, but in its being credible in the culture where it was developed and where it has provided solutions'*. To what extent would you agree with her?
>
> • Consider and weigh up both sides of the argument.
>
> • Develop one or two specific examples to support each side of the argument.
>
> • What are the implications of your arguments for and against?

TASK: THINK ABOUT 9.3

If indigenous knowledge were to be classified as knowledge in a more general sense, what would be the consequences?

9.5 Methods and tools for developing indigenous knowledge

We have seen what indigenous knowledge is, but where does it come from? How do indigenous peoples come to know what they know?

Indigenous languages

Indigenous languages are important for developing and transmitting knowledge within the indigenous communities in which they are spoken. They are also important to the outside world in that they give a unique window into the conceptual worlds of the people who speak those languages. Indigenous languages often express ideas or concepts for which there are no equivalent words in other languages, and concepts that we might take for granted may be absent from indigenous cultures. For example, the languages of the Dani peoples of western New Guinea are said to only recognise two basic colours: *mili* for cool/dark shades such as blue, green and black, and *mola* for warm/light colours such as red, yellow and white. This raises the question of whether the Dani people see the same colours that other people see, and therefore impacts on a deep philosophical question about colour perception and more generally **qualia**. There are studies that suggest we can only see colours that we have concepts and language for, so the colours that we see depend upon the languages we speak.

> **KEY TERM**
>
> **qualia:** qualities or properties as perceived by a person

TASK: THINK ABOUT 9.4

If you drive through rural areas, do you see Friesians, Jerseys, Charolais, Simmental and Ongole, or do you simply see cows? In urban areas, do you see Persians, Siamese, Burmese, Bengals, Ragdolls and Munchkins, or do you simply see cats? What we see is largely dictated by our conceptual frameworks.

It is estimated that 95% of the world's 6,500 or so languages are spoken by no more than a cumulative total of 5% of the world's population. Some of these languages have fewer than 1,000 speakers, and many of them are unwritten because they have no formal script. In such languages, indigenous knowledge is passed orally from one generation to the next without being codified in writing or translated into any languages with wider access. This means that if an indigenous language is lost, the indigenous knowledge encoded in that language will be lost with it.

KEY POINT

It is generally believed that between 50% and 90% of the world's languages will be extinct by the year 2100. Preserving indigenous languages has become a priority for many people who wish to preserve indigenous knowledge.

TASK: ACTIVITY 9.2

Consider the following knowledge questions. Can you think of arguments and examples to support different points of view?

- Indigenous languages often embody indigenous knowledge concepts that do not translate well. In what way is this issue similar to or different from language issues in other areas of knowledge?

- Would introducing writing systems to people with unwritten languages help to preserve indigenous knowledge?

- To what extent could indigenous knowledge be preserved by translating indigenous languages into widely spoken languages such as English, Arabic, Mandarin or Hindi?

Praxis

Praxis refers to the established customs and practices of a group. In indigenous communities, skills and practical knowledge are passed on from one generation to the next through an apprenticeship-like system in which, typically, fathers teach their sons, and mothers teach their daughters. Among the Aboriginal people of Australia, girls are taken aside when they reach puberty to be taught 'women's business' by the womenfolk. This includes teaching them the knowledge and skills deemed necessary to prepare them for marriage and motherhood. Similarly, when the boys reach puberty, the men of their ethnic group put them through a series of initiation rites to prepare them for manhood. Women are not allowed to be party to these initiation rites, just as men are not allowed to know the secrets that are passed on to the girls.

TASK: THINK ABOUT 9.5

1   What assumptions might underlie the practice of dividing knowledge along gender lines?

2   In a world that is striving for universal human rights and gender equality, and even questioning the concept of gender assignment, how can we respond to indigenous gender roles respectfully without relinquishing the ideal of gender equality?

The skills that are passed on in any indigenous society may include hunting, cooking, farming, craftsmanship, where to find and access safe water, how to develop natural medicines, and so on. These are skills that can only be learned through experience and developed through practice.

TOK IN YOUR LIFE

Have you ever foraged for mushrooms or other wild foods? How do you know what to collect, especially when the consequences of eating the wrong things can be deadly?

Practising a skill allows our senses to sharpen. If we listen to birds in the forest with an expert, our ears will gradually become attuned to the different sounds that birds make, and we will begin to develop expertise. Similarly, if we pick mushrooms with an expert forager, we will learn to distinguish what is edible from what is potentially deadly.

Figure 9.2: Gamelan music players. Children learn traditional skills by practising them alongside their elders

---

TASK: ACTIVITY 9.3

Could you become a good footballer or musician by reading every *how to* book ever written but never actually playing? What kinds of skills can you can learn from reading manuals, and which must you learn through praxis? Write a brief paragraph on how book-learning and praxis can complement each other, using examples from your own experience.

TOK LINK: CORE THEME

How might indigenous knowledge systems expand your insights or deepen your awareness of yourself, others or the society and world in which you live?

Authority

It is common in many indigenous cultures for authorities such as elders, chieftains or shamans to act as **arbiters** and guardians of indigenous knowledge. These authorities determine what counts as knowledge, and have responsibility for developing, preserving and protecting indigenous knowledge. Indigenous leaders may be appointed, elected or attain their position through inheritance or common

KEY TERM

arbiter: a person who settles a dispute or has the final judgement and authority in relation to an issue

recognition. The indigenous knowledge they preserve may relate to areas as diverse as religious beliefs and practices, environmental knowledge, indigenous history, indigenous laws and indigenous crafts and skills. Authority figures are frequently responsible for decision-making, maintaining indigenous traditions and upholding cultural norms within their communities. They may be considered guardians of the collective memory.

In some cases, authorities within an indigenous group may forbid their knowledge to be shared outside the group. Elders of some Native American ethnic groups, for example, fear exploitation, and will disown any member of the group who shares their knowledge of indigenous medicines with outsiders.

TASK: THINK ABOUT 9.6

1   How can we be sure that indigenous authorities transmit indigenous knowledge accurately?

2   Could the ways in which authorities are appointed affect the reliability of the knowledge that is preserved?

REAL-LIFE SITUATION 9.1

In the South African Zulu culture, Zulus recognise herbalists and diviners as authorities in traditional medicines. The herbalists are rather like pharmacists; their role is to make traditional medicines and apply them to the patients. The diviners are the diagnosticians: they **divine** the causes of illness by throwing bones, shells, seeds and other artefacts onto a mat and observing how they land. Some diviners can also act as mediums, who consult with ancestral spirits to determine which medicines need to be prescribed.

1   What is the impact of culture on the production of knowledge?

2   To what extent does the evaluation of knowledge claims depend on culture or perspective?

KEY TERM

divine: in this context, to discover something in a supernatural way

The herbalists' and diviners' knowledge and skills are highly specialised and learned over many years through serving as apprentices. As a result, they acquire indigenous knowledge stretching back over many generations, and have a high status among their people. In urbanised Zulu communities, herbalists and diviners are able to attain relative wealth by selling their knowledge and skills.

TASK: THINK ABOUT 9.7

To what extent does the example of Zulu knowledge that appears to work beneficially for the Zulu community make the knowledge scientifically valid? Try to come up with arguments for both sides.

Faith

There is a strong connection between traditional medicines and belief systems in many indigenous cultures. People need to have faith in the stories and traditions transmitted by their communities in order to preserve them. The Bantu people who live in Zimbabwe, for example, have a holistic system of traditional medicine which considers illnesses in terms of physical, emotional, spiritual and environmental imbalances. Bantu healers often consult the spirit world to reach their diagnoses, and their medical practices are inseparable from traditional Bantu religion. The use of their medicines requires significant faith in both the spirit world and the ability of the healer to act as a medium.

> **KEY POINT**
>
> Indigenous knowledge is not static; it develops and changes over time. As indigenous peoples undergo different experiences, are exposed to changes in their environment and meet with people of different cultures, so their ideas, beliefs and practices change.

Storytelling

Storytelling is an important tool for the development and transmission of knowledge for many indigenous peoples, particularly those without a written language system. Indeed, an oral tradition was the norm in all cultures before written materials became widely available, and many of our most ancient texts are records of stories and events that had been passed down orally for generations before.

For indigenous peoples, stories are an effective way of teaching future generations knowledge that is essential to survival, as well as to teach knowledge deemed valuable to their culture.

The Dreamtime stories of Australian Aboriginals are a clear example of this. Many of the Dreamtime stories are about animals and people that can be seen as patterns in the stars of the night sky. These stories help people to remember and recognise certain stars. This knowledge then enables them to use these stars to navigate across the vast Australian bush and deserts. Accurate navigation is as essential to survival in the Australian outback as it is at sea.

> **TOK IN YOUR LIFE**
>
> Think about some of the narratives that you live by. They may be stories that come from your religious background, or they may be secular stories that have resonated with you. What is it about those stories that make them so meaningful to you, and how do they shape your perspectives?

As well as passing on knowledge useful for navigation, the Dreamtime stories also include important information about animal behaviour and habitats. This knowledge can be vital for the survival of people who live off the land.

Figure 9.3: The night sky in the Australian outback has inspired many stories

TASK: THINK ABOUT 9.8

Why might stories make it easier to learn and remember important information?

Reason

A great deal of knowledge is discovered by indigenous peoples as the result of inductive reasoning through regular and repeated observations of the local environment. For example, people may observe over the years that some local plants are more resistant to drought than others, or they may observe that animals behave differently under different weather conditions. Over time, these observations become regarded as truths, which help the holders of these truths to survive and prosper.

Sometimes the local knowledge acquired has global applications. For example, the Quechua peoples of Bolivia and Peru discovered the bark of the cinchona tree could be used to reduce fever and inflammation. When scientific studies were conducted, it was discovered that the tree bark produces a chemical we now know as quinine, which became the first effective treatment for malaria.

TASK: ACTIVITY 9.4

There are many *alternative* health care systems around the world, some of which are based on indigenous knowledge. These include Ayurvedic medicine in India and Sri Lanka, acupuncture and traditional medicines in China, and Native American medicines in North America.

CONTINUED

In pairs or small groups, prepare a debate on the knowledge question, *'To what extent should indigenous medical practices be subjected to scientific testing and expected to meet modern (western) medical standards?'*.

Whichever side of the debate you are on, develop one or two specific examples to support your argument, and think of counter-arguments to points that the opposite side might raise.

REAL-LIFE SITUATION 9.2

Aye-ayes are a type of lemur that are native to Madagascar. They are one of the world's rarest and most endangered species. As well as being under threat through habitat loss, they also suffer from the consequences of indigenous beliefs. Some indigenous Malagasy peoples believe that because of its strange appearance, the aye-aye must have been made by the devil. The Sakalava people claim aye-ayes enter houses at night and murder people in their beds. Other indigenous Malagasy villagers believe that they will die if an aye-aye looks at them. Evidence is presented in the form of anecdotes, such as the story of a woodcutter who had cut down a tree in which a female aye-aye and her baby were sheltering. The baby was killed but the mother managed to escape. About a month later, the woodcutter died unexpectedly, and a month after that, the woodcutter's son also died.

Many Malagasy believe that if an aye-aye is seen, it must be killed to avoid bad luck, and must then be hung on a pole by a crossroads so that strangers who approach it will carry any residual bad luck away with them.

1   Explain whether you think the villagers' evidence for the evil nature of the aye-aye is reasonable.

2   To what extent can the nature of what is reasonable be determined by cultural context? Try to find examples to illustrate different perspectives.

Artefacts

Artefacts exist within a social context, and only mean something within that context. For example, you may understand the significance of a wedding ring, but in societies that symbolise marriage in other ways, a ring on the finger may appear meaningless.

Cultural artefacts often give children their first experiences of the culture into which they were born. By playing with and exploring those artefacts, children discover different aspects of their culture.

Artefacts are manufactured objects, and they therefore inevitably indicate the knowledge and skills of those responsible for making the artefact. In this sense, artefacts can be seen as a method for collecting and preserving information and understanding, and can offer a window into the world of their makers. For example, archaeologists can learn a great deal about ancient civilisations by studying artefacts such as fragments of pottery, ancient coins and tools.

Interpreting an artefact involves considering the artefact's context to try to discover the knowledge it embodies. Techniques such as carbon-dating and being aware of where and how artefacts are discovered, help to provide a context which enables ancient artefacts to be interpreted.

TASK: ACTIVITY 9.5

Select an example of an indigenous artefact and consider its context. What information might it provide you about the people who made and used it?

TOK IN YOUR LIFE

Try to think of an artefact that best represents your life and/or culture. What is it about the artefact that is meaningful to you? If you were to show the artefact to someone from a different culture, what might they learn about you through studying it?

9.6 Ethics and indigenous knowledge

Indigenous knowledge is an area of knowledge that is rife with ethical issues. As well as ethical questions arising over who should be regarded as indigenous and what counts as indigenous knowledge, there are significant issues regarding the impact of colonialism and globalisation on indigenous communities, and the use of indigenous knowledge by people outside indigenous communities.

REAL-LIFE SITUATION 9.3

Among the Bhotia peoples of Uttar Pradesh, India, men traditionally herded sheep and grew cotton, while women wove carpets from the wool and tied it with home-grown cotton. In recent decades, synthetic materials and chemical dyes have replaced the natural materials, but the chemical dyes are carcinogenic and pollute the environment.

There is a programme underway to revive traditional carpet-weaving in the region, drawing upon the Bhotia people's indigenous knowledge of carpet-weaving, sheep-farming and cotton-growing. This programme is driven, in part, by the high demand for non-synthetic carpets in Europe, where natural carpets retail for three times the price of synthetic carpets.

1   Does encouraging indigenous peoples to continue their traditional practices limit their options for progress?

2   How ethical would it be for other communities to adopt the Bhotia methods of rug making?

Figure 9.4: Bhotia women making a traditional rug. Is the revival of such skills beneficial to indigenous peoples, or does it exploit them?

TASK: THINK ABOUT 9.9

The growing respect for indigenous knowledge is, in part, due to the recognition of the usefulness and commercial value of that knowledge. To what extent do you think the revival of indigenous knowledge is driven by a non-indigenous desire for greater profits? Does it matter?

Ethical issues also arise when indigenous knowledge and traditional practices conflict with a wider understanding of and striving for universal human rights. For example, the Emberá are an indigenous community in Latin America who traditionally build their houses along the banks of rivers, although most now live in villages, towns or urban centres. The Emberá are the only indigenous peoples in Latin America known to practise female genital mutilation (FGM) – a practice which is illegal in many countries around the world. The tradition was extremely secretive until an incident in 2007 in which a girl died as a result of FGM. Following this incident, there was a campaign to raise awareness of the dangers of FGM. By 2015, only 25,000 members (10%) had decided to discontinue FGM, which meant that, at that time, 90% still wanted to continue the practice.

In another example, the Dani people of New Guinea expect women to cut off the top part of their fingers when a relative dies as a sign of respect and grieving.

TASK: ACTIVITY 9.6

In a post-colonial and largely relativistic world, many of us are reluctant to suggest that some cultural practices are wrong. In small groups, discuss:

- Should people have the right to expect others to mutilate themselves or their children if it is part of their culture?

- Are there any ethical standards that you think all people should adopt, regardless of their cultural norms?

9.7 Knowledge questions

1   How can reason make sense in an indigenous context to someone without faith in the underlying indigenous cultural principles?

2   How can appreciation for indigenous knowledge lead to its exploitation?

9.8 Exhibition task

Consider how you might use a hand-woven rug as an item for your TOK exhibition. Which IA prompt question would you choose, and which theme would you focus on? Write 250–300 words on the real-world context of the rug and how it links to your chosen IA prompt.

9.9 Extended writing task

Write 450–550 words on one or more of the following questions:

1   To what extent can indigenous knowledge be applied to situations outside the environment in which the people who develop that knowledge live?

2   How might we evaluate a knowledge claim that is based on indigenous knowledge?

3   Could there be such a thing as global indigenous knowledge over the preservation and stewardship of the Earth's resources?

SKILLS SELF-ASSESSMENT CHECKLIST

Reflect on what you have learned in this chapter and indicate your confidence level between 1 and 5 (where 5 is the highest score and 1 is the lowest). If you score below 3, revisit that section. Come back to this list later in your course. Has your confidence grown?

	Confidence level	Revisited?
Can I articulate some of the difficulties that come with trying to define indigenous peoples?		
Can I compare the scope of indigenous knowledge with other areas of knowledge?		
Am I aware of some of the different perspectives on indigenous knowledge, and can I discuss their implications?		
Can I discuss some knowledge issues relating to indigenous knowledge, and am I able to provide some specific examples?		
Can I identify and evaluate some of the methods and tools used in producing and developing indigenous knowledge?		
Am I able to identify and evaluate specific examples of ethical issues relating to indigenous knowledge?		
Have I the skills necessary to weigh up ethical issues relating to indigenous knowledge?		

9.10 Further reading

To understand more about traditional medicine in Zimbabwe, read: Takawira Kazembe, 'Traditional medicine in Zimbabwe', *Rose Croix Journal 4*, 2007

To follow up on the way language affects what we see, read: Aina Casaponsa and Panos Athanasopoulos, 'The way you see colour depends on what language you speak', *The Conversation*, 16th April 2018

If you want to know more about Aboriginal storytelling, read: Helen McKay, 'The Dreamtime – Australian Aboriginal storytelling', *Bushcraft and Survival*, 16th June 2010

If you would like to know more about the plight of the aye-aye, read: Elwyn Simons and David Meyers, 'Folklore and Beliefs about the Aye-aye', *Lemur News* Vol. 6, pp11–16, 2001

To find out what the UN is doing to preserve indigenous languages, read: UN Human Rights Council, 'Many indigenous languages are in danger of extinction', *The Narcosphere*, 17th October 2019

Part 3

Areas of Knowledge

Chapter 10

History

LEARNING INTENTIONS

In this chapter, you will develop your skills to explore the knowledge claims made in history, learn how historical knowledge is produced, how it connects with knowledge in different areas of knowledge and the influence of ethical considerations. You will explore how, in our search for historical knowledge, we make use of various tools and methods, including language, memory, reason and imagination.

You will:

* develop the skills to investigate the scope of history, and evaluate the knowledge questions arising about the nature of historical knowledge

* improve your skills of interpretation, and appreciate why there are different historical perspectives

* foster the skills to evaluate the reliability of the tools and methods used in history, and the role of selection and interpretation of sources

* hone your writing skills, and in particular, your ability to use examples to support an argument about the nature of historical knowledge, and to discuss the implications that follow

* identify and evaluate different perspectives in response to ethical questions and issues associated with historical knowledge.

10.1 Introduction

History is one of the subjects in *Individuals and societies* – in Group 3 of the Diploma Programme (DP). However, for the purposes of TOK, history is dealt with separately from the human sciences. Our historical knowledge is arguably one of the most important bodies of knowledge, and our mechanism for passing on knowledge to future generations is one of our successes as a species. History studies the recorded past using a method that is based on the concepts of evidence, reliability and accuracy. We have an appetite for the past, shown by the popularity of historical novels, blockbuster films with historical themes, historical TV documentaries and the numbers of people who flock to museums, historical monuments and galleries. Furthermore, our own knowledge of the modern world depends on a good knowledge and understanding of our historical past. The identity of a country is shaped by its collective memory of its military, political and socioeconomic history.

TOK IN YOUR LIFE

What is the study of history about, and in what ways do you think it is important? Who in your TOK class is studying higher- or standard-level history? What are the topics they study, and why are they considered to be significant? Identify one or more specific real-life example.

10.2 The scope of history

The subject matter and scope of history include both the span of time – including the ancient, medieval and modern past – and the international history of the different continents and cultures across the globe.

Understanding this vast subject matter is made possible by the evidence-based historical method. Historical knowledge claims are based on an interpretation and selection of sources and evidence. On the one hand, there appears to be indisputable and objective historical facts which form part of our historical knowledge. For example, we can claim that the leader of the Indian independence movement, Mohandas Karamchand Gandhi (1869–1948), was shot on 30th January 1948. This is a historical fact that can be checked against sources.

On the other hand, we can make a very different type of claim by asserting that, '*The life and work of M. K. Gandhi paved the way for a modern Indian democracy, and without him, Pandit Jawaharlal Nehru* (1889–1964) *would never have become India's first prime minister in 1947'.* This claim is based on an interpretation of the evidence that weaves a meaningful narrative. Historical judgements like these might be less certain than basic facts because they are interpretations. It follows that some historical knowledge claims are contestable – where not everyone agrees with the same interpretation of an event.

Figure 10.1: The leader of the Indian independence movement, M. K. Gandhi, in November 1931 during his visit to the UK. To what extent are historical facts more certain than historical interpretations?

TOK IN YOUR LIFE

What do you think is a fact about your own past? What is an interpretation of your own past? Identify one or more specific real-life examples of each.

Write a journal entry that explores the distinction between historical fact and historical interpretation.

Historical explanations

One historical fact is that Singapore became independent from Malaysia on 9 August 1965. An explanation of why this happened would require interpretation of the evidence, and an understanding of the political and economic causes behind the event. There may be an infinite number of causes of a single event. If a historian sets out to read every primary source that is relevant to the study of an event from the past, how far back do they need to go before claiming knowledge and understanding? There has to be a limit to the chain of causation that can be explored as well as a limit to the sources that are thought to be relevant. Historians make a judgement about cause and effect relationships based on certain assumptions. These assumptions might include the idea that some causes are more significant than others, and that we can trace an event back to key evidentially supported causes. It is only often with the benefit of hindsight that judgements about significant causes can be made.

TASK: ACTIVITY 10.1

As a class, write down each of the following knowledge questions at the top of a piece of paper. Get into small groups. Pass the papers around the class so that each group makes a new contribution to each question.

To test your skills, you might develop this further – small groups could add a new idea such as: a new argument for, a counter-argument against, a new real-life example, a different perspective, an identification of assumptions made or a consideration of the implications.

Once finished, evaluate the responses on paper, and discuss the knowledge questions as a class.

1 Can we have certain knowledge of the past? Why? Why not?

2 Is history a science? Why? Why not?

3 Is eyewitness testimony a reliable source of evidence? Why? Why not?

4 How much source material and information needs to be gathered before we can claim knowledge and understanding of an event?

5 If a historical explanation relates to the concepts of cause, effect and motive, is this also the same when explaining phenomena in other areas of knowledge such as the natural and human sciences?

10.3 Historical perspectives

Historians take a global approach to studying the past. The vast subject content of history has enormous variety – including every time period in each continent throughout recorded human history. The selection of suitable topics for historians to study has changed over time. The past emphasis on the role of leaders in a country's military and political history has changed to include an understanding of the past through the eyes of women, ethnic minorities or indigenous peoples.

The selection of topics for their significance links to our perspective on the past. For example, historians might focus on understanding the causes and consequences of the division in 1945 between North Korea – supported by the Soviet Union – and South Korea – supported by the USA. Alternatively, historians might choose to focus on the history of popular culture in South Korea. Cultural historians might want to explain the rise of *K-pop* and the factors that have caused the global popularity of Asian bands such as *BTS*. This band, which formed in Seoul in 2013, has spread Korean culture and language to a global audience, and its members were included in *Time 100's list of the most influential people* in 2019.

Our perspective on the past is determined by what is considered to be significant in the present; people and events might be thought to be historically, culturally, economically or politically significant.

Figure 10.2: The South Korean boy band *BTS* performing in California in 2019. Cultural historians might want to understand the historical development and role of popular culture.

REAL-LIFE SITUATION 10.1

The assassination of US President John F. Kennedy occurred in Texas on 22 November 1963. It is an event that was captured on film, and broadcast on television around the world. We might think that *seeing is believing*. However, does it mean that your interpretation of an event is necessarily true or accurate just because you see it? Is it justified to assume that the eyewitness testimonies of the shooting of Kennedy are accurate and reliable as a source of knowledge? Our interpretation of events is shaped by the complex interrelationship between our sense perception, assumptions, memory and imagination.

'Inside' and 'outside' perspectives

When historians claim to know something about the past, they need to justify this on the basis of evidence or reports of what actually happened. For example, the assassination of President Kennedy was investigated by the Warren Commission, which produced an 888-page report and concluded that there was one assassin – Lee Harvey Oswald (1939–1963). The Warren Commission provided detailed records of what happened, but the findings have since been questioned. It would be very difficult to know what happened from the *inside*, meaning from the perspective of Lee Harvey Oswald, as this famous case never came to trial because Oswald was shot dead by Jack Ruby just two days after Kennedy was killed.

Historical events can be understood from different perspectives. Historian R.G. Collingwood (1889–1943) claimed that the task of the historian is to understand both viewpoints – the *outside* of a historical event as well as the *inside*. Collingwood makes the distinction between our knowledge of the outside of an action, in this case the shots fired, and the inside of an action, in this case the thoughts of the assassin who carried out the action.

The nature of historical knowledge: objective or subjective?

The German scholar Leopold von Ranke (1795–1886) was the founder of modern academic history. For him, the purpose of history was to *show what happened*. The historian G. R. Elton (1921–1994) also defended the idea that history is a search for the objective truth about the past, and that historical knowledge is out there waiting to be discovered.

A counter-argument was made by E. H. Carr (1892–1982) who challenged this traditional view of history. He wrote, *'The belief in a hard core of historical facts existing objectively and independently of the historian is a preposterous fallacy, but one which is very hard to eradicate'*.

Historians can may be able to get closer to objectivity if they understand the past from different perspectives. For example, the medieval Crusades might be understood from various viewpoints. A western or Christian view may have once been the dominant narrative of this conflict. However, the broadcasting network Al Jazeera has produced a 4-part documentary offering an Arabian perspective of the events, based on the book by Amin Maalouf, *The Crusades Through Arab Eyes*.

History is more than just assembling the facts of past events; it is an attempt to understand in a critical way the causes, course and consequences of those events, and to appreciate the different perspectives that the primary sources are based on. A good starting point is to consider the knowledge question: *'How can we be sure if our construction of historical knowledge is based on an accurate, objective view of the past, or on our own subjective interpretation?'*. Simply put, is history something we discover, or do we invent it?

KEY TERMS

objective view of history: the idea that truth or reality is independent of your own personal perspective; for example, the claim that *'there are objective truths about the past'*

subjective view of history: the idea that truth and reality depend upon your own personal perspective; for example, the claim that *'what I know about the past is based on my own thoughts, feelings, imagination and interpretation'*

CROSS REFERENCE

You can find out more about the study of historical perspectives, known as historiography, in Chapter 10 of the Course Guide.

KEY POINT

There are many factors that influence history. Remember that the historical periods and topics that are chosen to be taught in schools, and considered historically significant today, are influenced by multiple factors such as educational, cultural or political contexts. Moreover, the task of the historian is shaped by intellectual movements and key thinkers.

TASK: ACTIVITY 10.2

History textbooks used in schools in different countries might offer different accounts of the past. Think about what you have learned in your history lessons during your time at school. Identify and evaluate the different historical perspectives that you have been taught.

Individually or in pairs, produce a poster or timeline to show the history you have studied, and share it with your class. Compare your work as a class and use this as a basis for further discussion:

- How can we know which version or historical perspective is justified?

- What does our study of history tell us about the concerns, culture and context of the present day?

TASK: ACTIVITY 10.3

Discuss the following questions as a pair or small group. Think of one or two specific real-life or concrete examples that you could use to support the arguments for and the counter-arguments against. Then share your ideas with your class, and identify any bias behind your selection of examples, and consider the implications.

1 Is any account of the past justified? Why? Why not?

2 *'The belief in a hard core of historical facts existing objectively and independently of the historian is a preposterous fallacy...'* **E. H. Carr**. How far do you agree?

3 Is it possible for a historian to study the past from an objective and neutral perspective? Why? Why not?

10.4 Methods and tools in history

There are various methods and tools available to produce historical knowledge. All history must be based on a sound interpretation of the evidence. Historians use an empirical method based on interpretation of historical sources and have many tools at their disposal. Here we will consider four of those tools: language, reason, imagination and memory.

Language

Throughout history, there have been many *recorders* of history: the *Father of History* – Herodotus – lived in ancient Greece in the 5th century BCE, and was one of the earliest to record history. History can be described as the study of the recorded past, with written records and written documents forming the basis of much of the evidence. Historians also use non-written sources such as artefacts and archaeological finds.

The modern social history of the American West focuses on the ordinary lives of the settlers and the Native American Indians. To gain knowledge of this period from the 19th century, historians might select different types of **primary sources**: Native American artefacts such as headdresses and beadwork will be interpreted differently using written primary sources from the time, such as the diary of settler Laura Ingalls Wilder (1867–1957). Historians will interpret the sources, and check their reliability and accuracy.

Reason

A primary source might be an artefact or a written document from the time being studied. A historian's interpretation of a primary source can produce a **secondary source**, which is a source that presents information found elsewhere. A secondary source, written after the event, often includes historical interpretation, and may comment on primary materials. Our classification of sources as primary or secondary involves a judgement based on reason.

Historians use reason to evaluate sources, and also use reasoning as part of their method. Identifying particular pieces of evidence – such as archaeological finds – to form general conclusions about life in a specific era, is an example of inductive reasoning that historians use routinely.

> ### KEY TERMS
>
> **primary source:** a document or physical artefact that was created during the time of study
>
> **secondary source:** a document or physical artefact that was created much later than the time to which it relates, or by someone who was not directly involved

---

REAL-LIFE SITUATION 10.2

The Qin Shihuang UNESCO World Heritage site in Shaanxi province in western China is one of the world's richest archaeological reserves. The extraordinary terracotta warriors, horses and artefacts excavated there are primary sources used by historians to gain knowledge of Chinese emperors. For example, historians have analysed the statue army in the mausoleum, and have reasoned that it represents the exact number of guards in the imperial army at that time.

1   What can ancient artefacts tell us about the social and political world context of the time in which they were created?

2   How does art relate to power and politics?

Sometimes historians will formulate a general hypothesis based on some observations, and look for particular evidence to support it. One general hypothesis is that great people are the agents of change in history. Historian A. J. P. Taylor (1906–1990) identified Napoleon, Bismarck and Lenin as examples of great individuals who have changed the course of history. Taylor looked for evidence to show how these individuals changed the world.

Similarly, the revolutionary communist philosopher Karl Marx (1818–1883) proposed that economic and technological factors are the causes of change. Marx looked for evidence for his overarching theory to assess whether conflict between the social classes created a pattern of events which developed independently of the actions of individuals.

Figure 10.3: To what extent do you think change is caused by economic and technological factors or the actions of individuals?

You could readily spot evidence that might fit Marx's hypothesis today: global economic factors, the impact of the global Covid19 pandemic, or the rapid growth of digital technology might be identified as causes that determine change, rather than the actions of individuals. The danger of selecting evidence that fits is that it can lead to confirmation bias in which only evidence that supports the general hypothesis is considered.

Our view of the past depends on our rationality. The view that change is caused by *both* long-term social and economic trends *and* the actions of individuals is based on a rational judgement about the relative importance of different causes of events. Reason enables us to make sense of the past, interpret evidence and identify patterns in history.

TOK LINK: TECHNOLOGY

In the *information age* that we are living in, many people have access to vast amounts of historical sources, unlike in any other era in history. Does digital technology make the task of the modern historian easier or more difficult?

Imagination

Imagination might seem to be the enemy of the historian. Whereas a historical novelist can embellish the facts and be free to innovate beyond the evidence, historians are usually limited by their own conventions. In his 2006 book *Imperium*, novelist Robert Harris (1957–) writes literary fiction about the famous Roman orator and lawyer Cicero (106–43 BCE), and is not constrained by the same need to base his narrative on the evidence. 'Whilst Harris does not include anything that we know for a fact did not happen, and the reports of Cicero's speeches are consistent with the historical record, even if the dialogue between characters is imagined.

In contrast, the historian has a responsibility to stay true to the evidence. R.G. Collingwood commented that, *'As works of imagination, the historian's work and the novelist's do not differ. Where they do differ is that the historian's picture is meant to be true'*. On the other hand, some historians have used imagination as a tool for making the past more real and more immediate to modern readers. In his 2008 book *The Black Death: An Intimate History*, historian John Hatcher (1951–) combines history with fiction. He reconstructs the experience of ordinary people living in a Suffolk village during the time of the Black Death in mid-14th-century Britain, using a combination of archival evidence and his own imagination. Constructing history from the distant past where source material and artefacts are limited requires an empathetic and imaginative leap. To make the medieval period more accessible to his modern readership, he combines historical data with fictional conversations between people of the time.

Memory

People who were present at an event and experienced it first hand as eyewitnesses can give very important testimonies based on their direct memory, which can be very powerful. In this book *If This Is a Man* (1947), Italian–Jewish writer Primo Levi (1919–1987) offers a first-hand account of the inhumanity that he experienced having survived in Auschwitz from February 1944 until the concentration camp was liberated on 27 January 1945.

On the other hand, eyewitness testimony is not always a reliable source of information that can be taken at face value. People's memories may be inaccurate or unreliable. Memory can also be affected by **hindsight bias**.

Like all sources, memoirs and personal memories of eyewitnesses need to be interpreted. While they may appeal to our emotions and communicate the reality of an event very effectively, the historian needs to use their own judgement and consider them carefully. For example, a memoir by Albert Speer (1905–1981), Hitler's Armaments Minister between 1942 and 1945, has been challenged because it does not fit with other evidence. In his book *Inside the Third Reich* (1970), Speer gives his personal account based on his own memories, but glosses over his use of concentration camp slave-labour and therefore his own involvement in the Holocaust.

> **KEY TERM**
>
> **hindsight bias:**
> the tendency to imagine that events in the past were more predictable than they actually were. It is the thinking that goes along the lines of *'I should have known that ...'* or *'I knew it all along.'*

> **KEY POINT**
>
> Historians use different tools and methods to gain knowledge. A historian uses a number of key concepts, including continuity, change, causation, interpretation, evidence, reliability and accuracy. Tools and methods can interact; for example, a historian might use their reason as well as their imagination to understand the past.

Working individually or as a pair or small group, prepare a presentation to your class on one of the following knowledge questions. Analyse your chosen question with a particular focus on thinking through the implications.

1   In what ways do historians use reason as a tool in their search for historical knowledge?

2   In what ways might it be appropriate for a historian to use their imagination in their search for historical knowledge?

3   How far do you think our memory of an event can be reliable and accurate?

Consider and weigh up both sides of the arguments. Think through the implications of both sides:

• What follows?

• How does your argument link to knowledge and knowing?

• Link the argument back to what counts as historical knowledge.

One feature of analysis is to identify assumptions being taken for granted which are either hidden and implicit or more obvious and explicit. When analysing any work, try to identify any assumptions that are being taken for granted.

10.5 Ethics and history

Ethical questions arise in relation to the study of the past. For example, questions arise about how far historians have a responsibility to tell the truth about the past, the ethics of the victors of a battle writing their own version of history, or a political regime today using **propaganda** to twist or distort the past for their own purposes.

If history encourages understanding and compassion towards people living in different places, it might be said to play an ethical role. The issue arises as to whether historians are justified in making ethical judgements about the past. One argument is that where possible, neutral language can and should be used to describe the past, avoiding loaded terms such as *extermination* or *conqueror*. The counter-argument is that 'genocide' is an entirely justified word to describe certain atrocities committed. For example, from 1975–1979, the Khmer leader Pol Pot (1925–1998) caused the deaths of over one million of his people from starvation, execution and forced labour under his totalitarian regime. Historians are justified in describing these crimes against humanity as the Cambodian genocide. In their pursuit of historical knowledge, historians themselves might be committed to certain ethical standards, which assumes a responsibility to tell the truth.

propaganda: the distortion of information, usually for political purposes

The historian needs to conform to standards and conventions such as intellectual honesty, accuracy and sound judgement and interpretation of the evidence.

Ethics and knowledge claims

One reason why history is important to us as individuals is because we can learn from the mistakes of the past. The poem that opens Primo Levi's book *If This Is a Man* (1947) clearly indicates the moral purpose of remembering the Holocaust; his eyewitness account of his survival in Auschwitz points to the fact that the lessons learned should be passed down to future generations, never to be forgotten.

Another reason why history is important is because it can help us to remember and give us a sense of national or global identity. The historian can focus on Asian, Middle Eastern, West Indian, European, Australasian or Latin American history. However, there are ethical considerations which limit the scope of the enquiry. It would be unethical to make claims that are not based on a sound and reasonable analysis of the evidence. The following example illustrates why.

It is part of our shared knowledge that between 1939 and 1945, around 5.5–6 million Jews were killed in Europe – an act of genocide known to Jews as the Shoah but often referred to as the Holocaust. In 2000, David Irving (1938–) sued American historian Deborah Lipstadt (1947–) for libel. Lipstadt had claimed in her book, *Denying the Holocaust: The Growing Assault on Truth and Memory* (1993), that Irving had deliberately misinterpreted evidence and was a Holocaust denier. Irving took the case to court in an attempt to clear his name.

The case involved the court examining the evidence, which included not only Irving's personal interpretation of the Holocaust, but also evidence from others who did not share his extreme minority view. Irving claimed that historians can interpret evidence as they see fit, and are usually exempt from the rigours of a courtroom challenge and a need to prove their case. In this case, Richard Evans (1947–) – a historian from the University of Cambridge – was the expert witness. He showed that Irving had deliberately distorted the evidence, and Irving lost his case.

This shows that a historical interpretation is not necessarily justified when tested against the standard of the law. But history is seldom tested against this standard, and most historians would accept that their work should conform to certain commonly accepted standards and conventions, such as honesty, diligence and accuracy. Even before the court case, Irving was believed to have stepped outside of these boundaries in the opinion of his many critics. To deny the Holocaust is a highly offensive claim to make, and is illegal in some European countries.

TASK: ACTIVITY 10.5

Conduct a series of mini-interviews or a survey with different people in your class to find out their response to the following questions. In your mini-interview, develop your awareness of different perspectives and responses within the class. Then discuss the questions as a whole class, and reflect on what you have learned.

1   Should historians avoid using emotive words or value judgements to describe the past, such as *victor, heroine, slaughter* and *massacre, whistleblower, traitor, hero, coward*? How far can neutral language be used to describe the past?

CONTINUED

2   To what extent do historians have a responsibility to tell the truth about the past?

3   Is it ever justified to use propaganda to twist or distort the past?

4   How far does the study of history develop our understanding and empathy towards others?

Knowledge of patterns

Today, the ethical and political question remains: when and under what circumstances should the United Nations sanction military intervention by foreign countries? Our shared historical knowledge of foreign intervention might shape our understanding of what is an appropriate response. We might consider what has happened before – is there a precedent? We might compare similar situations and look for historical parallels – are there patterns that repeat themselves in history, and if so, can we avoid the mistakes of the past? Countries that have prompted debate about foreign intervention more recently include Iraq, Afghanistan, Libya, Syria and Mali. The counter-argument is that events are never identical, and the past cannot repeat itself; it follows from this that it makes no sense to assume that there are lessons from the past to learn.

Our historical knowledge and understanding might affect how we judge political situations today. For example, our interpretation of the Bulgarian Crisis of the mid-1870s, also known as the Balkan Crisis, might have an impact on how we judge a country's modern foreign policy. Bulgaria had been ruled by Turkey since the 14th century. In 1876, the Bulgarians revolted against Turkish rule, and in response, the Turks are reported to have killed between 10,000 and 25,000 Bulgarian men, women and children. The political response to this in the UK was mixed. On the one hand, British Prime Minister Benjamin Disraeli (1804–1881) was reluctant to believe the reports and intervene on behalf of the Bulgarian people. On the other hand, the leader of the Liberal Party, William Gladstone (1809–1898), was morally outraged by the atrocity, and supported intervention.

Similarly, the political climate of a country in the present might call for historical understanding if it is to be fully understood. For example, historians might want to understand the causes of the conflict that have led to the civil war in southern Sudan from 2013 to 2020.

10.6 Knowledge questions

1   Can we be sure whether the historian has the same methodological rigour as the experimental scientist?

2   How might the assumptions behind the historical method compare with the assumptions behind methods in other areas of knowledge?

3   Are historical explanations the same as scientific explanations? What are the similarities and differences?

10.7 Extended writing task

Write 400–600 words or more on one of the following questions:

1   What part does language play in producing historical knowledge?

2   Is our historical knowledge closer to our knowledge in science or literature?

3   How do we judge who decides which events are historically significant?

SKILLS SELF-ASSESSMENT CHECKLIST

Reflect on what you have learned in this chapter and indicate your confidence level between 1 and 5 (where 5 is the highest score and 1 is the lowest). If you score below 3, revisit that section. Come back to this list later in your course. Has your confidence grown?

	Confidence level	Revisited?
Can I discuss the scope of history, and identify arguments and counter-arguments about historical knowledge?		
Am I able to identify knowledge claims and arguments which make assumptions that are taken for granted?		
Can I construct an argument about the nature of historical knowledge?		
Can I identify and evaluate different perspectives of history?		
Do I have the skills to evaluate the reliability of the tools and methods used in history, and the role of selection and interpretation of sources?		
Am I able to offer examples or evidence to support or illustrate a point about historical knowledge?		
Can I identify and evaluate different perspectives in response to ethical questions and issues associated with historical knowledge?		

10.8 Further reading

For a recreation of life in a 14th-century village, read: John Hatcher, *The Black Death: An Intimate History*, Da Capo Press, 2008

For an account of a survivor of the Holocaust, read Primo Levi, *If This Is a Man*, Orion Press, 1947 (English translation 1959)

For a discussion of what counts as a justified account of the past, read: A. Megill, *Historical Knowledge, Historical Error: A Contemporary Guide to Practice*, University of Chicago Press, 2007

For a survey of the history of art in various countries and cultures across the globe, see the excellent series of BBC programmes *Civilisations* presented by Simon Schama, Mary Beard and David Olusoga

> Chapter 11
The arts

LEARNING INTENTIONS

In this chapter, you will examine knowledge in the performing arts, the literary arts and the visual arts. You will explore the scope of the arts and how the arts influence our identity; the relationship between cultural perspectives and the arts; the broad range of tools and methods used in both the creation of and the interpretation of the arts; and finally, ethical standards in the arts, the responsibilities and values of artists and the concept of censorship.

You will:

*   develop the skills to investigate the scope and limits of the arts

*   appreciate the different factors that influence the arts, such as technology

*   consider the value of the arts, including their commercial value

*   evaluate the role of the arts in your own life

*   consider how the arts can be viewed from different perspectives

*   foster the skills to identify the tools and methods used to interpret works of art

*   hone your writing skills, in particular, your ability to construct arguments, use examples in support of an argument and discuss the implications that follow

*   identify and evaluate different perspectives in response to ethical questions and issues associated with the creation and interpretation of art works.

11.1 Introduction

The instinct to create works of art is universal across cultures. Among the earliest known artistic masterpieces are the prehistoric cave paintings in Lascaux in France. This is one of the UNESCO World Heritage sites; the cave paintings are thought to date back about 20,000 years and are believed to possess 'outstanding universal value'.

11.2 The scope of the arts

Today, the arts have features in common, but are very broad in their range – from opera, dance and poetry to film, advertising, painting and music. There are certain features that artistic activities have in common. Works of art might demonstrate technical skills, contain truths, express emotions or attempt to imitate or resemble aspects of the world around us. For example, writing a novel might be thought of as a craft that uses language alone to fulfil all of these elements: the novelist has the technical skills to control the unfolding of a plot, to express a degree of truth about human relationships and emotions, and to create an imaginary world that has its own coherence.

If artistic tools offer the equipment to express abstract ideas, and artists possess skills and know-how to use these tools, then art might be thought of as a technology. Furthermore, technology gives rise to new art forms such as photography, film, computer art, computer games and computer music. Technology also allows art to be mass-produced to enable it to reach a wide audience.

It is, however, difficult to define the exact scope of art. Marco Evaristti's *Helena* (2000) is an installation that placed live fish in a liquidiser as a social experiment to see what would happen if visitors were given the option of pressing the button that would kill the fish. Is this in poor taste and animal cruelty, or is it acceptable if it is called art? Is it justified to call this art if the *installation* is by a recognised artist? On the other hand, might we be justified to claim that some so-called performance artists are pushing the scope of art to unacceptable limits. There is an important question here – who decides what counts as art? How do we know where art begins and ends?

Bill Posters is an artist-researcher who was once a street artist. He now explores the relationship between art, computational propaganda and political protest. Bill Posters and Daniel Howe are renowned for making a deepfake video of Facebook CEO Mark Zuckerberg, to raise questions about the responsibilities of technology giants.

1   How can imaginative processes in the arts lead to knowledge about the world?

2   What kinds of truth can the arts express?

TOP TIP

Sharpen your analytical skills by identifying the assumptions you have about what art is and what art is not. Would you classify a deepfake video either as a form of art or a tool for propaganda, or neither or both? Consider the factors that might influence your classification, and how your categorisation might influence your ethical view.

The arts extend our experience and enrich our inner lives. Our artistic tastes express our identity, and say something about who we are. By seeing films, reading novels, listening to music or going to art galleries, we increase our individual knowledge and insight into the world around us. We can learn about ourselves, our relationships and various cultures at different times.

If you watch a production of Shakespeare's play *Macbeth*, or the Indian adaptation *Maqbool*, you will gain an insight into the devastating consequences of ambition and power. If you see Michelangelo's sculpture *Pietà*, you might be overwhelmed by its realism. The arts help us to look at the world in new and original ways with fresh eyes. The Russian writer Viktor Shklovsky (1893–1984) observed that *'Art makes the familiar strange so that it can be freshly perceived. To do this, it presents its material in unexpected, even outlandish ways: the shock of the new'*.

Some people argue that we need to distinguish between "genuine" art and **kitsch**. Kitsch is sometimes thought of as pseudo-art because it is sentimental, clichéd or unoriginal, for example a photo of a kitten on a greetings card.

They argue that, unlike kitsch, "genuine" art can help us to make sense of the world and give our lives meaning. The arts can help us to feel more connected, understanding other people's emotions through empathy, and being able to live vicariously through novels.

KEY TERM

kitsch: derivative, clichéd art

TASK: ACTIVITY 11.1

Choose one of the following questions, and prepare and deliver a presentation to your class based on your analysis of the question. Focus on developing the skill of selecting and evaluating specific examples to support your analytical points. Select at least one or two specific concrete examples that you could use to support the arguments for and the counter-arguments against.

CONTINUED

1   Computer games entertain us with storytelling, music and pictures where we can experience a virtual world and another life. Do they expand or limit our imagination? Do you think that they are an art form, and if so, on what grounds?

2   What impact do you think technology is having, and will have, on the arts in the future?

3   Is there a point at which an artist is no longer doing art, if they go beyond certain conventions and boundaries? Who decides? How do we know what the scope and limit of art is?

Arts and commercial value

REAL-LIFE SITUATION 11.2

One morning in January 2007, a man on a subway platform in Washington, D.C. USA, played the violin. Many people passed him by in a hurry and failed to recognise who he was. He was one of the world's best violinists, Joshua Bell (1967–). Several nights earlier, he had performed in a concert for which tickets were sold at a high price. The subway experiment was set up by the *Washington Post* to discover whether, in an everyday environment, people would recognise a famous musician's talent. This was not intended to be a rigorous experiment, but it makes us think about how our sense perception is affected by various factors.

1   What is the role of context in making artistic judgments?

2   How does knowledge and prior experience influence our appreciation of art?

Art is not just about passively receiving sense data, in the same way that music is not just about hearing. The way we judge art is heavily influenced by its context and setting, as well as our own expectations and priorities.

There is a social status associated with the creation and ownership of art, and art has an economic value. Jackson Pollock's (1912–1956) painting *No. 5*, which he painted in 1948, sold for $140 million in 2006. Mark Rothko's (1903–1970) *Orange, Red, Yellow* sold in 2012 for $87 million. British author J. K. Rowling (1965–) made a fortune with her fictional creation of Harry Potter. If the creativity of individuals is driven by market forces, what are the implications? The market may be the final arbiter of the value of art, but is the value of art reducible to a sum of money?

REAL-LIFE SITUATION 11.3

Leonardo da Vinci's (1452–1519) painting *Salvator Mundi* (Saviour of the World) sold for $450 million in 2017. The value of the painting is linked to the **provenance** of the piece, which at the time of the auction was believed to be Leonardo da Vinci. Since then, some people have questioned the provenance of the piece. If the general view among experts was that da Vinci did not complete the entire work, the value of the piece would drop.

Can we distinguish between valuing a work of art and valuing an artist?

KEY TERM

provenance: the origin of something; in the context of art, the creator of a work of art

TASK: ACTIVITY 11.2

Why should the value of a work of art drop if another person from the same period as da Vinci were to have painted it? What does this say about how art is valued?

Discuss this question with a partner or in a small group, and identify and evaluate different perspectives.

Figure 11.1: A visitor photographs a painting entitled *Salvator Mundi* during the exhibition 'Leonardo da Vinci' at the Louvre in Paris, 2019

TOK LINK: OTHER AREAS OF KNOWLEDGE

The performing, literary and visual arts all have a very broad scope. How does this breadth and diversity compare with other areas of knowledge? Are other areas of knowledge similar in this respect?

11.3 Perspectives on the arts

The arts can be understood from various different viewpoints. The objective view of art is that our judgement of art can be based on criteria and qualities that are independent of the observer, whereas the subjective view of art is that our judgements of art are based on personal preference.

TASK: ACTIVITY 11.3

Leela and Naresh are discussing knowledge in the arts. What does each of them assume or take for granted about the arts? Evaluate which viewpoint, (if any) you agree with most, and why. Which, if either, do you think is justified?

Leela: How can the arts have anything to do with what we know? Surely music, painting and poems are there to be enjoyed and experienced? There is no knowledge involved.

Naresh: If you go into someone's house, they may have a picture up on their wall. We all know what looks good or sounds good. We all have aesthetic knowledge. It is a universal feature of what it is to be human.

Leela: No, art and literature are just a matter of preference. Liking or disliking a painting or a poem is no different from liking or disliking sushi. Both are just a question of individual taste!

Naresh: Then why are some works of art and literature considered greater than others? Leonardo da Vinci's *Mona Lisa* or *Salvator Mundi*, the plays and poetry of Shakespeare and Beethoven's symphonies have all stood the test of time. Even if we do not agree about what we like to look at or listen to, surely enduring art communicates some kind of universal and timeless truth which is agreed upon by different cultures?

KEY POINT

Some works of art are closely linked to the time, place and context in which they were created. It follows that the arts have the capacity to communicate or reflect something unique about a particular place, time and culture. On the other hand, good or great art, such as the plays and poetry of Shakespeare, seem to go beyond cultural and historical boundaries.

The arts and different perspectives

The instinct to create art has developed in all cultures; like language, the arts are universal. Some art forms are specific to particular cultures: the Japanese tea ceremony is an art form and a social activity; the Chinese dragon dance is a traditional part of Chinese culture; and the Keralan classical Indian dance-drama, Kathakali, is unique to southern India.

On the one hand, our preference for art is a matter of individual taste. On the other hand, the cultures we inhabit might determine and influence our artistic preferences. It follows that our artistic taste says something about who we are and the communities we belong to. The music you listen to and the books you read can help to define your identity and influence your perspective. What we like to read or look at tells others something about the sort of person we are, or the person we would like to become. So our individual perspectives, and our cultural and historical perspectives play important roles in the way that we judge art.

TOK IN YOUR LIFE

Think about your favourite film, poem, piece of music, novel or painting. How far do these reflect your cultural, social or gender identity? How have they expanded your knowledge or insight?

Keep a record of reading novels and poems, visiting art galleries or seeing theatre productions. You can use these examples to make analytical points in your TOK essays.

TOP TIP

You can further develop your analytical skills by comparing the scope of the arts with other areas of knowledge. Think about the following:

- The arts have a creative and imaginative motivation. How does this compare with other areas of knowledge? For example, the task of both an artist and a mathematician can be highly creative and imaginative, and the product of each arguably beautiful.

- How does the social function of the arts compare with that in other areas of knowledge?

Figure 11.2: The classical Keralan dance-drama, Kathakali, is deeply rooted in its Indian social and cultural context. Is it possible to know about the arts independently of their context?

The arts evolve and change over time. Our idea of beauty also develops over time, and can vary across cultures. The curvaceous figures of European women in the 18th and 19th centuries were considered beautiful, yet today in some countries, the fashion industry represents female beauty very differently. This raises the question: *'Does the fashion industry represent society's notions of beauty, or does it define beauty for society?'*.

Art is very accessible, since hearing music or seeing a sculpture is something we simply experience. Works of art stand alone, and the observer or interpreter of the work of art is free to make their own judgement. However, the arts are also arguably more **esoteric** than some other areas of knowledge. Knowing where Rothko fits in to the history of art, or where James Joyce's *Ulysses* fits in to English literature, requires knowledge and insight. To understand what is going on, we need background knowledge of the history, context and genre.

REAL-LIFE SITUATION 11.4

Plautilla Nelli (1524–1588) was the only known woman during the Renaissance who painted Jesus' Last Supper. Recently, her work – which was in a very poor condition – has been restored to be fully appreciated and, for the first time in 450 years, it is on public display in the Santa Maria Novella Museum in Florence.

Why might the discovery of past female artists and the restoration of their work be important today?

Knowing the context in which a work of art is produced can be the key to understanding its meaning or significance. Gabriel Prokofiev (1975–) composed *Concerto for Turntables and Orchestra* by combining his famous Russian grandfather Sergei Prokofiev's (1891–1953) classical music traditions with the rhythms of modern club music. Our knowledge and insight into artworks of the present can be informed by knowledge of the historical development of an art form. Artworks can be consciously created in relation to what has come before; they can inform the present and point forwards to the future.

TOK LINK: PERSPECTIVES

Is there such a thing as outdated knowledge in the arts? How might this compare with redundant or obsolete knowledge in other areas?

11.4 Methods and tools in the arts

Creative processes are required to produce works in the performing, literary and visual arts. The arts contain their own inner logic and coherence, and the creativity involved takes place within a framework using reason, structure and convention. For example, in poetry, there are 14 lines in a sonnet and 17 syllables in a Japanese haiku. We might assume that conventions or genres dictate artistic content to some degree. There is no single artistic method; rather, diverse methods based on the concepts of form, structure, genre and context. There are various cognitive methods and tools used to gain knowledge in the arts, as explored below.

Language

TASK: THINK ABOUT 11.1

How does language relate to knowledge in the arts?

The poet, painter or musician has many tools, and here we will consider language. The arts can communicate verbal knowledge, as in literature. Language in the arts can also be used metaphorically, namely in a non-literal sense. A simile compares two things using the words *like* or *as*: '*My love is like a red rose*'. A metaphor makes a comparison between two things more directly without using the words *like* or *as*: '*My love is a red rose*'. In Shakespeare's play *Antony and Cleopatra*, Cleopatra nostalgically refers to her lost youth as her *salad days*. This does not literally mean a time when she ate salad. Taken literally, it makes no sense, but taken as a metaphor, it means that she is remembering the freshness of her youth.

The artist Picasso (1881–1973) once claimed that, '*Art is a lie that brings us nearer to the truth*'. When novelists use fictional characters and imagined events to communicate an experience, they are inventing within known artistic conventions. If the experience connects with us, the fictional story can persuade or convince us that we are learning something genuine about the real world. We can relate to the characters' experiences. We know not to interpret the language in the arts literally.

If you have ever written your own poetry or fiction, you will know that finding the right words is difficult. The actor James Earl Jones (1931–) observed that, '*One of the hardest things in life is having words in your heart that you can't utter*'.

Non-verbal language offers an alternative expression for our knowledge. The arts, including dance, music, painting and theatre such as mime, can communicate non-verbal knowledge. For example, it is hard to put into words the feelings of listening to music such as Allegri's (1582–1652) *Miserere*, or watching an emotive dance. The arts help us to express things that we cannot say directly, and it might not even be necessary to say what art communicates. This opens up the arts to communicating a wide range of knowledge.

The non-verbal arts have their own language. A performance of classical ballet fits a particular genre, convention and form. A performance of the American composer John Cage's (1912–1992) piece *Four Minutes, Thirty-Three Seconds* requires the audience to watch a 'performance' which consists of silence. As with a conventional

KEY TERM

non-verbal language: communication without words

performance, there is an audience, as well as instruments on the stage, and players dressed appropriately for a concert. Even though the musical performance takes place in silence, it could be argued that it relies on a type of non-verbal language.

The non-verbal arts belong to one of the few areas of knowledge that can communicate knowledge without the spoken or written word. This invites you to consider what function language plays in these arts.

Emotion

> ## TASK: THINK ABOUT 11.2
>
> How far are the arts the language of the emotions?

The arts are sometimes called the language of the emotions. Music has a very direct emotional impact, and can affect our mood. If you listen to the fourth movement of Symphony No. 5 by Mahler (1860–1911), you might feel a range of emotions from sorrow to joy. Our feelings can also motivate us to create an artwork. The poet William Wordsworth (1770–1850) described poetry as *'emotion recollected in tranquillity'*. The arts can shape and change how we feel. An audience might respond emotionally to a work of art through its appeal to our shared emotions. Watching a performance of a tragedy on stage could move us to tears, and a comedy might make us laugh.

The arts can give us a feeling of transcendence – a sense of a metaphorical window on another world. Bengal in India has a rich cultural and literary heritage. Rabindranath Tagore (1861–1941), a Bengali poet and polymath who was the first non-European to win the Nobel Prize in Literature in 1913, wrote a collection of poems entitled *Gitanjali*. With its spiritual and philosophical themes, *Gitanjali* touches on universal emotions. But what moves one person emotionally might leave another feeling very little or nothing at all.

Neuroaesthetics, developed by Semir Zeki (1940–), attempts to understand our response to art from the perspective of our shared neuroscientific knowledge. His work aims to understand what is happening in our brains when we look at art. Dara Djavan Khoshdel (1988–) set out to investigate the science behind the claim that some paintings are expensive because we respond to them emotionally. He investigated the emotional response of participants to the artwork of Graham Sutherland (1903–1980) using a galvanic response monitor which measured their emotional response in relation to the small amounts of sweat they produced. He found that there was no link between the price of a painting and the participants' emotional response to it. His experiment indicated that if we know a painting is expensive, it does not follow that we will be more moved emotionally by it.

This raises questions again about what art is, and how and why we value it. Some people might assume that our response to art is automatic, subconscious and instinctive. However, our response to artwork is not a purely instinctive response, since it is shaped by various other factors, including our expectations, our education and our cultural context. We actively interpret our perception of art in the light of these complex factors.

Reason

TASK: THINK ABOUT 11.3

What is the role of reason, rationality or rational analysis in relation to the arts?

The evolutionary purpose of art and the precise role that the arts have played in terms of our survival is an important but disputed question. There is no Darwinian account of art that is agreed upon, but there is a significant question here about the extent to which art is natural or cultural, or both, and the implications of each position.

Our response to art is not just an automatic and unconscious instinct. We can stand back and rationally weigh up the content and form of a painting before arriving at a judgement. From a young age, we can appreciate music, and the whole purpose of the arts is that they are accessible – anyone can enjoy them. Although judging art might seem more of a matter of the heart than the head, the arts are open to rational criticism and interpretation. Reason provides a framework for the imagination.

Figure 11.3: If someone claims that this picture depicts a snow scene, they are clearly wrong. As interpreters of the arts, we need a degree of competence to make sound judgements. Is any interpretation of art acceptable?

In the arts, there are rule systems for analysis. The use of literary devices in poetry and prose can be analysed as tools that create an artistic effect. Similarly, the visual arts can be analysed using various concepts such as perspective, form, composition, colour, line, contrast and shadow. Prizes in the arts such as the Man Booker Prize, the Man Asian Literary Prize, the Pulitzer Prize and the Turner Prize indicate that we can make judgements about the arts based on criteria in which our reason and rationality are involved.

When it comes to interpreting art, you might consider the expertise of literary critics or art critics. Some people might argue that the knowledge and expertise of a critic makes their interpretation more authoritative. However, the relationship between the audience and the arts is also an important one, and others might claim that the arts should be accessible in such a way that everyone can make a justified and informed judgement.

TOK IN YOUR LIFE

In your IB Diploma Programme studies, you are interpreting a range of literary texts. Think about the different texts that you are studying, and how they relate to the concept of interpretation.

Imagination

TASK: THINK ABOUT 11.4

How far do the arts depend upon imagination?

Art can be a form of escapism where we can let our imagination loose. The arts enable us to travel inwardly, and so expand our horizons. Reading literature from a range of cultures can widen our understanding of those cultures. We can also touch an experience of another person across time. Reading the poetry of Rumi (1207–1273) gives us a great insight into the Persian spiritual wisdom of the past. By reading literature, we can know more about our own mental narratives by comparing them with those of others, even if those in literature are invented. The American novelist Anne Tyler (1941–) observed, *'I write because I want more than one life; I insist on a wider selection. It's greed, plain and simple'*.

TASK: ACTIVITY 11.4

As a class, select around ten images of visual works of art. Start working in a pair or small group, ranking the art works in order according to which you judge to be the best – where ten is the highest score and one is the lowest. Each pair then shares their ideas with the class, leading to a whole-class discussion of the following questions:

- What criteria can you use for judging the visual arts?

- What tools and methods are relevant when judging art?

- Was there agreement in your class about what counts as good art? Why? Why not? Would we expect a consensus? What are the implications?

- How do you know which is the best art?

You could develop this activity further by either creating and judging your own artworks or by judging alternative examples, such as music or literary arts, and reflecting on whether you arrive at the same conclusions.

TOK LINK: OTHER AREAS OF KNOWLEDGE

How do the tools and methods used in the arts compare with those used in other areas of knowledge? How far is imagination and creativity important in areas of knowledge beyond the arts?

11.5 Ethics and the arts

Should art ever be censored on ethical grounds? What is the relationship between the arts and ethics? In *The Republic*, written by the Greek philosopher Plato around 360 BCE, Plato suggested that the arts should be censored by the state in people's best interests. Today, the question about the ethical limits to our knowledge in the arts remains unresolved, and we debate issues of standards of decency and taste. Artists explore the boundary between what is acceptable and unacceptable, often to make a point. For example, the artist Jill Greengrass photographed children who were upset and crying. Earlier in the chapter, we considered Marco Evaristti's *Helena* – the installation which placed fish in a liquidiser. Another example is Sruli Recht who used his own skin in the creation of a piece of jewellery known as *Forget Me Knot*.

TASK: THINK ABOUT 11.5

Is it ethically justifiable to call acts of cruelty art?

There is an important relationship between the arts and education. Potentially the arts have a civilising effect; they broaden our perspective, and may open our eyes to social and ethical issues. The arts can communicate knowledge that will educate and inform. In the mid-19th century, the pre-Raphaelite painters in Britain were controversial for exposing the social ills of poverty, prostitution and hypocrisy. Their art set out to shed light on these social problems. Art that is considered shocking today might not be considered controversial in the future.

Art can touch on messy and complicated ethical themes. For example, Shakespeare's play *Romeo and Juliet* deals with the stresses of family feuds and falling in love with someone who is considered unsuitable. The ethical dilemma that Juliet faces when she discovers that the man she has married – Romeo – has killed a member of her family reads like a plot from a television soap opera. People enjoy the thrill of a narrative based on an ethical dilemma.

We might also question the ethical behaviour of artists. Adolf Hitler (1889–1945) painted pictures, and yet was responsible for the deaths of over 6 million people. The painter Caravaggio (1571–1610) committed murder, and yet is considered a great artist, and the novelist Charles Dickens (1812–1870) was not thought to be a good husband and yet is considered a great writer. We might consider whether a person's character detracts from their artistic ability, and how these two elements connect.

Another question concerns the suitability of artistic content and subject matter. **Censorship** is a restriction on what is considered decent, justified or acceptable, suggesting that the arts should be limited on ethical grounds.

KEY TERM

censorship: the suppression or limitation of any material or views and beliefs that are considered to be unsuitable or inappropriate

TASK: ACTIVITY 11.5

As a class, write down the following questions at the top of a piece of paper, ready to evaluate them.

1   Should we value art created by a person who we believe has acted unethically? Why? Why not?

2   In what circumstances, if any, should the arts be censored or restricted on ethical grounds, and if so, why?

3   How do we know if the role of the arts is to support or challenge the existing values of a society and culture?

4   What role, if any, should the arts play in developing a person's moral character?

Then get into small groups. Circulate the questions around the class so that each group contributes a new point in response to the question, and continue until you have fully considered each one. To develop your skills of analysis further, you might add new ideas including: a new argument for or counter-argument against, a new real-life example, a different cultural, social or political perspective, an identification of any assumptions made or a consideration of the implications. Then evaluate your class responses on paper, and discuss the questions as a whole group.

Figure 11.4: The Mandelbrot set forms a beautiful and intricate two-dimensional shape. The arts and mathematics both require creativity and imagination. What do you think are the connections and links between these two areas of knowledge?

TOP TIP

When you write about the arts, avoid making general claims that are difficult to support, such as *the arts are just a matter of personal preference and contain no knowledge.*

Think about the ways in which the arts contain more knowledge than we might first assume. For example, they may offer insight into human relationships or the world around us.

11.6 Knowledge questions

1   What criteria need to be met before we are justified in claiming that we know something is *good art* or *good science*?

2   To what extent do two areas of knowledge *tell us the truth*?

3   Can we be sure if ethical considerations should limit the knowledge pursued in two areas of knowledge?

11.7 Extended writing task

Write 500 words or more on one of the following questions:

1   What, if anything, can we learn from the performing arts, the visual arts and the literary arts?

2   Do we need to know the context in which an artwork was produced in order to claim that we have knowledge of that artwork?

3   What ethical responsibilities do artists have when producing art?

SKILLS SELF-ASSESSMENT CHECKLIST

Reflect on what you have learned in this chapter and indicate your confidence level between 1 and 5 (where 5 is the highest score and 1 is the lowest). If you score below 3, revisit that section. Come back to this list later in your course. Has your confidence grown?

	Confidence level	Revisited?
Am I able to discuss the scope and limits of the arts?		
Can I appreciate the role of the arts in my own life, the value of the arts for me and the communities that I belong to?		
Can I appreciate how the arts can be viewed from different perspectives which have developed throughout history and across cultures?		
Am I able to analyse the tools and methods used by artists to create works of art and interpret works of art?		
Can I use specific examples to support an argument?		
Am I able to weigh up and evaluate arguments and counter-arguments in relation to knowledge questions?		
Do I have the skills to think through and consider the implications that follow from an argument?		
Am I aware of the relationship between the arts and ethics, and the ethical considerations, responsibilities and value of artists?		

11.8 Further reading

For a discussion of the 'renaissance genius', read Charles Nicholl, *Leonardo da Vinci: The Flights of the Mind*, Penguin, 2005

For an exploration of brain function in relation to literature, art and music, read: Semir Zeki, *Splendors and Miseries of the Brain: Love, Creativity, and the Quest for Human Happiness*, Wiley-Blackwell, 2008

For an explanation of truth and art, see BBC *Civilisations*, which takes a global perspective on the origins and development of the human instinct to create works of art

Mathematics

12.1 Introduction

Mathematics could be regarded as the most perfect system of knowledge we have. It is elegant, beautiful, simple, systematic, readily repeatable and many of its theorems are supported by proofs. But the price of its perfection is that it is largely disconnected from the world. As Einstein (1879–1955) once put it, *'Insofar as the statements of mathematics are certain, they do not refer to reality; and insofar as they refer to reality, they are not certain.'* One of the purposes of this chapter is to explore what implications such claims have for mathematical knowledge. Another is to develop your analytical skills to help you to feel more confident discussing mathematics as an area of knowledge.

12.2 The scope of mathematics

Thinking of mathematics, we primarily think of numbers (arithmetic), shape (geometry) and deduction (logic). However, the scope of mathematics could be seen as much broader because mathematical skills help to underpin our reasoning skills, creativity, abstract thinking, problem-solving and communication skills. All of us use the skills and products of mathematics in our daily lives, therefore Einstein's claim above may strike you as strange. As you look around you, may see fifteen fellow-students in your class; you may be sitting at a rectangular desk, having travelled to school in a vehicle with round wheels. Perhaps last night's homework was done on a computer controlled by operations in binary arithmetic and logic gates. Number, shape (geometry) and logic seem to be as rooted in the real world as anything could be. The problem is that instances of mathematical concepts in the world are only ever approximations.

TOK LINK: KNOWERS AND KNOWLEDGE

How important is personal experience in mathematics compared with other areas of knowledge?

TASK: THINK ABOUT 12.1

1 Is mathematics a body of knowledge or a method for creating/ discovering knowledge?

2 To what extent must mathematics be used in conjunction with other areas of knowledge to provide knowledge of the world?

Numbers

Counting is a human activity believed to extend back well before written history began. It is an activity that we tend to take for granted, and yet number theory is perhaps one of the most difficult aspects of mathematics. Some ancient peoples, and even some ethnic groups today (such as the Piraha of Brazil), only had words for *one, two* and *many*.

We now mostly count in groups of 10 (what we call the decimal system), but it has not always been so. The Babylonians, for example, used the sexagesimal system based on groups of 60. The first evidence we have of a decimal system comes from Aryabhata, a Hindu mathematician born in 476 CE. Our number systems are a product of history and culture.

> **REAL-LIFE SITUATION 12.1**
>
> Ali has two bars of chocolate and Risa has one bar. We might say that Ali has twice the number of chocolate bars as Risa, and there are three chocolate bars altogether. However, if they break up all the chocolate into equal-sized squares, Risa has more pieces than Ali. Although Risa had fewer chocolate bars than Ali, she had more chocolate.
>
> To what extent does counting relate to quantity?

The way we learn about numbers shapes the way we think of them. Take, for example, the natural numbers: 1, 2, 3, ... which are so familiar to us. Small children learn to count by applying them to objects like bricks, balls or apples.

TOP TIP

Many students like to give *1 + 1 = 2* or something similar as an example of mathematical truth. This is *not* recommended because it is a cliché, and an example of truth by definition rather than truth created or discovered by mathematics. If you are going to write about mathematics in your TOK essay or presentation, you should use examples from your mathematics lessons and your own experiences.

Figure 12.1: Counting objects such as apples is how many of us first learn about numbers but this can be misleading

Look at the three apples in Figure 12.1. If you added two more, there would be five apples; if you ate two, there would be one. But what happens if you eat four? Immediately there is a problem: you cannot eat more apples than you have; the natural numbers do not extend simply to negative numbers. You need a different kind of concept before you can deal with negative numbers. Some people struggle all their lives with negative numbers and algebra, because of the strong associations they have built between numbers and objects.

TASK: THINK ABOUT 12.2

1   Why do we need negative numbers?

2   How might our world be different if we only had number words for *one*, *two* and *many*?

3   Do numbers and concepts such as zero and infinity exist only in human imagination?

If you look at any three actual apples, they will not all be the same. Every apple is unique, so what we are counting are three *similar* things belonging to a particular class that is an **abstraction** from the world of apples. It is the ability to work with abstractions that gives mathematics its power.

Numbers like π and $\sqrt{2}$ have the property that they are *irrational*: their decimal expansions go on forever without ever repeating. Therefore, the number π requires an infinite number of bits of information to express it, which means we could never write it all down.

> **KEY TERM**
>
> **abstraction:** a generalised concept usually derived from many specific instances

---

KEY POINT

We can manipulate irrational numbers like $\sqrt{2}$ and π, but we can never fully know what they are.

Geometry

We all know what a circle is; we can draw one using a compass, and some of us can write down the equation of a circle. We can see many apparent circles in the world around us, but although the equation is precise, a drawing of a circle is only an approximation, and the wheels on the school bus are very poor approximations of circles. Instances of circles in the real world are imperfect examples of a hypothetical perfect circle.

In **Euclidean geometry**, a triangle on a plane can be shown to have the property that its angles add up to 180° using a mathematical proof based upon Euclid's five axioms. Whether there has ever been or could ever be such a triangle outside the mind of the mathematician is an entirely different matter to which mathematics has no answer.

> **KEY TERM**
>
> **Euclidean geometry:** the study of plane and solid figures on the basis of axioms and theorems derived by the Greek mathematician, Euclid. It is the form of geometry commonly taught in secondary schools around the world

---

KEY POINT

Euclidean geometry, in which the properties of shapes are explored with great ingenuity, is a fiction in the sense that none of these objects exists except in our minds. It follows that abstraction and imagination are key elements of mathematics.

So far, we have seen that the trouble with mathematics is that the things it studies and whose properties it explores with such great certainty do not actually exist. To this extent, mathematics justifies the first half of Einstein's claim, *'Insofar as the statements of mathematics are certain, they do not refer to reality.'* But what about mathematics when we apply it to the *real world*? All around us, we see examples of constructions and technologies that would not be possible without mathematics.

Applied mathematics

When engineers build bridges and other constructions, they use mathematical theories and formulae. To support traffic of a certain mass, a bridge needs to be made of girders of *this* density, *this* length, *this* breadth and *this* thickness connected by welds and bolts of *this* strength which will, when assembled, comfortably support traffic of *this* total mass doing *these* speeds with *these* impact characteristics. Engineers try to make sure that bridges do not suffer from the kind of defects that led to the 2007 I-35W bridge disaster in which a bridge over the Mississippi river collapsed in the USA without warning, killing 13 people and injuring 145 others. The reason for the collapse was that the plates holding the bridge beams were only half the thickness that they needed to be.

Figure 12.2: On 1st August 2007, the I-35W bridge collapsed without warning because the margins of error were not sufficient

Although all characteristics of bridges or any other engineering projects use mathematical quantities and theories, they are all *approximate*, and succeed only because of generous *tolerances* which usually ensure that whatever imperfections there may be in the theory or the manufacture of the components, there is a huge margin for error between the theoretical maximum load on the bridge and the actual breaking-strain.

TASK: THINK ABOUT 12.4

To what extent does the value of mathematics lie in its applicability to problems in the *real world* compared with the value of other areas of knowledge?

Neither mathematics nor engineering describe the world *precisely*: they aspire to describe it as well as they can while leaving plenty of margin for error. Mathematics is an incredibly useful tool that underpins most of the research in the natural and human sciences, but its certainty is found in the abstract, rather than in the real world.

Using applied mathematics has led to impressive constructions and innovative technologies that have changed the world we live in, but there is always a trade-off between safety, cost, precision and margins for error. We could, for example, build cars as strong as tanks; they would be much safer to drive in, but they would be so slow and expensive that few people would buy them. Mathematics helps us to say what the optimum trade-offs are, and what the margins of error should be, but only as a best estimate and not as an absolute certainty. So we have seen – at least in these examples – that the second half of Einstein's statement is also justified: '*Insofar as the statements of mathematics refer to reality, they are not certain.*'

TASK: THINK ABOUT 12.5

Compare the extent to which the individual knower is significant in mathematics with the importance of individual knowers in other areas of knowledge.

TOK IN YOUR LIFE

Calculating the time you need to get to school each morning involves applying mathematics to a real issue. You need to leave a margin for error if you want to avoid being late. Even then, an unexpected traffic jam, a delayed bus or a puncture in your bicycle tyre may still make you late if your margins are not big enough.

What other calculations do you make that require margins of error? (Think about practical work in the science laboratory or cooking dinner.)

12.3 Mathematical perspectives

There is a tendency for many people to think that mathematical knowledge is beyond culture; that it is *true* for all people and at all times, whether they understand the mathematics or not. But like all areas of knowledge, mathematics is a human enterprise with a long history, and throughout that history, different perspectives from different cultures have contributed to creating the academic discipline that we know today.

Generally speaking, mathematics has long been regarded as a cultural element. This means that the mathematics of a culture is one of the features of that culture. However, there are a growing number of voices arguing that mathematics is a cultural system in its own right.

In *Mathematics as a Cultural System*, the mathematician and philosopher Raymond L. Wilder (1896–1982) discusses the relationship between individuals within cultures and the collective of the culture, and makes the point that individuals can only make changes to cultural systems with the cooperation of others within the culture. To make any new mathematical breakthroughs, mathematicians must draw on the learning of their predecessors and contemporaries, and such breakthroughs usually happen when the culture has evolved to the point where a breakthrough is likely. This is why a number of mathematicians may make similar breakthroughs at the same time even though working independently of each other; a phenomenon often seen in the natural sciences as well.

The question of the relationship between the individual and culture is complex. While individual mathematicians can influence and shape mathematical culture, mathematical culture makes the individual mathematicians. When breakthroughs occur, it is up to the mathematical community whether or not they embrace the changes into the culture. Often, there is a **cultural lag** when there is a strong resistance to innovation. For example, there was a long delay before many mathematicians were willing to accept imaginary and complex numbers into the culture of the mathematical community.

> ## CROSS REFERENCE
>
> You can discover more about the history of mathematics in Chapter 12 of the Course Guide.

> ## KEY TERM
>
> **cultural lag:** the idea that culture takes time to catch up with technological and other innovations

---

TASK: ACTIVITY 12.1

Compare the historical development of mathematics with the historical development of other areas of knowledge. In small groups, discuss one of the following questions:

- How does the creation or discovery of mathematical knowledge differ from the creation or discovery of knowledge in other areas of knowledge?

- To what extent does mathematical knowledge change over time, and what are the implications for mathematics and other areas of knowledge?

To develop your analytical skills, evaluate different perspectives in your discussion and try to reach a conclusion.

Figure 12.3: *Sangaku* enabled non-mathematicians and even children to understand and work on sophisticated geometric problems without access to calculus

During the Edo period (1603–1868), Japan had no access to the 17th-century European developments in calculus. During this time, Japanese mathematics evolved differently from mathematics elsewhere, and *sangaku* were developed. These were a collection of geometric theorems and problems, typically involving tangent circles or tangent spheres, painted on wooden tablets.

These tablets were works of art, religious offerings and public announcements of the latest mathematical discoveries. *Sangaku* were dedicated to gods, and placed inside Shinto and Buddhist shrines as thanks for the discovery of a theorem, and to ask for help with making further mathematical progress. Proofs of *sangaku* theorems were rarely given; instead, they posed a challenge to others to prove them.

In the mid-19th century, Japan opened up, and gradually Japanese mathematics adopted more international methods. Changes were made to mathematical scripts, so very few people now know how to interpret the *sangaku* tablets that survive.

1   To what extent is mathematical knowledge embedded in particular cultures or traditions?

2   What might be lost and what might be gained when traditional ways of doing mathematics are given up in favour of a universal approach?

KEY TERM

sangaku: Japanese temple geometry problems and theorems produced on wooden tablets

12.4 Mathematical methods and tools

Mathematics employs a wide variety of methods to solve problems and model the world. Some would say that mathematics is itself a method of problem solving. Rather than addressing specific mathematical methods such as algebra, geometry and calculus, we will look at the methods and tools that underpin mathematics more generally.

Mathematical proof

Mathematical knowledge is thought to be certain because it is subject to rigorous forms of deductive reasoning to provide us with mathematical proofs. Only when something in mathematics is proved do we grant that it is true, and call it a mathematical theorem.

People often think that proof establishes truth, but in reality, mathematical proofs do no more than *preserve* truth. If you make assumptions and apply the laws of logic (deductive reasoning) correctly, the conclusions you come to will be as true as those assumptions.

TOP TIP

Be very careful of using the word *proof* in anything but a mathematical sense. Mostly when people say they have 'proved' something, they really mean they have provided evidence for it. However, evidence does *not* constitute proof.

TASK: THINK ABOUT 12.6

If proofs do not tell us anything new, why are they so important in mathematics?

Axiomatics

Mathematicians like to reduce the number of assumptions in a mathematical subject to as small a set as possible. These assumptions are called **axioms**. Axioms are often thought to be self-evidently true. In other words, they seem so obviously true that people do not question them. One example of an axiom is the principle of contradiction, which states that a statement and its opposite cannot both be true at the same time and place.

However, sometimes mathematicians start with a set of axioms and see what happens to the original system if they change one or more of them. It was making changes like this that led to non-Euclidean geometries, in which some results of classical Greek geometry are no longer true. In spherical geometry, for example, it is not true that the angles of a triangle must add up to 180°.

KEY TERM

axiom: a starting point in reasoning that is accepted as self-evidently true within a particular mathematical system

TASK: THINK ABOUT 12.7

A riddle: Imagine you leave your house and walk 10 km due south. You then turn 90° left and walk 20 km due east before turning 90° left again and walking 10 km due north, only to find a bear on your front doorstep. What colour is the bear?

The point of the riddle in Task 12.7 is that it neatly illustrates different axiomatic systems. If you were to sketch these instructions on a plane as you do in Euclidean geometry, you would end up 20 km east of your starting point and the riddle would make no sense. But if you apply spherical geometry and start at the North Pole, you end up back at the same point. Knowing this is what tells us that the bear must be a polar bear, and so the answer is white.

Mathematicians do not usually just make up a set of axioms and see what they can prove from them. Instead, they tend to take an extended system and reduce it to axioms. Then they try to show that all of the original theorems can be proved from those axioms. This helps to ensure mathematical consistency within the system.

Different axiomatic assumptions give rise to different types of mathematics. But if we can pick and choose between sets of axioms, how can we say that one set of true statements proved from one set of axioms is better than an incompatible set of true statements proved from another set of axioms? In fact, mathematical truth is only true in the system in which it is established, and it is not necessarily a truth about the world.

Logic

Logic is the study of valid forms of reasoning. There are different types of logic defined by different rules of inference. Deductive reasoning is one form of formal logic. Take the following example:

> Premise 1: All rectangles have four sides.
>
> Premise 2: A square is a rectangle.
>
> Conclusion: Therefore, a square has four sides.

This is a very straightforward example, and it is true *as long as both premises are true*. It offers us certainty, but does not tell us anything that we do not know or assume to start with.

Not all logic is quite so straightforward. Some logics (called modal logics) address things like *possibility*, where the logical connections between *certain*, *possible*, *likely* and so forth are built into the deductions. A simple example might be:

> Premise 1: Some quadrilaterals are trapezoids.
>
> Premise 2: This shape is a quadrilateral.
>
> Conclusion: Therefore, this shape could be a trapezoid.

This time, there is no certainty – only a possibility, and again we do not learn anything new. These are simple examples, but the same considerations hold true for more complex mathematical problems.

TOK LINK: LANGUAGE

What difference will it make to our conclusions if our premises begin with *all, many, some, only, few* or *no*?

Although most school mathematics follows the rules of deductive reasoning, mathematical problem-solving involves something more. Good mathematicians, when seeing a new problem, will imagine what the answer must look like before working their way to it using deduction and providing a formal proof.

Sometimes, however, logic can be counter-intuitive. We know, for example, that it is possible to make statements that we know to be true but that are not provable within a mathematical system. This was shown by *Gödel's incompleteness theorems*, which shook the mathematical world when they were first published in 1931. They show that the truth of something need not depend upon the ability to prove it.

There are many things in mathematics that are believed to be true but no one has yet been able to prove: for example, that every even number greater than 2 is the sum of two prime numbers (known as *Goldbach's conjecture*).

TASK: THINK ABOUT 12.8

If you are given the pattern: 1, 2, 3, 4, ... and asked to give the next entry, the expected answer is probably '5'. But there are infinite *logical* possibilities that could go there. If we mark '5' as correct and other answers wrong, are we really testing people's ability to reason, or are we testing their conformity to shared assumptions?

Mathematical imagination

Imagination is an important tool often used by mathematicians. The problems with numbers that we considered at the beginning of this chapter may be helped by imagining a number line with different numbers represented by different locations along it. We can imagine the line extending indefinitely in both directions, although the line and the points along it have neither depth nor height. Although the Pythagoreans used number lines in ancient Greece, it was not until the 7th century CE that Brahmagupta, an Indian mathematician, wrote the first comprehensive rules for working with zero and negative numbers.

Mathematicians can solve problems in *n* variables by imagining them as the dimensions of an *n*-dimensional space, so although we may find it impossible to imagine what a six-dimensional figure might look like, we can explore its properties using mathematics.

In your mathematics classes, you may be introduced to what are called *complex numbers*. Complex numbers are created by altering the usual rule that negative numbers do not have square roots. Examples of complex numbers are *2 + 3i* or *4i*. What makes them complex is that they combine real numbers with an *imaginary number – i,* which represents $\sqrt{-1}$.

As strange as they may seem, imaginary numbers have turned out to have important applications to many real situations such as fluid dynamics, electromagnetism, quantum mechanics and fractals. Without $\sqrt{-1}$, our physics would be much poorer and our mathematics incomplete.

TASK: THINK ABOUT 12.9

1   Many mathematicians regard imagination as an important tool in mathematics. Compare its importance in mathematics with that in other areas of knowledge.

2   Deductive reasoning is an essential skill in mathematics. To what extent is it necessary in other areas of knowledge?

When comparing methodologies, try to come up with specific examples, preferably from your IB Diploma Programme classes, to illustrate your points.

Paradoxes of infinity

Most of us can understand that there are an infinite number of even numbers and an infinite number of odd numbers, and if we add them together we still have the same number of numbers – that is, an infinite number of them. We can even think of counting to infinity *theoretically*, even though we could never actually reach it: 1, 2, 3, 4, ..., ∞. But this is only one kind of infinity.

What is far more difficult to grasp is that there are an infinite number of different infinities, and some kinds of infinity are bigger than others. Some kinds of infinity are countable, and there are some that cannot be counted, even theoretically.

TASK: ACTIVITY 12.2

Watch the Ted-Ed™ video on *'How big is infinity'* and the *Guardian*™ video, *'Marcus du Sautoy counts from zero to infinity'*.

TASK: THINK ABOUT 12.10

What does it mean to have infinite types of infinity in a finite universe? Consider an infinite non-recurring decimal such as $\sqrt{2}$ or π. If it goes on forever and never repeats, must it eventually contain everyone's telephone number? Most people intuit yes, but the answer is no. Can you explain why?

Computational mathematics

Computational mathematics solves mathematical problems by computer simulation. It has wide-ranging applications – from analysing data to developing accurate and efficient methods for making complex physical and biological models, and so on.

Computational mathematics has given rise to new fields within mathematics. For example, meteorologist Edward Lorenz (1917–2008) ran a simple weather program, and discovered that by reducing the initial start-up data to three decimal places from six, the program predicted completely different systems of weather. This discovery gave rise to *complexity theory*, sometimes called *chaos theory*, which explains the sensitivity of non-linear mathematical systems to tiny variations in their starting conditions. We now know that many systems are so sensitive that *any* change in the starting conditions will produce divergent behaviour. Since we cannot input starting conditions with *infinite* accuracy, we cannot project the paths of these systems with any reliability; we can only say whether the behaviour will lie within certain limits and with what probability, and even that cannot be said for some systems.

REAL-LIFE SITUATION 12.3

When Pakistani and Indian farmers started to use the anti-inflammatory drug diclofenac to treat their cattle in 1993, 97% of Indian vultures were wiped out over a period of 15 years. This led to an increase in other scavengers such as rats and feral dogs, which in turn led to an increased risk of diseases such as tuberculosis, rabies and anthrax, and water being contaminated by rotting carcasses.

CONTINUED

New drugs are tested on animals, and the results are analysed mathematically to see if they are safe for use on different species of animals.

1   Why might the testing and statistical analysis of diclofenac not have predicted its environmental impact?

2   Why can we never know what all the effects of a particular intervention might be?

Figure 12.4: A lone vulture where once there might have been hundreds

KEY POINT

> For want of a nail the shoe was lost.
> For want of a shoe the horse was lost.
> For want of a horse the rider was lost.
> For want of a rider the battle was lost.
> For want of a battle the kingdom was lost.
> And all for the want of a horseshoe nail.
>
> **Anonymous**

The children's rhyme, 'For want of a nail' effectively illustrates how a very small initial starting condition (a missing nail) can have a dramatic impact on the path of a system – in this case the outcome of a battle, leading to the loss of a kingdom.

TASK: ACTIVITY 12.3

Watch Nicolas Perony's TED™ Talk, *'Puppies! Now that I've got your attention, complexity theory'* to explore some applications of complexity theory.

TASK: THINK ABOUT 12.11

Economic systems, ecological systems, the brain, developing embryos and our own immune systems are all examples of complex systems that cannot be modelled with any precision.

1   What are the implications of complexity theory for understanding these systems?

2   Why can we not put in all the starting conditions with *infinite* accuracy?

3   How can a model be false but still useful?

12.5 Ethics and mathematics

Mathematicians have influential roles in many aspects of society, including science, industry, the military and national security. As data is accumulated and analysed using mathematical techniques, mathematicians have an ethical obligation to ensure that their automated systems do what they are believed to do, and to try to eliminate any bias that may have inadvertently been programmed in.

Statistics is an area of mathematics renowned for being misused, whether by error or through deliberate attempts to mislead people. One practice that is frequently found is **data dredging**. This is when researchers look through vast amounts of data to try to uncover patterns without first having a hypothesis. While looking for patterns is a legitimate exercise in any mathematics, it is wrong to test a **hypothesis** on the same data that led to the construction of the hypothesis. An associated error that many people make is confusing **correlation** with **causation**. For example, if you compare ice cream sales and the number of deaths from drowning, you may find a correlation: the more ice creams that are sold, the more people drown, but this does not imply one causes the other. There are a number of ways this relationship could be explained.

- Eating ice cream makes it more likely you will drown.
- If someone drowns, grief causes people to eat more ice cream.
- A third unknown factor (such as hot weather) leads to people eating more ice cream and behaving in ways that make them more vulnerable to drowning (such as swimming).

KEY POINT

Correlation can appear as a result of causation, but it also occurs for many other reasons. If a correlation is found, extensive research needs to be undertaken to determine whether or not there is a causal relationship.

KEY TERMS

data dredging: scanning data for a pattern and presenting them as statistically significant when there is no real connection

hypothesis: a proposed explanation made on the basis of limited evidence as a starting point for further investigation

correlation: a relationship between two or more variables

causation: a relationship in which one thing or event causes another thing or event

TASK: ACTIVITY 12.4

Watch the Khan Academy video called *'Correlation and causality'* on YouTube™.

In pairs or small groups, try to find a similar news item, and analyse the way in which the article tries to use statistics.

1   Is the article trying to convince you of something?

2   Does the article confuse correlation with causation?

Discuss: How are practices such as 'data dredging' used to manipulate and mislead people?

Not all mistakes with statistics are deliberate. Sometimes, well-meaning people can make mistakes if they do not take appropriate steps to check their calculations.

REAL-LIFE SITUATION 12.4

In 1999, a young solicitor was wrongfully convicted of murdering her two young sons because the prosecution had given flawed statistical evidence in her trial. Both boys had died of Sudden Infant Death Syndrome within a few weeks of their birth. In 2003, the mother's conviction was overturned on appeal after it was discovered that the boys had died of natural causes. The Royal Statistical Society issued a statement arguing that there was no basis for the statistical evidence presented at the original trial, and expressed concern about the misuse of statistics in the courts.

In small groups, discuss:

1   Why are so many people willing to accept statistical evidence without critically evaluating it?

2   In what circumstances and to what extent do we have an ethical responsibility to critically evaluate statistics before using them to support our arguments?

While it is very easy to see how statistics can be misused, deliberately or inadvertently, some people say that **pure mathematics** is a harmless exercise, and that most of its ethical issues are related to plagiarism and the publication of work. However, some people have questioned whether the enterprise of pure mathematics is ethical because it engages intelligent people who might otherwise use their intelligence in ways that are more immediately useful to society. Others point out that many mathematical theories that were once regarded as pure mathematics have come to be extremely useful. For example, factoring large **integers** was once a pure mathematical enterprise, but it is now the basis for a **cryptosystem** used to maintain security over the internet.

KEY TERMS

pure mathematics: the study of abstract mathematical concepts independently of practical applications

integer: a whole number along the number line: …, −3, −2, −1, 0, 1, 2, 3, …

cryptosystem: a series of algorithms for encoding and decoding information to prevent unauthorised access

TASK: THINK ABOUT 12.12

To what extent is it ethically justifiable for mathematicians to research areas of mathematics that do not have immediate and obvious applications?

12.6 Knowledge questions

1   If mathematical modelling cannot make reliable predictions about complex systems, why are mathematical models regarded as so important in the human and natural sciences?

2   To what extent does the analysis of statistics depend upon human interpretation?

3   To what extent are we justified in believing that mathematical knowledge is certain?

12.7 Extended writing task

Write 500 words on one or more of the following questions:

1   To what extent is certainty achievable in mathematics?

2   Are mathematical concepts discovered or invented?

3   To what extent is mathematics dependent upon culture?

SKILLS SELF-ASSESSMENT CHECKLIST

Reflect on what you have learned in this chapter and indicate your confidence level between 1 and 5 (where 5 is the highest score and 1 is the lowest). If you score below 3, revisit that section. Come back to this list later in your course. Has your confidence grown?

	Confidence level	Revisited?
Can I discuss the scope and limitations of mathematics?		
Could I articulate the relationship between certainty and abstraction in mathematics?		
Am I able to discuss different cultural influences on mathematics?		
Can I discuss mathematics as a cultural system?		
Can I compare and contrast methods and tools used in creating mathematical knowledge with those used in other areas of knowledge?		
Can I explain the difference between correlation and causation?		
Am I able to critically evaluate news articles that cite statistical evidence?		
Am I able to explore ethical issues relating to mathematics?		

12.8 Further reading

To discover more about how our number system evolved, read: Calvin C. Clawson, *The Mathematical Traveler: Exploring the Grand History of Numbers*, Perseus, 1994

To know more about the cultural nature of mathematics, read: Raymond L Wilder, *Mathematics as a Cultural System*, Pergamon Press, 1981; and Helaine Selin (ed), *Mathematics across Cultures*, Kluwer Academic Publishers, 2018

To explore the mathematics underlying the natural world, read: Ian Stewart, *Nature's Numbers*, Hachette UK, 1995; and Ian Stewart, *Professor Stewart's Cabinet of Mathematical Curiosities*, Profile, 2008

To investigate mathematical paradoxes, read: Stanley Farlow, *Paradoxes in Mathematics*, Dover Books, 2013

To discover more about some of the assumptions and concepts that underpin mathematics, read: Bertrand Russell, *Introduction to Mathematical Philosophy*, Spokesman Books, 2008 (first published in 1919)

> ## Chapter 13
The natural sciences

LEARNING INTENTIONS

In this chapter, you will explore the scope and limits of science, and consider how scientific knowledge changes. Throughout the chapter, you will develop skills to help you critically evaluate competing scientific knowledge claims.

You will:

- develop an awareness of the scope and limitations of the natural sciences, and learn to distinguish science from pseudoscience

- consider how personal and cultural perspectives can influence the natural sciences

- learn about some of the methods and tools used in creating scientific knowledge

- develop analytical skills to help you to critically evaluate scientific knowledge claims

- learn about some of the ethical issues relating to the natural sciences.

BEFORE YOU START

1   Do the natural sciences provide us with truth and certainty?

2   How might politics and economics influence the pursuit of knowledge in the sciences?

3   To what extent should ethical considerations influence progress in the natural sciences?

13.1 Introduction

The natural sciences cover a broad area of knowledge, including chemistry, biology and physics, which you might study in Group 4 of your IB Diploma Programme. Arguably, we rely on scientific knowledge more than other areas of knowledge in our daily lives, yet we can sometimes find ourselves surrounded by conflicting information that *claims* to be scientifically *proven*. Developing skills to help us evaluate scientific claims is important for navigating a path through conflicting claims, and assessing the extent to which scientific knowledge is reliable.

13.2 The scope of the natural sciences

The natural sciences involve the systematic study of the natural world and its properties. It could be argued that any studies of human behaviour are a subset of the natural sciences. However, when we speak about the natural sciences, we generally refer to the physical sciences, the earth sciences and the life sciences, although the divisions between these branches are not always clear-cut.

The natural sciences have changed over time. Theology was once the queen of the sciences because, in medieval times, pursuing theological knowledge was a major pre-occupation of those who wanted to understand the world. Indeed, throughout the ages, many theologians have made important contributions to what we might regard as science today. For example, Nasir al-Din al-Tusi (1201–1274) was a Persian theologian who is often considered the father of trigonometry, and Gregor Mendel (1822–1884) was an Augustinian friar and the founder of modern genetics.

TASK: THINK ABOUT 13.1

1   How might a religious belief in the natural order of the world have motivated the study of science in medieval times?

2   To what extent would you regard mathematics as a science?

TOK LINK: LANGUAGE

What we understand by *science* has changed over the centuries. Could there be disciplines that we regard as science now that might not be regarded as science in the future?

Important to the scope of the natural sciences is the distinction between science and **pseudoscience**. Karl Popper (1902–1994), a philosopher of science, identified the difference between science and pseudoscience as one of attitude. While science sets out to challenge scientific knowledge claims, pseudoscience sets out to find supporting evidence. According to Popper, only a claim that is **falsifiable** can be considered scientific. This means that a scientific claim must be capable of being shown to be wrong. For example, the claim that *'Holly bushes are evergreen'* could be falsified by someone producing a deciduous holly bush. The claim that *'There is a monster living in Loch Ness'* is not scientific, because although it could conceivably be true, the claim cannot be falsified. The inability to find a monster could be dismissed by saying, *'it was hiding'*, or *'people were not looking in the right place'*.

TASK: ACTIVITY 13.1

In pairs, discuss the following claims. Which are falsifiable and which are not?

1   All crows are black.

2   Male birds have two Z chromosomes (ZZ), and females have a Z and a W chromosome (ZW).

3   Unicorns exist.

4   All metals expand when heated.

5   Some zebras have spots.

If you think some of the claims are not falsifiable, identify why.

TASK: THINK ABOUT 13.2

Is being falsifiable but not falsified the same as being true? Is being unfalsifiable the same as being untrue? What are the implications for scientific claims?

13.3 Perspectives in science

Many people think of science as a discipline that produces objective knowledge. However, like all other areas of knowledge, the natural sciences are as influenced by different perspectives. Characteristics such as gender and culture can affect what scientists choose to study, and what they see. For example, until Jane Goodall (1934-) began observing chimpanzees, almost all primate studies had been done by male scientists who focused on male competition for access to females. The men had largely ignored the female primates during their field studies, and assumed that the females simply accepted winning males as their mates. It was only when Goodall and other women began studying primates that it was discovered that female primates are often dominant in their relationships, take an active role in deciding which males they mate with and sometimes mate with several males.

Similarly, while western primatologists tended to focus on male dominance and dominance hierarchies, Japanese primatologists such as Kinji Imanishi (1902–1992) focused on status and social relationships, and therefore found different characteristics. As Johann Wolfgang von Goethe (1749–1832) once pointed out, *'We only see what we know'*. Our expectations act on our perceptions in ways that are measurable and yet imperceptible to us. This is a form of **confirmation bias**.

TASK: THINK ABOUT 13.3

1 How might confirmation bias affect the design and interpretation of experiments in the natural sciences?

2 Why is it important to have diversity in science?

Paradigm shifts

Occasionally, perspectives in science undergo a **paradigm shift,** when usual perspectives and expectations give way to new ways of thinking. These paradigm shifts often occur in response to new discoveries, and are sometimes referred to as *scientific revolutions*.

The paradigm shift model of science suggests that science extends knowledge by adding detail to prevailing paradigms. However, as it does so, certain **anomalies** occur. This leads to the questioning of the paradigms and generates a number of new, competing ideas until new paradigms are established.

> ### KEY TERMS
>
> **paradigm shift:** a significant change in approach and underlying assumptions
>
> **anomaly:** something that deviates from what is expected

REAL-LIFE SITUATION 13.1

In 2018, the European Research Council awarded a grant to researchers at the University of Oxford for a project that investigates how structural complexity can give materials new properties that are not possible in materials with simple structures.

The researchers claim that the aim of the project is to create a paradigm shift in the way that chemists design materials, in order to produce materials with entirely new behaviours.

1 Is scientific revolution the same as scientific progress?

2 To what extent can there be scientific progress without paradigm shifts?

One of the implications of changing perspectives and paradigm shifts is that our view of the universe changes with time. What were once thought to be 'final' theories of science have repeatedly been superseded.

TASK: ACTIVITY 13.2

In pairs, create a 3-minute video to present to your class in response to one of the following questions:

- How much of what we currently believe to be true in science might be superseded or even overturned in the future?

- Identify a few specific examples of how scientific knowledge has changed over time, for example our understanding of the atom.

- What are the implications of changing scientific knowledge?

13.4 Methods and tools of the natural sciences

The **empirical method** of science requires that scientific theories be *tested* in ways that are *repeatable*, and produce *consistent* results regardless of who conducts the experiments. As a result, scientific knowledge is often regarded as more certain than other areas of knowledge.

Scientific knowledge has helped to provide us with new technologies, chemical compounds and procedures that have helped to improve our standards of living. Computers, aeroplanes, plastics, medicines and surgical procedures are just a few examples of some of the innovations provided through advances in scientific knowledge. Science has also provided us with new insights into life, our planet and the universe.

KEY TERMS

empirical method: using experimental data to develop or evaluate a theory

verify: confirm by use of evidence

> **TASK: THINK ABOUT 13.4**
>
> To what extent is science seen as setting the standard for all knowledge?

People will often ask of a truth claim, *'Is it scientifically proven?'*. Commercial products are frequently advertised as *'scientifically proven'* to give you whiter teeth, cleaner laundry, clearer skin or glossier hair. Perhaps this is because many people view *'scientific proof'* as a stamp of authenticity. But what does this really mean?

Early scientific methods set out to **verify** scientific theories, but verification is often too ambitious. How, for example, would we verify a statement such as, *'There is no planet in the universe made entirely of green cheese'*? Verification by experiment would involve testing every planet and showing that it was not made of green cheese. This is not practically possible. Even though the statement is believed to be true, it cannot be verified.

Figure 13.1: Many commercial products claim to have 'scientifically proven' benefits? Do they? How can we know?

TASK: ACTIVITY 13.3

In pairs, look at the advertisement in Figure 13.1. What claims does the advertisement make, and what evidence does it provide to support those claims? Do you think the evidence offers proof? What evidence would you need to accept the claims?

Evaluate some examples of modern advertisements that make *scientific* claims.

An intense debate has arisen around the issue of verification. **Positivists** insist that a statement that cannot be verified should be rejected as meaningless. This includes all references to God, ethics and many other things of a speculative nature.

In *The Logic of Scientific Discovery*, Karl Popper argues that verification expects too much of scientific methods, and that we should embrace statements as scientific provided that they are falsifiable. For example, if we make a knowledge claim, *'There is no planet in the universe made of cheese'*, the discovery of any planet made of cheese would falsify the claim. Therefore, according to Popper, the claim can be regarded as scientific. On the other hand, the claim, *'There is a planet in the universe made of cheese'*, is not falsifiable because no matter how many planets we find that are not made of cheese, the claimant could say that the planet is still out there – we have just not found it yet. This makes the claim unfalsifiable, and therefore unscientific.

> **KEY TERM**
>
> **positivism:** the belief that the only valid knowledge is that which is based on sensory evidence

TASK: THINK ABOUT 13.5

There are some scientific beliefs – for example, the core of the sun has a temperature of approximately 15.7 million kelvin – that we do not have the technology to verify, but we may be able to verify in the future.

Can we regard such statements as scientific *knowledge*?

The scientific method

There are numerous versions of the scientific method. They usually start with a question which may come from observation or general research. For example, you may ask, *'Why do some chilli plants grow more chillies than others?'*.

The next step is to construct a hypothesis. You may have noticed that chillies grow well in sunny places, so your hypothesis might be, *'The more sunlight a chilli plant gets, the more chillies it produces'*.

You would use your hypothesis to plan an experiment and predict an outcome. You might decide to grow chillies in varying positions: some in sunny spots and some in shady spots. Your prediction might be *'The plants in the sunniest positions will produce the most chillies'*.

You would conduct the experiment, trying to control other variables as much as possible by making sure that all of your plants come from the same healthy stock, are planted in the same soil and receive the same amount of water.

Once you have conducted your experiment, you would need to analyse your data to see whether or not it supports your hypothesis. If it does, it strengthens your hypothesis, but it does not *prove* it.

TASK: THINK ABOUT 13.6

If you conduct an experiment and the results match the prediction, why does this not prove your hypothesis?

Data analysis

Scientific experiments and field observations generate large amounts of data which are analysed to support or falsify hypotheses. One of the most difficult questions in science concerns the relationship between experimental data and theory. The problem is that for any set of data, there will be an infinite number of theories that can explain it. Scientists will nearly always choose the simplest – or most elegant – theory to explain their data if it fits within a network of associated theories.

KEY POINT

Occam's Razor states that when choosing between possible hypotheses, we should choose the one that makes the fewest assumptions. Scientists adopt the simplest explanations first, and will only accept a more complex explanation if it has greater explanatory power.

TASK: ACTIVITY 13.4

Plan a response to the following question: To what extent does science follow the 'scientific method' commonly found in science textbooks?

In your plan, develop some arguments and counter-arguments, and find examples from your Group 4 subject in support of both.

Repeatability

Science generally insists upon repeatability as a criterion for truth. However, some of the most significant events in the world are not repeatable. For example, scientists trying to learn more about the spread of Covid19 must largely rely on data collected by governments, and they cannot create duplicate conditions for testing their hypotheses. It is only within a laboratory, with its controls and limitations, that more-or-less repeatable conditions can be achieved. However, the more controlled the environment, the less like the real world the experiment is.

In one sense, there is no such thing as a repeatable experiment. At the microscopic level, there will always be small variations, and we know from Chapter 12 on mathematics that small variations can lead to wildly different behaviours in complex systems.

TASK: THINK ABOUT 13.7

It is often said that scientific results must be repeatable. To what extent is this possible or even desirable in other areas of knowledge?

By restricting the number of variables that affect the outcome of an experiment, laboratory experiments limit the applicability of their results to non-laboratory situations. We know from our experiments how things work under ideal conditions, but not how they work in reality. However accurate they may be, scientific theories can only model the world approximately.

Although we say that science is empirical/experimental, a great deal of its power comes from the *coherence* of the worldview it presents to us. Experimental results that go against a popular theory are often assumed to be the result of an error. Moreover, any set of experimental data will usually have some results that do not fit the theory; for example, data plots may cover an area rather than fitting a line or predictable curve. Typically, we ignore the rogue results – calling them *outliers* – and we plot a smooth curve or line through the middle of the data, because we insist on the simplicity and geometry of the theory.

TASK: THINK ABOUT 13.8

1   When you are asked to draw a *line of best fit* for a science experiment, how many of your results sit on that line?

2   To what extent can we understand the world if we ignore results that do not fit our theories?

Scientific models

We need simple ways of visualising the universe to help people come to terms with its vastness, and we also need simple ways of visualising the tiny atoms and molecules that make up the universe as we know it, so that we create models. But these models are simplistic, and do not show the world as it is.

The universe mapped out by Sir Isaac Newton (1643–1727) was a stunning intellectual achievement, and the Bohr–Rutherford model of the atom serves us very well in elementary chemistry. However, both of these models are false. The universe is not Euclidean as Newton assumed; atoms are not composed of protons and neutrons which are orbited by electrons in convenient shells as the Bohr–Rutherford model describes. The reality is much stranger than these models suppose.

TASK: THINK ABOUT 13.9

1   Why are models always relatively simplistic?

2   In what ways can models help and hinder the production and communication of knowledge?

TASK: ACTIVITY 13.5

Select one of the following questions, and brainstorm some ideas to plan a response. Find some specific examples from science and one other area of knowledge to support your arguments.

CONTINUED

1   How important are the use of models in science and one other area of knowledge?

2   Why is it regarded as helpful to teach physical laws and models that we know are not true? Are there parallels in another area of knowledge?

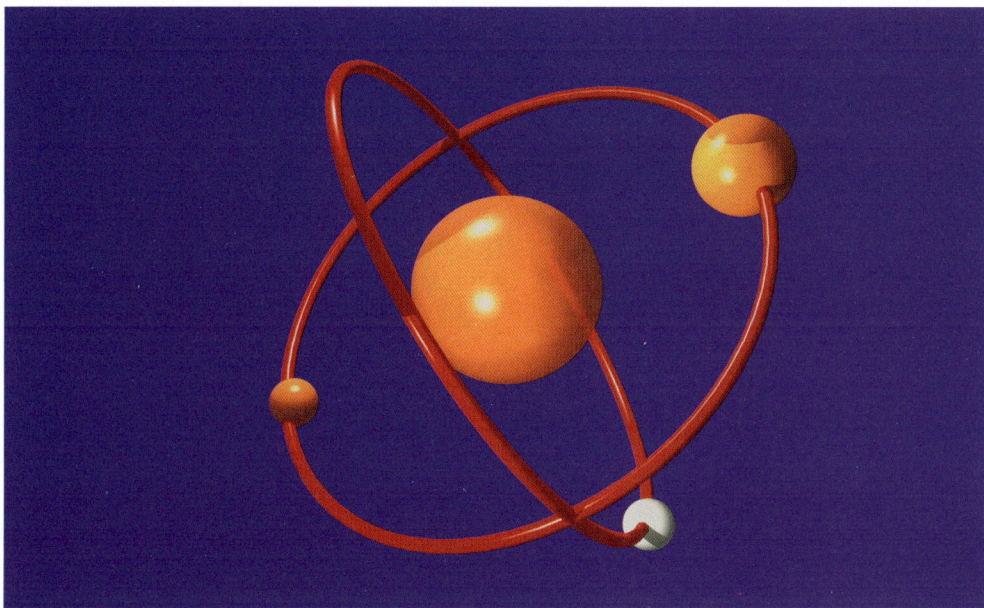

Figure 13.2: A model of an atom. To what extent is it more important for a model to be useful than to be accurate?

Scientific theories

Scientific theories could be said to operate as tools in science, in that they provide a framework within which experiments are designed and results are interpreted. Two of the strongest reasons to accept scientific theories are that they *explain* known behaviour and *predict* future behaviour. A well-founded scientific theory tells us what to expect, and experiments confirm that what we expect to happen does indeed happen. For example, in chemistry, our theory about acids and bases says that if we add an acid to a base, we will get salt and water. If we do an experiment to test this, the results should confirm our theory.

There are times when a theory may be accepted even if it seems strange to ordinary thinking and reason. For example, neither quantum theory nor general relativity seem to follow commonly understood patterns of reason, but they have been accepted by the scientific community because of their intellectual beauty and explanatory powers.

TASK: ACTIVITY 13.6

Look at the material on the 'Piltdown Man' on the Natural History Museum website. Discovered in the early-20th century, the skeleton had all the characteristics predicted of the 'missing link' in the theory of human evolution. However in 1953, despite having been accepted by scientists for more than 40 years, the remains were shown to be forgeries.

To what extent might the willingness of scientists to accept the Piltdown Man fraud have been the result of wanting to find evidence that fitted with their scientific theory?

TOK IN YOUR LIFE

Can you think of occasions when you have accepted evidence (not necessarily in science) because it confirms what you already believe?

To what extent do we sometimes accept evidence because we want it to confirm our theories?

Why is this tendency a form of pseudoscience?

Language

Language is an essential tool for scientists to formulate their theories and publish their results; it is also central to peer review – the practice that filters and controls what is published in scientific journals. Often, disciplines within science develop so many technical words that they seem to have a language of their own. Without knowing the technical language, it is difficult to understand the science.

KEY POINT

Defining scientific terms is very important in all branches of science. Scientists debate issues such as what a single organism is, what counts as a planet and what constitutes a substance.

REAL-LIFE SITUATION 13.2

The largest known organism is *Armillaria ostoyae*, otherwise known as a honey mushroom, an example of which covers 2384 acres in Oregon, USA. *Armillaria ostoyae* is regarded as the largest known organism based on the definition of an organism as something made up of genetically identical cells that can communicate and can at least coordinate themselves for a common purpose.

1 Why is it necessary for scientists around the world to work with agreed definitions?

2 What would the implications be if different scientists used different definitions?

Reason

In Chapter 12 on mathematics, we considered deductive reasoning when we explored mathematical proofs. The sciences also use deductive reasoning, but perhaps even more important is the use of **inductive reasoning**. This is when a general knowledge claim is made on the basis of repeated past experiences. Most – if not all – scientific claims are made on this basis. For example, grey whales are said to make the longest migrations of any mammal, travelling up to 20,000 km per year. This is based on past observations. However, there is no guarantee that they will continue to migrate such long distances in the future. Even scientific claims based on laboratory experiments assume that the ways substances react in the future will be the same as they have reacted in the past.

The problem with inductive reasoning is that no number of past experiences can prove anything. For example, scientists long believed that animals with different numbers of chromosomes could not be crossbred and give birth to fertile offspring. This has now been shown to be false. Goats and sheep have different numbers of chromosomes, and yet can produce fertile hybrid offspring who have gone on to produce live young of their own.

KEY TERM

inductive reasoning: when we predict future events on the basis of past experiences

Figure 13.3: A goat/sheep hybrid – an animal once thought by scientists to be impossible

Reason plays a central role in determining whether a new scientific argument or theory fits within the existing web of scientific ideas. If it does, it may be accepted; if it does not, it is much harder to overthrow established thinking.

TASK: THINK ABOUT 13.10

1   If we have only ever observed black crows, does this mean that all crows are black?

2   Space travel was once thought to be impossible. What things do we currently regard as impossible? Could they be possible in the future?

Creativity and imagination

Creativity and imagination are powerful tools in scientific development. They allow science to reach into the microscopic world, where we can speculate about quarks and gluons that nobody can sense directly, and out into the universe to other galaxies, pulsars, quasars and black holes, the properties of which challenge the very foundations of physics.

They can also play a part in the more everyday world of science. While experiments are often seen as the key to science, many scientific experiments are conducted in the mind rather than in a laboratory; these are called *thought experiments*, and they have been key to many great discoveries.

The Italian physicist Galileo Galilei (1564–1642) conducted one of the earliest famous thought experiments by imagining tying objects with different masses together and dropping them from a great height. By using his imagination and thinking it through logically, Galileo was able to show that the speed of a falling object is not dependent upon its mass.

Albert Einstein (1879–1955) credited his work on special relativity to a thought experiment he did as a boy, when he imagined himself chasing a beam of light through space at the speed of light.

Science fiction has often anticipated scientific advances long before they were technically possible. Writers such as Jules Verne (1828–1905) and H. G. Wells (1866–1946) in the nineteenth century used their creativity to predict submarines and spaceships, just as Leonardo da Vinci anticipated manned flight with his designs for bird-like wings and helicopters. Imagination stimulates scientific research: once something is thinkable, others will try to make it possible.

TASK: THINK ABOUT 13.11

1   To what extent are scientific models imaginary?

2   Would our technology be different if we had not had creative writers like Jules Verne?

13.5 Ethics and the natural sciences

There are three main strands of ethical issues in science: issues about what knowledge is pursued, how knowledge is pursued and whether knowledge is pursued and constructed fairly.

What is being investigated?

Ethical issues in science can be very contentious. Some people argue that all scientific progress is valuable, and that the generation of new knowledge is self-justifying. Others believe that some types of knowledge are too disturbing or destructive to pursue. One area of contention is in genetics. While the genetic study of diseases is generally applauded, the genetic study of behaviour can be very contentious, for example, when certain genes or combination of genes appear to predispose individuals with those genes to aggression and violent behaviour, raising a number of ethical questions.

Those who argue against such research fear that the implications of the research could lead to prejudice or even **eugenics**. On the other hand, a deeper understanding of genetics can lead to improved health care and better understanding of human behaviour.

Another form of science that some would regard as unethical is the development of chemical and biochemical weapons. While most people would agree that chemical weapons should not be used against people, the science behind those weapons is also used to kill other creatures considered by many to be *pests*. The use of chemical sprays and fertilisers in agriculture and gardens is thought to be responsible for much of the loss of biodiversity around the globe, and also linked to many diseases in animals and humans. However, some people would argue that without chemical sprays and fertilisers, it would be difficult to produce enough food to feed the human population.

TASK: THINK ABOUT 13.12

1   Is there any knowledge that scientists should not pursue?

2   What would the implications be if all human behaviour were found to be genetically based?

3   Is the fear of implications sufficient reason to restrict the pursuit of some types of knowledge?

How knowledge is pursued

This is the area of ethical issues that people tend to be most aware of. Historically, barbaric experiments have been carried out on people and animals in the name of science. Now, there are international guidelines set up to protect the dignity, rights and welfare of human research subjects, but the question of using animals is still hotly debated. Also debated is how drugs should be tested on humans. Even when a drug is found to be safe for other animal species, it is not necessarily safe for humans. Human 'volunteers' are often paid for participation in drug trials. Those who volunteer are often students and others who need money. Many trials are carried out in **least developed countries**, which can be seen as exploiting the very poor, as well as a way of trying to evade some health and safety regulations.

REAL-LIFE SITUATION 13.3

In January 2016, a French company, Biotrial, which was set up to run pharmaceutical trials, recruited 128 healthy paid volunteers to test a new drug. After the volunteers had been given a small dose of the drug with no reported side effects, the dosage was increased. Five participants became ill and were sent to hospital. One of these patients, a man in his late 20s, was declared brain dead just two weeks after starting the trial. The four other patients sent to hospital may have suffered irreversible brain damage.

1   The health advantages of modern drugs are indisputable. Occasional deaths and health problems created by testing new drugs on humans for the first time are inevitable. We may believe that the risks are outweighed

KEY TERM

eugenics: controlled breeding to improve a population

KEY TERM

least developed countries: low-income countries that have severe structural obstructions to sustainable development

CONTINUED

> by the potential benefits, but is it ethical that the bulk of those risks are taken by the poor?
>
> 2 Although the participants would have given *'informed consent'* to take part in the trial, how is it possible to give 'informed consent' when the outcomes are unknown?

Another concern for the practice of science is that ethical issues proliferate as science progresses. For example, now that we have the ability to alter genes to protect against – and even eliminate – some diseases, questions arise over how far we should be willing to go. For example, we might agree to edit genes that lead to children dying in infancy, but what about genes that predispose them to depression or aggression? Eliminating a genetic disorder does not involve the same individual living without the disorder; instead, it means a different individual living a different life.

REAL-LIFE SITUATION 13.4

In 2018, it was claimed that the first two gene-edited children had been born. Scientists used a gene-editing technique to edit the genomes of twin embryos to protect them against the HIV virus. The embryos were then implanted into the mother, who subsequently gave birth to twin daughters. One of the concerns with carrying out this research is the risk that gene-editing could cause unintended mutations elsewhere in the genomes of the children.

1 Why might procedures that are regarded as risky and unethical now be common-place in the future?

2 What would the implications be if we could modify children's physical and psychological profiles before birth?

3 How might developments in science lead to changes in ethical values?

Keeping science fair

Scientists are only human, and sometimes they may subconsciously look for results that will support their theories, even while trying to be fair. Sometimes, the choice or design of their research may inadvertently reflect their own biases.

Excluding obvious wrongful practices such as fraud and plagiarism, there is a more insidious issue involving politics and funding. While scientists generally acknowledge their sources of funding, this can be incomplete. For example, in 2006 a radiologist published a paper suggesting that screening smokers with CT chest scans could dramatically reduce the number of lung cancer deaths. However, the paper potentially trivialised the impact of lung cancer, and did not acknowledge that the research had been funded by a tobacco company.

REAL-LIFE SITUATION 13.5

A 2012 study into the effects of eating genetically modified (GM) crops found that there was a significantly higher incidence of cancer in rats fed GM crops compared with the control group. This finding led to an emotional outcry within the scientific community, with pro-GM scientists accusing the research team of having an anti-GM bias. The researchers were accused of using a breed of rats that is highly susceptible to cancer, and using biased data analysis.

1   How might strong personal beliefs lead to a skewing of experimental results?

2   In what ways is emotion necessary for developing new knowledge in science?

TOP TIP

News media are excellent sources of TOK material in all areas of knowledge. Drawing on real-life situations and examples from news stories will help you to avoid using common or stereotyped examples in your TOK presentation.

Figure 13.4: When you look through a microscope, identifying cells and cell components is not always clear cut

Although the **peer review** system helps to provide checks and balances, studies have shown that reviewers tend to be more critical of competitors and women, and less critical of senior scientists. Even computer algorithms can have inadvertent bias programmed into them. For example, a lot of data from pharmaceutical studies contains gender bias because most studies have been conducted on men. It is only recently that scientists have become aware of gender differences in the ways that people respond to some drugs.

KEY TERM

peer review: the evaluation of academic or scientific work by others working in the same field

TASK: ACTIVITY 13.7

Analyse the following knowledge question: In what ways might ethical considerations influence the pursuit of knowledge in the natural sciences?

1   Identify specific real-life examples for different sides of the argument.

2   Consider the implications of claiming that a) scientists should be able to pursue knowledge at any price, b) scientists have a responsibility to pursue knowledge ethically.

3   Come to a conclusion – should ethical considerations constrain science? Who should decide what is acceptable?

CROSS REFERENCE

You can learn more about the peer review system and its issues in Chapter 13 of the Course Guide.

TASK: THINK ABOUT 13.13

To what extent is it possible for science to be value free?

13.6 Knowledge questions

1   Are the natural sciences bodies of knowledge, systems of knowledge or a set of methods for producing knowledge?

2   How do scientists try to prevent errors in their research?

3   To what extent do the natural sciences rely on assumptions that cannot be proven by science?

13.7 Extended writing task

Write 500 words on one or more of the following questions:

1   To what extent is scientific knowledge certain?

2   In what ways do our beliefs and cultural assumptions determine what we accept as knowledge in science and other areas of knowing?

3   To what extent must claims in any area of knowledge be falsifiable if we are to regard them as knowledge?

SKILLS SELF-ASSESSMENT CHECKLIST

Reflect on what you have learned in this chapter and indicate your confidence level between 1 and 5 (where 5 is the highest score and 1 is the lowest). If you score below 3, revisit that section. Come back to this list later in your course. Has your confidence grown?

	Confidence level	Revisited?
Am I able to distinguish science from pseudoscience?		
Am I able to articulate how personal perspectives and cultural perspectives can influence the natural sciences?		
Can I discuss some of the methods and tools used in creating scientific knowledge, and can I compare them with methods and tools used in other areas of knowledge?		
Will my analytical skills help me to critically evaluate scientific knowledge claims?		
Am I aware of some of the ethical issues relating to the natural sciences?		

13.8 Further reading

To find out more about the demarcations between science and pseudoscience, read:

Janet Stemwedel, 'Drawing the line between science and pseudoscience', in *Scientific American*, 4th October 2011

To read more on how perspective affects science, read: Douglas Medin, Carol Lee and Megan Bang, 'Point of View Affects How Science Is Done', in *Scientific American*, 1st October 2014

To find out more about drug testing in less economically developed countries, read: Rebecca Robbins, 'Most Experimental Drugs are Tested Offshore – Raising Concerns about Data', in *Scientific American*, 10th September 2017

> Chapter 14
The human sciences

LEARNING INTENTIONS

In this chapter, you will develop skills to help you evaluate the tools and methods used to produce knowledge within the scope of the human sciences. You will explore some of the different perspectives, as well as some of the ethical issues that arise.

You will:

- investigate knowledge questions arising from the human sciences

- be able to discuss and evaluate different perspectives on the human sciences

- discover and assess the tools and methods used for developing knowledge in the human sciences, and weigh up their reliability

- understand some of the difficulties in developing knowledge within the human sciences

- consider how to use examples or evidence to support an argument about knowledge in the human sciences, and the implications that follow

- develop an awareness of some of the ethical issues that may arise when developing knowledge in the human sciences.

14.1 Introduction

Human science has perhaps the broadest scope of all of the IB's areas of knowledge, and covers a diverse range of subjects. It is the study of the social, cultural and psychological aspects of human beings; at its most fundamental level, it addresses the question of what it is to be human.

14.2 Scope of the human sciences

The human sciences include most of the subjects in 'Individuals and societies', which is Group 3 of the IB Diploma Programme. All subjects that focus on human and the human world, such as psychology, economics, geography and anthropology, are regarded as human sciences. However, for the purposes of TOK, world religions, indigenous societies, politics and history – which would generally be classed as human sciences – are considered as separate areas of knowledge or optional themes.

> **KEY POINT**
>
> The human sciences overlap considerably with all other areas of knowledge in terms of the questions they investigate, the knowledge claims they make and the methods and tools they depend on to develop their knowledge. You can use the knowledge framework to help analyse these connections.

14.3 Perspectives in human sciences

There are as many different perspectives on the human sciences as there are people on the planet. Different opinions on fundamental issues about the human condition will lead to very different perspectives on issues in the human sciences. For example, beliefs about whether **human nature** is naturally good or inherently aggressive, or whether there is no such thing as human nature, will lead to different perspectives on the political and psychological issues. Significantly, the perspectives that human scientists have can potentially influence the types of research they do, how they frame their research questions, their choice of methodologies and the ways in which they analyse and interpret their data.

> **KEY TERM**
>
> **human nature:** characteristics and behaviours that are believed to occur naturally in human beings; the essence of being human

The nature versus nurture debate

The nature versus nurture debate questions whether human behaviour is primarily a product of our genetic make-up, or whether it is more strongly influenced by our up-bringing. While there is no definitive answer, there are a multitude of perspectives on the issue. Advances in understanding gene function continue to offer new scientific perspectives. Wherever you stand in relation to this debate, your ideas on it are likely to influence your perspectives on many different issues within the human sciences, and may also affect the way that you would choose to conduct research and evaluate knowledge in the human sciences. For example, if you believe that human behaviour is largely determined by genetic factors, you might want to run studies that take account of the genetic profiles of the subjects being studied, and you might be dismissive of studies that do not attempt to account for genetic differences. Whereas, if you are of the view that up-bringing is a major factor in determining human behaviour, you might be more interested in considering environmental factors.

Of course, the nature versus nurture debate is not as straightforward as it may sound, and few people would argue fully one way or the other. However, even with a nuanced view which agrees that both nature and nurture affect human behaviour, there are many different perspectives on which aspects of human behaviour are most affected by nature or nurture, and to what degree.

TASK: THINK ABOUT 14.1

1   What type of evidence would you need to decide whether a kind temperament is genetic or the result of nurture?

2   What challenges would you face if you tried to investigate?

3   How could you distinguish between genetic, social, cultural or other factors?

TOK LINK: OTHER AREAS OF KNOWLEDGE AND OPTIONAL THEMES

To what extent might developments in the natural sciences impact on how we understand human nature and behaviour?

14.4 Methods and tools of the human sciences

A significant difference between the human and natural sciences is that experiments in natural sciences are usually repeatable by other scientists in tightly controlled laboratory studies. This is rarely true in the human sciences, where new knowledge often relies on isolated case studies, non-repeatable studies or studies that have far too many variables to control properly.

Scientists and philosophers of science have many different opinions on what constitutes a scientific method, but there is general agreement that for human sciences to be regarded as *sciences*, the methodologies used to study them must meet certain standards in terms of a *systematic* approach.

In practice, the study of individual or group behaviours is often done by conducting studies of large numbers of individuals or groups, and analysing the behaviours statistically to try to determine trends that will allow researchers to make predictions based on probabilities. For example, after analysing the behaviour of different investors in multiple situations, economists might predict a rise in stock prices following growth in the **gross domestic product (GDP)**. This prediction will be based on investor behaviour in similar circumstances in the past. Political analysts make predictions about electoral results based on extensive polling of the population. Many times, their predictions are realised; but sometimes they are not. Increasingly, technology and big data are used to analyse voting trends. Look back to Chapter 5 to see how technology is used to produce knowledge.

TASK: THINK ABOUT 14.2

1   Why must we be cautious about predicting investor behaviour for the current year based on investor behaviour in any other years, even if the financial circumstances seem similar?

2   Why can circumstances only be *similar* and not the *same*? Think about all the changes that happen in the world. How might these affect investor behaviour?

Large-scale observations are not the only way of gathering data for the human sciences. Other methods include case studies, observations of knowing participants, non-participatory observations, surveys, statistical analysis, case studies, controlled experiments and thought experiments. We will examine each of these tools and methods.

Figure 14.1: People watch the super moon behind a War Memorial in Fremantle, Australia. What are the various tools and methods used in the human sciences to observe and understand human behaviour?

Participatory observations

Psychology, business management, anthropology, geography and other disciplines may all, in different circumstances, use studies in which the individuals or groups they are studying *know* they are being studied; these are called **participatory observations**. There are many different types, and they vary in the degree to which the observers interact with those being observed. For example, an anthropologist may spend months or even years living with a remote ethnic group to study their customs and culture, and to try to get an 'inside perspective' on everyday life for that group. In other instances, a psychologist, sociologist or educationalist may run a series of 30-minute focus groups to study people's responses in an interactive environment, or to gain access to the thoughts and opinions of different social and cultural groups.

Clinical drug trials are another type of participatory observation. Often, these are run as *double-blind* trials. This means that neither the people taking the drugs nor the researchers giving the drugs know which people are in the treatment group and which are in the control group. This is to eliminate both the **placebo effect** in patients and any subconscious bias on the part of the researchers in the way that they treat the patients, or the way in which they interpret results.

In some cases, an observer may simply watch and record behaviours. Some people regard these as non-participatory observations because the observer does not directly interact with those being watched. However, the knowledge of being observed is itself an interaction that has noticeable effects on the behaviour of those being observed.

KEY TERM

participatory observation: when the people being observed know they are being observed, and willingly participate; these observations usually involve some kind of interaction between the researcher and those being observed

placebo effect: when patients show an improvement in their condition because they think they have been given an effective form of treatment

REAL-LIFE SITUATION 14.1

A long-term research project by Harvard Business School in 1927–1932 sought to find what physical and psychological factors in the working environment of the Hawthorne plant of the Western Electric Company helped to increase worker productivity. It was discovered that, whatever factors were adjusted (e.g. heating, lighting, working hours) and whether they were increased or decreased, productivity increased. This became known as the Hawthorne effect – productivity increases as a result of the workforce receiving greater attention.

To what extent do you think the Hawthorne effect might account for athletes breaking records during the Olympic Games?

TOK IN YOUR LIFE

Think about how the Hawthorne effect can affect you in your life:

• Do you work harder when you know your teacher is watching you?

• To what extent do members of your family behave differently when you have visitors?

• Do you make more of an effort when you know your work will be assessed?

Figure 14.2: Do you eat differently when you have guests?

TASK: THINK ABOUT 14.3

To what extent can we learn about the behaviour of people by observing them when they know they are being observed?

TASK: ACTIVITY 14.1

Develop a series of three or more points or examples (from your own experience or IB Diploma Programme studies) to support an argument in favour of one of the following:

• We cannot accurately describe or explain the behaviour of humans if they know they are being observed.

• We can accurately describe or explain the behaviour of humans even if they know they are being observed.

Now compare your work with a partner, and ask them to evaluate your points.

Non-participatory observations

If you ever listen in to a conversation when the people who are talking do not realise you are listening, you are being a non-participatory observer. Psychologists often use **non-participatory observations** to study the behaviour of children and animals. This might include them being watched through one-way windows or hidden cameras in a variety of situations.

It is more difficult to make non-participatory studies of adult humans because of ethical considerations. Whereas parents may give consent for their children to be studied, adult humans must usually consent to being studied. By giving their consent, adults become knowing participants. One way that psychologists try to get around this problem is to invite people to volunteer for psychological tests, and then test those who have consented in ways they are not expecting.

Sometimes, non-participatory observations may be made in a *covert* manner. This means that people do not know they are being observed. In most cases, it would be unethical for a researcher to do this, but in some circumstances, it is regarded as acceptable for people, such as undercover police officers or undercover agents. These covert observations are interactive in that the undercover agent must effectively join the group he or she is observing and be accepted as one of them. An example of non-participatory observation is when a police officer pretends to be a drug dealer to infiltrate a drug-smuggling organisation. Only then can observations be made without the group realising it is being observed.

> **KEY TERM**
>
> **non-participatory observation:** when those being observed are unaware that they are being observed

TASK: THINK ABOUT 14.4

In the human sciences, the process of making observations alters the practices being observed. To what extent is this true in other areas of knowledge?

TOP TIP

Be careful not to become confused by terminology when doing research, particularly in the human sciences. Not all people use the same definitions. For example, some people will describe non-interactive observations (such as school inspections) as non-participatory even though the subjects know they are being observed. When comparing types of research, you need to be clear how you are using the different terms, and use them consistently.

Surveys

Surveys are a popular method of research in the human sciences. Surveys obtain responses from a sample of individuals in a population, from which they try to make statistical inferences about the whole population.

There are many different types of survey: some ask open questions which respondents can answer in any way they wish; others ask closed questions which may be answered with one of a few choices (usually two to five options). Surveys can be done over the phone, by mail, in person, online, and so on. Each of these methods has several advantages and disadvantages. There is usually a trade-off between the complexity of the survey, ease of administration, the numbers of completed surveys, costs and the reliability of the results. Many survey methods skew the results simply by their collection method. For example, if a company puts an online survey on its website, the people who respond will be the type of people who enjoy filling in surveys, and who were on the website in the first place. However many responses the company eventually gets, they will be from a particular section of the community.

A good survey is not easy to devise. People's opinions can be swayed by the ways in which questions are asked, and even by the order in which they are asked. Consider the differences in language in the following:

Students should be severely punished for handing in late work	*Yes / No*
There should be consequences for students who hand in late work	*Yes / No*
Students should get off scot-free for handing in late work	*Yes / No*

The way in which a statement is worded might influence the responses received. Which words used in each of the sentences above most influence your choice of answers?

CROSS REFERENCE

You can find out more about how questions can influence surveys in the Course Guide.

REAL-LIFE SITUATION 14.2

A study conducted by Lars Hall, Petter Johansson and Thomas Strandberg at Lund University in Sweden in 2012 asked people to fill in a survey about their moral principles and their thoughts on current moral issues. The people were then asked to defend their positions. However, they were tricked by having two of their written responses reversed. Interestingly, 69% of participants did not notice at least one of the two changes and went on to argue the opposite of the position they originally claimed to hold.

1   Is this survey method ethical? Can someone give informed consent to participate in a survey in which they may be tricked?

2   If survey results are easily skewed and people's opinions are easily swayed, how much credibility can we give to surveys?

3   Can you think of some of the advantages and disadvantages of some of the different survey methods you have encountered?

Statistical analysis

Although statistical analysis is listed as a methodology for the human sciences, it is not an independent method; statistical analysis requires data, and the data are provided by other methods such as those already outlined.

Statistical analysis is very useful, but it is only as good as the data it is applied to. If irrelevant factors are observed or relevant factors are observed badly, if poor questions are asked or good questions are classified poorly, then the conclusions of any analysis will be unreliable.

Also, statistical analyses always require interpretation, and interpretation is always based on assumptions. As we saw in the chapter on mathematics, however accurate the reasoning process, the conclusions we draw are only as good as the assumptions on which our reasoning is based.

TOP TIP

If you use a survey for your extended essay, you might make use of this advice to help create it.

TOK IN YOUR LIFE

When filling out a survey, have you ever found yourself ticking answers that you do not really agree with because there is nothing closer to the answer you want to give? How much can we rely on data generated by such surveys?

Case studies

Case studies involve detailed analysis of single individuals, groups or events, usually over a long period of time. Case studies may look at subjects as diverse as the management structure in a particular organisation, an innovative therapy in a particular care home or the life of an individual person. They rely heavily on observing details in the life of the individual or collective being studied, asking questions then interpreting and analysing responses.

Case studies are prone to particular challenges. In some cases, particularly in long-term studies, the researcher might develop an attachment to the subject. An example is a psychiatrist who writing up the case study of a long-term patient. In other instances, the researcher may have a vested interest in interpreting results and reporting a case in a way that is consistent with their preferred theories. This may not be a deliberate bias; it may be a tendency of the researcher to select, reject or interpret data because they may think in a certain way.

Subjects for case studies are rarely typical. They tend to be selected on the basis that they offer an interesting and unusual perspective on a particular area of research. For example, a researcher into marketing strategies might conduct a case study on a company that has had a remarkably successful marketing campaign in order to try to discover which factors led to the success of that campaign.

TASK: THINK ABOUT 14.5

1   Why might it make more sense for a marketing researcher to study one very successful campaign than to compare several campaigns by different companies, selected randomly?

2   'We see what we know' is a popular truism. How might case studies compound this?

TASK: ACTIVITY 14.2

With a partner, prepare a presentation to your class on one of the following questions. Be sure to use your skills of analysis: identify arguments and counter-arguments, develop specific real-life examples, consider different perspectives, reach a conclusion and consider the implications. Present your ideas and lead a class discussion on the question.

1   Is the fact that knowledge in the human sciences changes over time a strength or a weakness?

CONTINUED

2   To what extent can we eliminate our cultural biases and ideological beliefs when doing research into the human sciences? Should we even try to?

3   What are the dangers when experts studying rare cases have particular, preferred theories? To what extent can we guard against such dangers?

While ethical considerations can limit the kinds of experiment that can be conducted on human beings (for example, we cannot remove or damage parts of human brains to see what effects it causes), case studies can sometimes provide information that cannot ethically be obtained through experiment. For example, we can study people whose brains have been injured through accident or essential surgical procedures. Such case studies have provided neuroscientists, psychologists and philosophers with invaluable insights into the workings of the brain.

REAL-LIFE SITUATION 14.3

In 1953, a man had a large portion of his brain surgically removed in an attempt to cure him of severe epilepsy. The surgery cured his epilepsy but left him unable to create new memories. He was able to remember events that occurred before his surgery, but could not recall anything that happened after. He could only remember new pieces of information for approximately 20 seconds. Despite this, he was able to learn and remember new skills. As a result of studying this man, neuroscientists and psychologists learned a great deal about which parts of the brain are involved in long-term and short-term memories, and how different types of memory are processed and stored in different areas of the brain.

1   How much can we rely on knowledge that is drawn from a sample of one?

2   How might the personal involvement of doctors in cases like this affect the knowledge produced?

TASK: ACTIVITY 14.3

Change blindness is an interesting phenomenon. It means that major changes can happen in a person's visual field without the person recognising that any change has happened. View the psychology experiments on YouTube™ entitled *Experimental psychology – change blindness – selective attention* by Marcus Chalmer (Daily Motion 11 September 2015)

1   Do these experiments follow the scientific method? Try to think of reasons to support why it might *and* might not follow the scientific method.

2   What hypothesis might you develop after this experiment, and how would you go about testing it? What controlled variables could you use?

Controlled experiments

Controlled experiments are largely perceived as being the domain of the natural sciences, but, as we saw in Chapter 13, not all natural science is based on controlled experiments. Similarly, not all controlled experiments are done in the field of natural sciences. Experiments are a widely accepted research method in psychology, sociology, economics and other branches of the human sciences.

The simplest models of human experimentation divide subjects into two groups: a control group and a test group. Subjects in both groups are treated alike, except for the stimulus or condition being tested for. For example, if we were to run an experiment to test whether background noise during examinations can affect students' results, we could take a pool of students studying a subject at the same level and randomly divide them into two groups. Both groups would sit the examination in similar environmental conditions (ie same temperature, light conditions, etc) but the control group would sit in a quiet room and the other group (the test group) would be subjected to the sound of a lawnmower outside their examination room. If the exam results of the students in the noisy room were to be significantly lower that those of the control group, this would support the hypothesis that noise distractions can affect test results. As with such studies in the natural sciences, no controlled experiment can eliminate all variables, and results must be statistically analysed. A significant difference between running human experiments and natural science experiments is the ethical dimension. Human experiments are subject to much more stringent regulations than other types of experiments. These regulations state that human subjects must give informed consent, their privacy must be respected and they must be allowed to withdraw at any time. In addition, the experiment should demonstrably involve greater potential benefits than risks.

REAL-LIFE SITUATION 14.4

Although drug studies are generally considered the domain of the natural sciences, they can also involve the human sciences, particularly economics and politics. Many new drugs are tested on subjects in less economically developed countries (LEDCs); the informed consent they sign is often in a language they do not understand. This raises serious ethical questions about exploitation. Often these subjects bear all the risks of experimentation, yet if the drug eventually comes to market, they cannot afford to use it. Of course, if drugs are not tested, we cannot know if they are safe to use.

1   Why do you think many drug trials are carried out in LEDCs?

2   Would paying people to take part in potentially dangerous experiments make the studies more or less ethical?

3   Should new drugs be tested on healthy volunteers knowing that these might cause harmful side-effects? Or should they be tested on people who are going to die anyway? What effects might a subject's overall health have on the efficacy of the drug being tested?

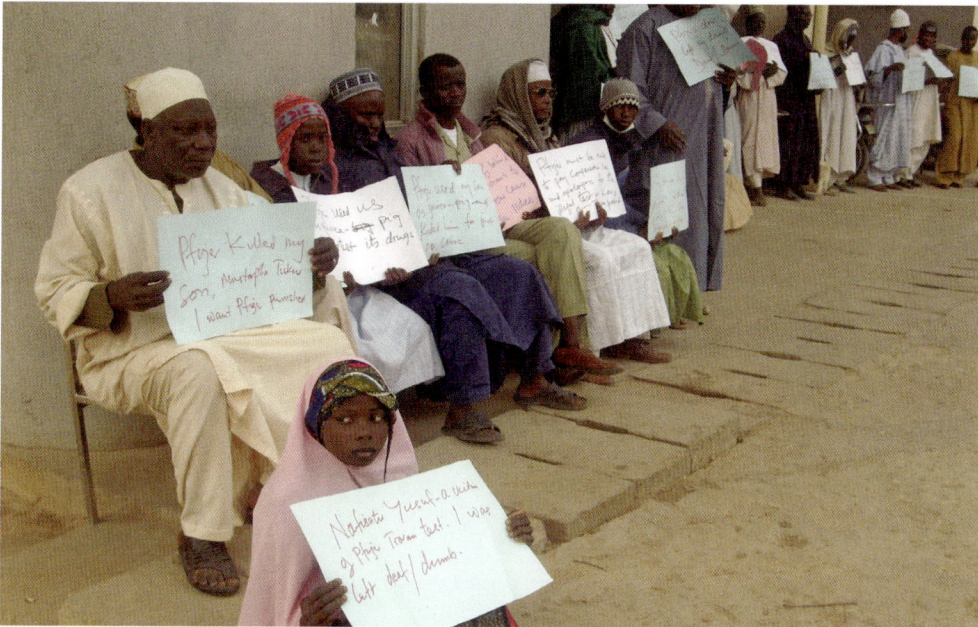

Figure 14.3: In 2010, the US Supreme Court allowed a civil lawsuit against pharmaceutical giant Pfizer for allegedly carrying out non-consensual drug tests in 1996 on Nigerian children in which some children died

Thought experiments

Thought experiments are perhaps most commonly associated with philosophy and physics, but also have a place in law, ethics, psychology, economics, cognitive science, business studies, political science and other fields within the human sciences. As we saw in Chapter 13, a thought experiment uses an imaginary situation to try to understand a real issue. By applying reason to an imaginary situation, the researcher can challenge current theories and further understanding. One famous example from philosophy is the *Ship of Theseus*. The experiment describes a wooden ship that has been preserved for hundreds of years, thanks to regular repairs and maintenance. As old planks rot, they are replaced with new ones, until a time comes when not one part of the ship is an original fitting. Is this still the Ship of Theseus? If it is not, when did it stop being the same ship? Many philosophers have developed the *Ship of Theseus* thought experiment, and there are several modern equivalents exploring the concept of identity.

Figure 14.4: The Ship of Theseus. How much of the original ship can be changed before it ceases to be the same ship?

TASK: THINK ABOUT 14.6

1   What are the advantages and disadvantages of thought experiments compared with practical experiments?

2   To what extent do the methods in the human sciences determine the reliability of the knowledge produced?

REAL-LIFE SITUATION 14.5

Migration is an issue that affects every country in one way or another. Some countries have large numbers of immigrants; others have large numbers of people emigrating. Some countries have large numbers of people moving around within the country. Even countries with relatively stable populations find that tourism and/or agricultural work can create seasonal migrations.

There are several different types of migration, and many different reasons for each of them. All of the methods outlined in this chapter have been employed in some ways to study human migration.

1   What would be the advantages and disadvantages of each of these methodologies if you wanted to learn more about human migratory patterns?

CONTINUED

2 What would be the advantages and disadvantages of each of these methodologies if you wanted to understand the motives behind human migration?

3 If you wanted to explore the issues related to refugees, what methods of investigation might you employ, and why?

4 How might personal assumptions, past experiences and personal preferences affect choices of methodology?

14.5 Ethics and the human sciences

Ethical considerations influence what knowledge is pursued in the human sciences, and how it can be pursued. When conducting research in the human sciences, there can be conflicts of interest between scientific interests in generating new knowledge and the rights and interests of those who are the subjects of the research or who are affected by it in some way. Researchers need to be aware of potential conflicts of interest, and a number of guidelines have been established (such as the **Nuremberg Code** and the **Declaration of Helsinki**) to help safeguard the interest of human subjects.

A major ethical concern for research in the human sciences involves the requirement for **informed consent**. While in some circumstances this may be straightforward, it can be very complex if research is to be conducted on groups of vulnerable people or minority groups. This may become even more of an issue if research is conducted through social media. All human science research must be carefully planned and conducted in a way that respects the integrity of those who participate, and does not cause inadvertent harm or distress to anyone.

KEY TERMS

Nuremberg Code: a set of principles developed in response to atrocious human experiments during the Second World War (1939–1945). It provides guidelines to help protect human experimental subjects from injury, disability or death

Declaration of Helsinki: a statement of ethical principles for medical research involving human subjects developed by the World Medical Association

informed consent: permission granted by participants in full knowledge of what is involved and how data collected will be used

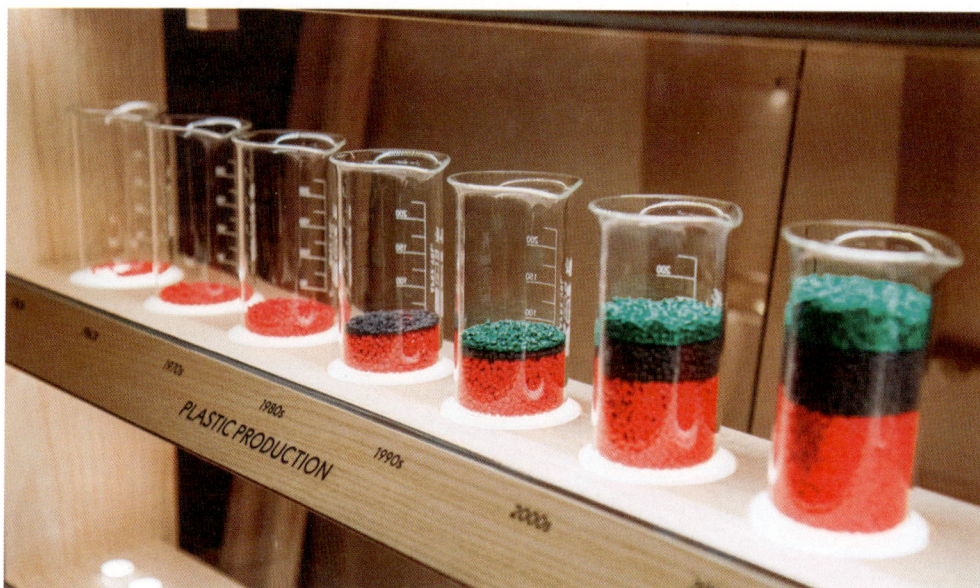

Figure 14.5: *For the Greatest Benefit to Humankind*: an exhibition in Sweden in 2019 to celebrate Nobel-Prize winning achievements

TASK: THINK ABOUT 14.7

1   How might the study of human nature and behaviour help us to solve local, national and global problems?

2   Should there be limits on the studies that can be done in the pursuit of knowledge in the human sciences, even though the studies might benefit all humankind?

KEY POINT

Remember that what can be done today in the human sciences is influenced and sometimes limited by ethical considerations.

TOK LINK: OTHER AREAS OF KNOWLEDGE

Researchers in the human sciences use a number of key concepts including: correlation, interpretation, evidence, bias, statistical significance and reliability. How do these key concepts compare with those used in other areas of knowledge?

14.6 Knowledge questions

1   To what extent is our knowledge in the human sciences shaped by the methodologies we choose?

2   To what extent should ethical considerations influence the pursuit of knowledge in the human sciences?

3   To what extent can any consent be *fully* informed?

14.7 Extended writing task

To further develop the quality of your writing, write 500 words on one or both of the following questions:

1   To what extent are the 'human sciences' really *science*?

2   To what extent can we make observations without affecting what we observe?

SKILLS SELF-ASSESSMENT CHECKLIST

Reflect on what you have learned in this chapter and indicate your confidence level between 1 and 5 (where 5 is the highest score and 1 is the lowest). If you score below 3, revisit that section. Come back to this list later in your course. Has your confidence grown?

	Confidence level	Revisited?
Am I able to support an argument about knowledge in the human sciences using examples, evidence or reasons?		
Am I able to identify different perspectives in the human sciences?		
Can I identify and evaluate the methods and tools used to produce knowledge in the human sciences?		
Am I aware of some of the difficulties in developing knowledge in the human sciences?		
Can I offer examples or evidence from my own IB Diploma Programme experience to illustrate a TOK point?		
Am I able to evaluate how ethical considerations might influence the methods used and the knowledge we pursue in the human sciences?		

14.8 Further reading

To understand how humans have adapted to environments around the globe, watch David Attenborough, *Human Planet*, BBC DVD, 1996

For human sciences used to explore the concept of self, and identity, read: Julin Baggini, *The Ego Trick*, Granta, 2011

For an exploration of the nature of human nature, read Steven Pinker, *The Blank Slate*, Penguin, 2002

For discussion of human behaviour and the nature-nurture debate, read: Matt Ridley, *Nature via nurture*, Fourth Estate, 2004

For an examination of human nature and why we behave the way do, read Dexter Dias, *The Ten Types of Human: A New Understanding of Who We Are, and Who We Can Be*, Cornerstone 2017

Assessment

The TOK exhibition

15.1 Introduction

The Internal Assessment (IA) for TOK is the exhibition, in which you show how TOK issues are **manifest** in the world around you. Planning and **curating** your TOK exhibition offers an exciting opportunity to explore links between TOK concepts in your daily life.

The exhibition is assessed and it is expected that you will exhibit the work you have curated and produced for an audience, it is expected that you will exhibit the work you have curated and produced for an audience. Your school will arrange an opportunity for you to display your work, along with that of the other TOK students in your school. The exhibition could be open to other year groups, to parents or even to a wider audience on an occasion such as an open day.

KEY TERMS

manifest: clear or obvious

curate: select, organise, and present

15.2 Understanding the assessment requirements

You are required to create your own exhibition, and are expected to complete this during the first year of your IB Diploma Programme course. You cannot produce this work in pairs or groups.

You must base your exhibition around one of the IA prompts published by the IB Diploma Programme, and select three objects that relate to it. Your exhibition must include your three objects – or images of these objects – with a written commentary on each one.

You will also need to submit an electronic file that includes:

- a title that clearly identifies your chosen IA prompt

- an image of each of your three chosen objects

- three written commentaries of no more than 950 words in total (about 310 on each). Each commentary must identify the real-world context of the object it refers to, and your justification for how the object links to the knowledge prompt

- references to cite the sources of your objects, and any sources you may have used for your commentaries.

You are then expected to showcase or exhibit your work. However, the exhibition itself is not assessed. Instead, your exhibition file will be marked by your TOK teacher, and moderated by the IB. Your work will be marked out of 10, and is worth 35% of your total mark for TOK.

KEY POINT

Your exhibition should show your three objects or their images, along with their accompanying commentaries, and any references. You can use actual objects for the exhibition, but you need to supply digital photographs of your objects for your exhibition file.

Assessment criteria

Holistic marking – also known as global impression marking – is based on the overall quality of your exhibition work. Your work will be awarded one of six levels of achievement, depending on its quality, with 'Excellent' being the highest level (worth 9–10 marks) and 0 being the lowest. The IB Diploma Programme publish descriptions for each level. Examiners will be looking to see how successfully you have shown that TOK issues are evident in the world around you.

To this end, they will ask themselves if you have:

- understood the knowledge prompt

- chosen three objects that are clearly relevant to the knowledge prompt

- identified and articulated the real-world context of your three objects

- written a clear justification, explaining how each of your three selected objects relate to your chosen IA prompt

- written well-explained, relevant points that are supported by evidence

- communicated how TOK connects with the world around us.

15.3 What should be the focus of my exhibition?

The expectation is that your exhibition will focus on either the core theme or one of the five optional themes. Try to choose a theme that particularly interests or appeals to you, because that will make it both easier and more engaging. If, for example, you belong to an indigenous community, you may find yourself appreciating your culture even more after exploring knowledge and indigenous societies through the lens of one of the IA prompts. If you live in a richly multicultural society, you may have an avid interest in the different religious perspectives and traditions around you, and choose to explore knowledge and religion. Perhaps your society is in the grip of a political dilemma that you would like to gain a better understanding of by focusing on knowledge and politics. Or you may have a keen interest in technology that you would like to develop even further by opting for the knowledge and technology theme. You may be a linguist, and want to explore the fascinating relationship between knowledge and language.

If you choose to focus on the core theme: *Knowledge and the knower*, you will have the opportunity to reflect on yourself as a knower and thinker, and consider the ways in which the communities that you belong to influence what you know. One of the exciting things about the exhibition is that virtually any interest you might have could be considered through one of these themes.

> **TOP TIP**
>
> Your teacher will have access via 'My IB' to a resource entitled, 'Theory of Knowledge student assessed work' for first assessment 2022. This contains 10 samples of exhibition work with examiner comments. It would be very useful to read the examiner comments about various exhibitions so you can better understand what makes an excellent TOK exhibition.

> **KEY POINT**
>
> The expectation is that your exhibition will focus on one particular theme. You might want to revisit these chapters when deciding on the focus of your exhibition. Chapters 1–4 outline the core theme: *Knowledge and the knower*, which invites you to think critically about your own perspective and the impact of the communities that you belong to. Chapters 5–10 outline the optional themes. Make sure that you play to your strengths and select the theme that interests you most.

15.4 Choosing your IA knowledge prompt

Once you have chosen the thematic focus of your exhibition, your next step is to select a knowledge prompt. Each IA prompt offers you an opportunity to explore the nature of knowledge and knowing.

Analysing and unpacking knowledge prompts

There are 35 different IA prompts, and they are all written in the form of knowledge questions that can be applied to any of the themes. Your teacher will make these available to you, and they will be the same set of questions for the duration of this TOK specification. You should choose your prompt according to your particular interests. Whether you want to explore what counts as knowledge, how knowledge is created, how knowledge is shaped and influenced or perhaps investigate the relationship between ethics and knowledge, there will be IA prompts that suit.

> **KEY POINT**
>
> The knowledge framework is a tool that will help you to explore any knowledge prompt. Think of how you can sharpen your analysis of a knowledge prompt using elements of the framework: scope, perspectives, methods and tools, ethics.

Studying the knowledge prompt: language and key concept

Each knowledge prompt is a question that contains various features: a command word and a TOK concept. It is worth identifying and exploring what these are. The following examples are *not* official IA prompt, and so you cannot choose them for your IA. However, they will help you to practise unpacking the IB's official IA prompts:

1   How do we know if *evidence* is needed for knowledge?

2   How do our *values* influence the knowledge we pursue?

3   What counts as *certain* knowledge?

4   Can we be sure if an *explanation* is justified?

5   Is *bias* a barrier to knowledge and knowing?

The words in italics identify the TOK concept. You might then think about how this concept relates to the theme you have chosen. For example, the concept of evidence might relate closely and in obvious ways to the themes of knowledge and politics, knowledge and indigenous societies, or knowledge and religion. However, you might also think of unusual and original pairings, such as knowledge and technology and bias.

TASK: ACTIVITY 15.1

Reflect on the theme you have chosen, and consider the concept that you would most like to explore within that theme. With that in mind, go through the 35 IA prompts to decide which one best fits your strengths and interests. Once you have settled on your IA prompt, you are ready to select your three specific objects.

KEY POINT

Consider the IB's IA exhibition knowledge prompts. It is important to pick the one that interests you most, and which you can respond to best.

15.5 Selecting and justifying your choice of objects

When you select your objects, it is important that you choose objects with specific real-life contexts. Objects can range from physical objects – such as water bottles distributed by your school as part of an environmental initiative – to a digital object such as a specific Tweet. If you want to use a photograph of, perhaps, a bird, think carefully about the photograph that you choose: why that particular photograph? Why that particular bird? A specific photograph that you have taken, or even someone you know has taken, will provide you with a real-life example that you can discuss with authenticity, unlike a generic photograph taken from the internet. The expectations of your commentaries include that they identify the real-life context of the objects you have selected, and explain clearly how your objects are linked to your chosen IA prompt and are connected through your chosen theme.

Figure 15.1: A photograph I took of a male blackbird that lives in my garden. It raises a question about the certainty of the knowledge that adult male blackbirds are all black except for their yellow beaks and eye-rings

Justifying your choices

Each object you include in your exhibition needs to be justified. This means that you are able to explain how each object links to your chosen IA prompt, and how it contributes to your exhibition and analysis of the IA prompt.

Justification requires giving some support for your ideas, such as reasons or evidence. There is no one correct way to justify the objects that you decide to include in your exhibition. The justifications will depend on what the object is, the context in which it is situated, your relationship with the object and the prompt that you are responding to.

TASK: ACTIVITY 15.2

Read the following justification written about a photograph of a marae in response to the indigenous societies theme, and the imagined IA prompt: *How does culture shape knowledge?*

Answer the questions below.

As someone who identifies as Maori, this *marae* is the very heart of my *whanau*, which is my extended family community. A *marae* is far more than a meeting house, which is the way the word is usually translated; it is our spiritual home, the home of our *whakapapa* (our ancestors). In our *marae*, I learn the stories of my people. Belonging to this *marae* helps me to know my ancestors, my *whanau* and ultimately, who I am. It shapes the way I view the people and the environment around me.

CONTINUED

1   Does the response clearly identify the object and its context?

2   Is there a clear link between the object and the IA prompt?

3   Is the choice of object justified?

4   What else should this commentary include to provide a clear analysis of the knowledge prompt?

Objects and their real-world context

It is a good idea to use objects that are relevant to you in the context of your IB Diploma Programme studies or in your life experience, so that you can demonstrate your ability to apply your TOK skills in your daily life. The exhibition is intended to give you the chance to explore the links between TOK and the world around you.

The objects need to be specific and not general. For example, your own particular bottle that you have had since your school's environmental campaign is more appropriate than any water bottle. Likewise, a specific article that you read in a higher-level geography class, published with a date and predicting the impact of climate change on a particular indigenous society is more suitable than any unspecified *article on climate change*.

For an exhibition on technology, objects might include the equipment or practical tools that you use in your IB Diploma Programme Group 4 science class to perform experiments. In an exhibition on language, you could select an object such as a specific book you have read as part of your IB Diploma Programme studies.

For an exhibition on politics, an object might include a photograph of a painting that uses propaganda. For example, it might be appropriate to select an object or work of art with a specific context that you may have studied in higher-level history, such as a painting of Napoleon by Jacques-Louis David (1748–1825) which is positive propaganda representing his power, or a negative representation of Napoleon depicting his weakness by Paul Delaroche (1797–1856). Both images could be used to link to the concept of propaganda.

KEY POINT

When selecting objects, avoid general objects, and instead choose specific objects that have a real-life context in the world around you.

TASK: ACTIVITY 15.3

Choose either the core theme or one of the optional themes.

1   Develop your skill to identify and select objects that belong to the theme. Make a list of different examples of objects that relate the theme to some of the following:

• people or places, either past or present

CONTINUED

- something of local, national or international interest

- a recent event in the news

- something invented or discovered

- a method or process for acquiring knowledge

- past knowledge or something that develops through time

- a different cultural perspective

- values, ethics and responsibilities.

2   Practise the skill of linking TOK themes to TOK concepts. Choose five concepts from the following list, and consider how they might relate to each of the themes. Do some themes fit more comfortably with particular concepts than others?

3   Practise the skill of linking TOK concepts to objects. Choose one or two concepts from the following list that would fit with your theme, and then try to link those concepts with some of the objects you identified above. Again, the official IA prompts are not limited to these concepts.

ambiguity

applications and usefulness

acquisition of knowledge

beliefs

bias

certainty and uncertainty

classification or label

communication

communities

constraints

context

culture

current knowledge

doubt

ethics

evidence

experts

CONTINUED

explanation

historical development

ignorance

imagination

interaction

interpretation

justification

knowledge

unknowable knowledge

objectivity

opinion

ownership

past knowledge

personal experience

perspective

power

production of knowledge

reliability

responsibility

material tools

truth

values

15.6 Writing commentaries

A significant aspect of the exhibition is the **commentary** you must write for each of your objects. The total word count for your exhibition file cannot be more than 950 words, (not including acknowledgements or references). This means that you should aim for just 300 words for each of your commentaries.

At first glance, the commentaries might seem an easy task because there are not many words to write. However, the commentaries are in many ways more difficult to write than a longer writing task because you need to make sure that every word counts. A 310-word limit for each commentary needs to be a summary, which does not give

KEY TERMS

commentary: generally, an expression of opinions or offering of explanations about an event or situation; in this case an explanation of each object you are exhibiting and its contribution to your analysis of the knowledge prompt

TOK exhibition commentary: a summary of the real-world context and justification for your choice of object, in around 300 words

you any room for waffle or wasted words if you are to do justice to the IB Diploma Programme requirements that you:

- clearly identify each object and its real-world context
- clearly explain links between the three objects
- clearly explain links between each object and the IA prompt
- justify the inclusion of each object by making clear and explicit references to the IA prompt, and supporting your points with evidence.

TASK: ACTIVITY 15.4

Below you will find six scenarios featuring different core or optional themes and different knowledge prompts. In all cases, the knowledge prompts are not official IB Diploma Programme IA prompts; rather, they are similar prompts that allow you to practise your skills.

Choose one of the scenarios to complete the following tasks:

1 Think about how you might outline and describe the specific real-world context of each object.

2 Think about how you might link the three objects to each other.

3 What reasons might you give to justify how each object connects with the knowledge prompt?

4 Respond to the individual 'think about' tasks. These invite you to discuss how you might explain the specific context of each object, and the reasons you might give to justify how it connects with the knowledge prompt.

Core theme 1: Knowledge and the knower

Imagine that you choose the core theme for your exhibition theme, and select the following (imagined) knowledge prompt: *What impact might a community have on what you know?*

1 You might first select an object that belongs to the local church you belong to – a silver chalice inscribed with the date 1660, which is used to share wine every week in the context of the worshipping community remembering the last supper of Jesus. This will be used to make a link to the religious community you belong to, which links you to a world-wide community following different Christian traditions.

2 Your second object might be an article found on a website that makes predictions about the political climate of the country you live in. This will be used to make a link to the national community you belong to.

3 Your third object might be a photo of you helping elderly members of your community at a weekly meeting, offering tea and light-entertainment as part of your CAS project. This will be used to make a link to the local community that you belong to.

How could each object be used to make different analytical points about the relationship between your knowledge and the communities you belong to?

Core theme 2: Knowledge and technology

Imagine that you choose technology for your exhibition theme. You are responding to the following (imagined) knowledge prompt: *Does the fact that knowledge changes over time undermine the confidence that we place in our present knowledge?*

1   You might select Ian McEwan's novel *Machines Like Us* (2019) which explores various ethical dilemmas and the capacity of a machine to understand the human heart.

2   You might then choose a specific news article on 'Transhumanism', about the people who choose to 'upgrade' their range of perception by implanting chips into their bodies.

3   Your third object could be your Fitbit™, which monitors your pulse and the number of steps that you take each day.

TASK: THINK ABOUT 15.2

How might these objects be used to make analytical points about changes in knowledge over time and the factors that influence our evaluation of our own present knowledge?

Core theme 3: Knowledge and language

Imagine that you choose language for your exhibition theme. You are responding to the following (imagined) knowledge prompt: *Can we gain reliable knowledge?*

1   You might first select a Tweet by the President of the United States that expresses an opinion about climate change, which came into your Twitter feed.

2   You might also choose a novel on the theme of climate change that you have studied in your Higher-Level English, for example *The Wall* by John Lanchester (2019).

3   Your third object might be the speech given by the activist Greta Thunberg (2003–) to the United Nations in 2019 that you watched on the news.

TASK: THINK ABOUT 15.3

How could each object be used to make different analytical points about the relationship between language and reliable knowledge?

Core theme 4: Knowledge and politics

Imagine that you choose politics for your exhibition theme. You are responding to the following (imagined) knowledge prompt: *Is all knowledge inevitably biased?*

1   You might choose a TV guide showing a televised debate scheduled.

2   You could also choose a political flyer posted through your letter box in support of a candidate in an election.

3   You might also choose a more modern example of computational propaganda, by Bill Posters and his creation of deepfake art which you read about on social media.

> **TASK: THINK ABOUT 15.4**
>
> How might you explain how the specific context of each object connects with the concept of propaganda, and how they could be used to make analytical points about how they have contributed to political knowledge?

Core theme 5: Knowledge and religion

Imagine that you choose knowledge and religion for your exhibition theme. You are responding to the following (imagined) knowledge prompt: *Do our values affect the knowledge that we seek?*

1   You might first select a Tweet by the Pope – the leader of the Roman Catholic faith – on the theme of peace that you read on Twitter.

2   You might also choose a news article based on an interview with the Aga Khan, the spiritual leader of Ismaili Muslims, which was in your local newspaper.

3   Perhaps you could also select your Extended Essay, which investigates attitudes to war and peace in the Hindu scripture *The Bhagavad-Gita.*

> **TASK: THINK ABOUT 15.5**
>
> How might these objects be used to make analytical points about how our values affect the knowledge that we seek?

Core theme 6: Knowledge and indigenous societies

Imagine that you choose knowledge and indigenous societies for your exhibition theme. You respond to the following (imagined) knowledge prompt: *How does culture shape knowledge?*

1   You might first select a photograph of scarification as a means of showing indigenous identity for the Great Andamanese people, which you found when studying indigenous societies in your TOK class.

2   You might also choose the *marae* that you belong to in New Zealand.

3   Perhaps you also select a photograph of one of your *whanau* (extended family) wearing *Ta Moko*, a Maori facial tattoo.

How might these objects be used to make analytical points about how our culture can influence how we perceive the world and shape our knowledge?

Citations and references

As with all of your academic work, it is important that you acknowledge any sources that you use when preparing your exhibition. This includes, but is not limited to, sources you may have cited or paraphrased. If you are using a photo that someone else has taken, or if you have borrowed an object, you should again acknowledge your sources. References and acknowledgements are not counted in your 950-word limit, but they should be displayed along with your objects and exhibition commentaries, and included in your exhibition file.

It is required that you offer specific details about the sources of your objects and images. An appropriate reference would include details that would enable you to find out more about the original source of the object. Clearly not all objects can be cited in the same way. If your selected object is either a piece of art you have produced or your own Extended Essay, a sentence to confirm that it is your work produced at a particular time and in a particular place would be sufficient. Here are two examples for an exhibition on politics.

Object: A book I studied on political philosophy when we studied human rights: Thomas Hobbes' *Leviathan*.

Citation: Thomas Hobbes originally published *Leviathan* in 1651. In my Higher-Level Philosophy class, we have read extracts from Noel Malcolm's edition published by Oxford University Press in 2014.

Object: My 4000-word scholarly Extended Essay which investigates the question: *'What did Thomas Hobbes mean by 'Laws of Nature'?'*

Citation: This Extended Essay is my own original work, supervised by my teacher, which I drafted in the summer of 2020 at my school in Singapore.

Authenticity and guidance

As with every piece of IB Diploma Programme coursework, the work for your exhibition must be authentically yours. Your teacher will use up to 8 hours of lesson time, in which you are expected to become familiar with the requirements, and begin planning your exhibition. However, your teacher can only give feedback on one draft of your work. Your teacher will also be checking for the authenticity of your work by monitoring the progress of your exhibition through all the stages, from planning to writing about and then exhibiting your work. The exhibition is an individual task, and while you may end up choosing the same knowledge prompt as another member of your class, you cannot choose the same objects. You must produce an exhibition that is unique to you, and is entirely the product of your own efforts.

15.7 Summary

For quick reference, this is a summary of the main points addressed in this chapter:

- Your TOK exhibition is an opportunity to explore the connection between a TOK IA prompt and the world around you.

- The focus of your exhibition can be on either the core theme, or any of the optional themes: technology, language, politics, religion or indigenous societies.

- You are required to select one from a list of IA exhibition knowledge prompts as the basis for your exhibition.

- A knowledge prompt is a question about knowledge and knowing, which includes a TOK concept such as certainty, bias, or evidence. All knowledge prompts are provided by the IB. You cannot make up your own.

- Your task is to select and justify three objects that relate to your knowledge prompt.

- You need to identify the specific real-world context of your object, and give a clear justification for how the object links to the knowledge prompt.

- You submit a file of your work which includes the following: your chosen IA prompt, images of your three objects, a written commentary about each object and appropriate referencing and citations.

- Your teacher marks your work, and the IB Diploma Programme moderates it.

- Your exhibition is then displayed and shared with others in your class or school.

The TOK exhibition is:

- an opportunity to highlight a TOK issue in the world around you, and demonstrate your analytical skills

- focused on either the core theme or one of the five optional themes

- an analysis of the connections and links between your three objects and a knowledge prompt.

Assessment

Who assesses the exhibition?	Internally assessed by your TOK teacher, and externally moderated by an IB Diploma Programme examiner using e-marking
What is the word limit?	950 words for the three commentaries
How is the essay marked?	Holistic/global impression marking
How much it is worth?	35% of the total marks for TOK
What is the maximum score?	10 marks
How many IA knowledge prompts are there to choose from?	35
How is the exhibition file submitted?	It is uploaded electronically.

SKILLS SELF-ASSESSMENT CHECKLIST

Reflect on what you have learned in this chapter and indicate your confidence level between 1 and 5 (where 5 is the highest score and 1 is the lowest). If you score below 3, revisit that section. Come back to this list later in your course. Has your confidence grown?

	Confidence level	Revisited?
Am I familiar with the requirements for a TOK exhibition?		
Can I link a TOK IA prompt and an object from the world around me?		
Can I identify and articulate the real-world context of an object?		
Do I have the skills to link objects to TOK concepts?		
Can I select appropriate objects and justify my choices?		
Am I able to articulate the ways that TOK manifests itself in the world around me?		
Do I have the writing skills needed to produce a TOK exhibition commentary?		

Chapter 16

The TOK essay

LEARNING INTENTIONS

In this chapter, you will cover what is required in a TOK essay. The chapter will help you to understand the assessment criteria, and to develop an awareness of the key features and characteristics of an excellent TOK essay.

You will:

- appreciate what is required in a TOK essay, and how it will be assessed
- develop your essay planning skills
- hone your writing skills, including your construction of an argument to support a thesis
- develop your analytical skills
- learn how to write an introduction and conclusion
- learn how to avoid plagiarism.

16.1 Introduction

A TOK essay is *an investigation or enquiry* into a knowledge question, rather than a research essay. There is no prescribed content, however, your essay needs to answer a prescribed title, and demonstrate your critical thinking. This chapter offers advice which may be helpful, but there is no ready formula for a successful essay.

16.2 Understanding the assessment requirements

In each examination session, the International Baccalaureate (IB) publishes six prescribed titles (PTs) for the TOK essay. You must choose one from the list, and answer it in no more than 1,600 words. If you are taking your IB Diploma Programme examinations in May, the titles are published in the previous September. For the November session, the titles are available from March.

The essay is submitted electronically. It is externally assessed by IB Diploma Programme examiners using holistic/global impression marking, and is worth 65% of your final TOK score.

Assessment criteria

Holistic marking, also known as global impression marking, is based on the overall quality of your essay. Your essay will be awarded one of six levels of achievement, depending on its quality – with 'Excellent' being the highest level (worth 9–10 marks) and 0 being the lowest. The IB Diploma Programme publish descriptions for each level.

Examiners will be looking to see if you have clearly written a coherent and critical examination of your chosen prescribed title. To this end, they will ask themselves if you have:

- understood the essay title
- developed a thorough and well-argued response to the knowledge question
- presented clear arguments are supported by specific examples
- carefully evaluated a number of counter-arguments
- considered the implications of your arguments
- raised other perspectives
- reached a clear and convincing conclusion.

TASK: ACTIVITY 16.1

Think of your essay title in relation to other aspects of TOK thinking. Make notes on:

- the connections between the prescribed essay title and parts of the knowledge framework

- connections and links with areas of knowledge

- any specific real-life examples that might support your analysis of the question.

16.3 Exploring your knowledge question

The examiner will make an overall judgement about your essay based on your ability to present a critical, well-argued exploration of your chosen essay title. Because your chosen prescribed title is the question you must answer, you must not deviate from it in any way.

TOP TIP

Some characteristics and features that may be found in a TOK essay include:

- exploration of the essay title

- analysis and evaluation rather than description

- assumptions identified

- clear and coherent arguments supported by specific, real-life examples

- counter-claims evaluated and implications considered

- links and comparisons within and between areas of knowledge

- analytical connections made with scope, perspectives, methods and tools, or ethics

- awareness, investigation and evaluation of alternative perspectives or viewpoints.

TOP TIP

Your teacher will have access via 'My IB' to a resource entitled, 'Theory of Knowledge student assessed work' for first assessment 2022. This contains 10 sample essays with examiner comments. It would be very useful to read the examiner comments about various essays so you can better understand what makes an excellent TOK essay.

There is no rigid list of features necessary to achieve a high mark. Examiners will judge your overall performance using holistic or global impression marking. It is worth looking carefully at the IB Diploma Programme descriptions of the six levels of performance, so that you understand them.

Depth and breadth

The balance between breadth and depth varies between essay titles, but whichever essay title you choose, your writing needs to demonstrate *both* depth and breadth of thought.

Depth of understanding refers to detailed knowledge within an area of knowledge. For example, a deep understanding of history might involve making a distinction between historical facts and historical interpretations. In the natural sciences, you might compare the scientific method in biology and physics.

Breadth of understanding includes making connections, links and comparisons with other areas of knowledge. By comparing similarities and differences in different areas of knowledge, you can explore concepts in different contexts. For example, facts in history might include dates that can be checked against the evidence, whereas facts in the arts might include a work's genre or its historical context.

TOP TIP

Making *distinctions* within an area of knowledge or between areas of knowledge is one way of showing your depth of understanding.

TASK: ACTIVITY 16.2

Consider the following list of concepts. Think of ways in which you might make distinctions between some of these pairs in an area of knowledge.

- certainty and ambiguity
- fact and interpretation
- nature and culture
- authority and power
- values and responsibilities.

16.4 Analysing knowledge questions

Analysis is essential to a good essay. Your TOK essay will need to demonstrate strong analysis of your prescribed title, and evidence of incisive critical thinking. Your essay will need to make relevant connections and comparisons with different areas of knowledge, and show that you are aware of your own perspectives, as well as the perspectives of others.

Analysis over description

If you were to write a descriptive essay, you might give an account of a topic; but to write an analytical essay, you need to show critical thought. Good analysis involves weighing up evidence behind the different positions, and assessing the relative merits of each to reach a balanced judgement. A good analytical essay, unlike a descriptive essay, will demonstrate your **higher-order thinking skills**.

This does not mean that you should not have any descriptive elements. You may need to describe subject-specific examples (for example science experiments, or books you have studied), but it is important that you relate them back to the TOK question or concepts you are exploring. In this way, your essay connects knowledge questions and TOK thinking to the ordinary world.

KEY TERMS

higher-order thinking skills: critical thinking skills including analysis, evaluation, and synthesis

KEY POINT

Careful analysis of knowledge questions will achieve strong marks under the holistic marking scheme. Essays that are too descriptive often gain poor marks.

Unpacking knowledge questions

When you choose your title, think carefully about the wording of the question, and make sure that you understand what the title means. Decoding the **command words** and **key concepts** in the title will give you a strong clue. Consider the following essay title: *'To what extent is truth different in two areas of knowledge?'*. Here, the key TOK concept is 'truth' and the command words are 'to what extent'.

This title requires you to form a judgement about the relative extent to which the concept of truth is different in two areas of knowledge. Other command words might include *evaluate, consider, discuss* or *examine*. Take time to understand the meaning of the words in the context of the essay question. The command words need to be understood in relation to the particular question.

Definitions of some command words

Evaluate	weigh up and form a judgement
Consider	think critically about, give critical thought to
How important	form a judgement about relative importance (very important / not that important)
On what grounds	consider what the criteria would be or reasons
To what extent	evaluate and form a judgement about the relative extent (to a large extent / to a limited extent) supported by sound arguments
Discuss	look at different perspectives and come up with your own answer
Examine	look at and consider critically

When you choose your essay title, play to your strengths. If you are inspired to write it, you are likely to write an engaging essay. Whichever title you choose, you need to be able to interpret the title in an open-minded way, and you will need to consider it from different perspectives.

The emphasis of titles can vary. Look carefully at the language used in the title, and make sure you understand the important terms. Some focus explicitly on one area of knowledge, for example science or history. Other titles might focus on an aspect of the knowledge framework, such as scope.

KEY TERMS

command word: instruction that tells you what to do in the essay; for example, *'to what extent'* or *'on what grounds'*

key concept: some essays have a central concept to explore, such 'explanation' or 'certainty'

Introducing analysis

When unpacking your knowledge question, give thought to the areas of knowledge that you might choose to refer to. The knowledge framework is a very useful tool for helping you to decide because it gives you reference points with which to compare different areas of knowledge.

TASK: ACTIVITY 16.3

For both essay titles below:

1 Identify the command words and key concepts.

2 Try to explain in your own words what the essay title is asking you to do.

3 Think about which areas of knowledge you might compare.

- *How far is it possible to gain certainty in two areas of knowledge?*

- *To what extent is it possible to avoid bias in the pursuit of knowledge?*

16.5 Planning and writing your essay

Before you begin writing, it is important to plan your essay. You will need to develop a **thesis** and a strong, coherent line of argument, which involves selecting appropriate examples and using them effectively. It also means writing a clear introduction and a compelling conclusion.

TASK: THINK ABOUT 16.1

1 How might you structure a coherent argument or sequence of ideas in support of a thesis?

2 How could you develop your planning, writing and editing skills to produce a strong essay?

3 How can you communicate your ideas clearly?

Developing a thesis

Your essay must respond to the knowledge question, and your thesis statement should sum up your answer with clarity and precision. Depending on how you decide to structure your essay, it is possible to place your thesis in your introduction or conclusion.

Consider the knowledge question: *'To what extent is it important to justify what we know on the basis of evidence in two areas of knowledge?'*.

Because it is a 'to what extent' question, you are being invited to answer with something along a continuum that extends from, *'It is not at all important'* to *'It is extremely important'*. Given that it is explicitly stated, you should consider two areas of knowledge in your response to shed light on the connections and contrasts between them.

Once you have decided which areas of knowledge you would like to explore in your essay, you may want to decide on your thesis. For example, you may wish to respond using history and the natural sciences, and argue that it is very important to justify what we know on the basis of evidence.

In some cases, however, you may want to delay deciding on your thesis until you have explored the question more thoroughly. For example, you might want to consider the question in mathematics and the arts, and only after looking at different claims and counterclaims might you reach a thesis, which might be to respond that justification on the basis of evidence is very important in some instances but less so in others.

Focus your time and attention on developing the quality of your arguments, and your thesis will follow naturally from your thought process. What you decide to argue is much less important than how you construct your arguments. Your thesis may change over time as a result of thinking the knowledge question through.

TASK: ACTIVITY 16.4

Choose an essay title from the list of six titles prescribed for your own examination session. Write a draft thesis statement for the title by summing up your answer in one or two sentences.

Constructing an argument

Your TOK essay can be thought of as an extended argument that answers the prescribed title in a way that leads to a clear and compelling conclusion. In order to get from the title to the conclusion, your essay needs to show a clear line of points and count which you must evaluate.

TOK LINK: LANGUAGE

Points and counterpoints are often referred to as arguments and counter-arguments, because each point is a minor argument that supports or counters your main argument.

Presenting a strong argument will demonstrate that you can organise your ideas in an original, coherent and creative way.

TASK: ACTIVITY 16.5

Choose an essay title and a thesis that you wish to argue. Write some points and counterpoints on different cards, and experiment with changing the order so that the argument flows coherently. You may want to take some cards out and add some new cards so that each stage of your argument follows logically.

Share your ideas with a partner, and give each other feedback on how well the argument flows.

Structuring your essay

A plan is a series of rough ideas to organise your thoughts so that you know what you are going to write before you start. It is a good idea to focus your plan on the structure of your argument, the supporting evidence and the different perspectives you will consider. Begin with your sequence of points and counterpoints, and develop a paragraph plan. As a rough guide, you will need about 12 paragraphs. A few either side is fine, providing you do not exceed the word limit or write too little.

Depending on your prescribed title, there are numerous ways to structure an essay. As long as your ideas are well organised and present a coherent argument, no one way is better than another.

Possible structures include:

- *By area of knowledge*: in which you answer your question in relation to one area of knowledge and then another. You might then go on to extend your analysis and make further comparisons. This structure can produce an excellent essay if it includes a good level of analysis.

- *By concept*: in which you explore the key concept in relation to two areas of knowledge, and then apply the deeper understanding of the concept to the knowledge question in the context of two areas of knowledge.

- *By thesis, antithesis and synthesis*: this structure looks at one possible answer (thesis), then a second contrasting answer (antithesis) and then raises a third possibility (synthesis) which establishes your own new thesis.

TASK: ACTIVITY 16.6

For homework, a class has been asked to plan an essay based on an essay title, *'To what extent is evidence required as justification for knowledge?'*.

Having discussed the title in class, the students come up with a plan. Ameena is planning to write her essay with plenty of descriptive examples to illustrate how we use evidence. She wants to gather many examples from different areas of knowledge. Sakura is taking a theoretical approach with lots of philosophical references to key thinkers with different views about the role of evidence. Paulo is planning an analytical essay looking at different positions he could take on the question, exploring the various 'sides' to the question and making use of personal examples from his IB Diploma Programme subjects.

Compare the different approaches to the question. What advice would you give to each student about their plan?

TASK: ACTIVITY 16.7

Select an essay title from this book. Experiment with different structures and make a draft plan. Share your plan with a partner and give each other feedback.

TOP TIP

Avoid the extremes of blind scepticism and blind acceptance of knowledge claims, which lead to naïve, uncritical essays. Your essay needs to tackle the complex and challenging grey areas in between.

Paragraphs

Plan your paragraphs so that each paragraph develops a single point or counterpoint. It is helpful to begin each paragraph with a topic sentence that indicates the theme of the paragraph, such as: *Religious knowledge may be a way of establishing and preserving culture.* When your argument moves on, you can make this clear with transition statements such as: *'On the other hand, …'*, or *'Having considered …'*.

TASK: ACTIVITY 16.8

1   Look at some exemplar essays and compare the different approaches.

2   Using an exemplar essay, identify the topic/theme of each paragraph, and look at the flow of the paragraphs. How do the paragraphs effectively move the argument on? Look at the use of topic sentences and transitions.

Figure 16.1: Support the analytical points you make by using real-life examples. In 2018 the artist Banksy produced a piece of art 'Love is in the Bin' which self-shredded soon after it was sold.

Developing analysis

There are a number of ways you can develop the level of analysis in your essay.

Using examples

Examples are an excellent way to illustrate your points and counterpoints, and to help explain concepts. The effective use of examples will develop your analysis, help to clarify your ideas and support your argument, so choose them carefully.

You can select examples from the bank of personal experiences that was suggested in the introduction to this book, or from class notes or media sources. Avoid using examples that are generalised or vague; specific examples will better support your analysis. Personal examples are preferable to examples taken from textbooks because they will be original.

Identifying assumptions

Another way to develop your analysis is to identify assumptions. Considering different perspectives is one way to help you identify them. For example, if you are assessing how much evidence is needed to justify belief, you might argue that the body of scientific evidence supports belief in climate change. You might then consider the perspective of a conspiracy theorist who argues that scientific evidence for climate change is fabricated or distorted for political and financial reasons. These two claims illustrate two different assumptions: the first, that science is rigorous, trustworthy and independent; the second, that some governments or organisations are so powerful and corrupt that they can cause scientists around the globe to fabricate a climate panic. You can then evaluate the different assumptions and decide which is more reasonable.

Assumptions can also be found in knowledge questions. For example, in the knowledge question: *How can we know when we have sufficient evidence to justify a belief?*; there is an implicit assumption that at least some evidence is necessary. This is based on a deeper assumption that humans are largely rational beings.

TASK: ACTIVITY 16.9

Try to identify implicit assumptions in the following knowledge questions:

1   How difficult is it to establish universal truths in different areas of knowledge?

2   What makes progress seem easier to identify in the natural sciences than in the arts?

Considering implications

In some prescribed titles, considering the implications of points and counterpoints can be a useful way of developing your analysis. In most titles, it is often worth considering the implications of your conclusion. For example, if you were to conclude that a knowledge of the arts is at least as important as a knowledge of mathematics, what might be the implications for education?

You could develop the implications by considering how they might apply to other areas of knowledge. For example, '*If our scientific knowledge is incomplete, to what extent is this also the case in other areas of knowledge?*'.

Sometimes, you might look at what is not implied. For example, '*If the arts are open to interpretation, it does not follow that any interpretation of art is acceptable*'. You might develop this further by considering whether there are limits to acceptable interpretations in other areas of knowledge.

> TASK: THINK ABOUT 16.2
>
> Consider the implications of the following:
>
> 1   If we accept that mathematics and science are the most certain areas of knowledge, does it follow that knowledge in the arts has less value?
>
> 2   If principles of right and wrong vary from person to person, does it follow that any behaviour is acceptable?

Bringing in different perspectives

Your analysis should include points from different perspectives, including your own.

For example, you might support the knowledge claim: *'The fact that there are prizes awarded for art suggest there are standards that can be used to judge whether some artworks are better than others'* with a perspective such as that of Hugh Moss, the author of *The Art of understanding Art* (2015), who claims the best art is that which affects you as an individual: it must catch your attention, draw you in and move you in some way.

You might then counter this with another perspective, such as that of art historian Bendor Grosvenor (1977–), who argues that we have collectively lost the ability to assess art for ourselves on its own merits. Instead, we follow such indicators as fashion, price and hype.

You could then bring in your own perspective, such as: *'Personally, although I accept that there are some standards by which to judge art, I believe the standards are arbitrary, and I do not believe there is any 'correct' way of judging art, so the notion of 'good art' is ultimately subjective'.*

> KEY POINT
>
> As well as using your own perspective to evaluate a knowledge claim or counter-claim, you can use examples from your personal experience to ensure that your *knower's voice* is clearly heard.

Writing the introduction and conclusion

Introduction

The introduction is where you set out the scope of your essay, give your interpretation of the question, define your terms and outline how you intend to approach the question. Depending on your preferred style, you may also wish to include your thesis statement.

Your first sentence needs to catch the reader's attention and demonstrate that you have thought long and hard about the question. Do not use dictionary definitions because they cannot communicate the richness of TOK concepts; it is better to explain key concepts in your own words, saying how you intend to use the term in your essay. For example, *'For the purposes of this essay, I will take 'progress' to mean an improvement or a change for the better'*. Immediately, you can see that this raises knowledge questions such as *'better for whom?'*.

Avoid wasting words with sentences like, *'Because this title raises such complex issues, we can only answer this question after careful consideration of the alternative perspectives'*. This says nothing about the question, and adds nothing to your analysis. Instead, say something interesting about the issues or the perspectives you will be considering.

It is often best to leave writing your introduction until last, or to start by writing a rough introduction which you later go back and refine. This is because your essay may have taken some unexpected turns since you wrote your plan: perhaps you decided to use history rather than mathematics as one of your *areas of knowledge*, or perhaps you planned to respond with one thesis, but after evaluating the evidence, you decided on a different thesis.

TASK: ACTIVITY 16.10

Write two possible introductions for one of the essays you planned earlier. Discuss them with a partner. Can you agree which is the most effective? Are there elements in either introduction that would be better moved to the body of the essay, or removed altogether?

Conclusion

Your conclusion needs to summarise your argument and provide a clear answer to the question in the form of your thesis. It is arguably the most important part of your essay because it leaves the examiner with a lasting impression.

Avoid weak endings that sum up with something like, *'Having looked at all the difficulties with answering the question, we have to accept that scientists and historians need to agree to disagree'*. Rather, say something along the lines of, *'Having examined [points 1, 2 and 3], and considered [counterpoints 1 and 2], we can see that…..'*.

After summarising your argument, end with an evaluation of your thesis, consider the implications and possibly raise further knowledge questions that lie outside the scope of your essay.

KEY POINT

Remember that your conclusion is a *summary*; it is *not* the place for last minute thoughts. Your conclusion should *not* introduce any new arguments or examples. It must only refer to arguments and examples you have used in the body of your essay.

Once you have finished writing your essay, wait a few days and then read through it carefully to make sure that you have answered the question directly. Check that your conclusion is consistent with what you have argued in the essay.

TOP TIP

After you write your conclusion, it is good practice to go through your introduction again. Sometimes, you may find that your essay has introduced perspectives that were not anticipated initially. If you are happy with your sequence of arguments, but the introduction does not match what your essay actually does, you should alter your introduction accordingly.

Other considerations

As well as technical details, there are a number of things to keep in mind when you prepare your essay. For example, do not assume that the examiner will know what a *marae* is, or is familiar with Holy Communion. If you use an example that is only familiar to people with a similar cultural perspective to you, make sure that you explain it clearly.

Style

Avoid a writing style that is too casual, or copying an academic style which might be confusing. Adopt a style that feels comfortable and allows you to make your points clearly and succinctly.

Think carefully about your use of pronouns. It is appropriate to make use of first person singular (I) when giving your own perspective or drawing a conclusion. However, your essay should also include other perspectives when you might use third person singular or plural (he, she, they), or first-person plural (we) if you are speaking about something generally agreed. For example, *'We often think of mathematics as rigorous'*.

Avoiding plagiarism

It is absolutely necessary that your TOK essay is your own work, showing your ideas, skills and understanding. Always make a clear distinction between your own ideas and those of other people. You could do this by paraphrasing or using quotations.

When you paraphrase, you should acknowledge the author and express their ideas in your own words. For example, *'In "On Liberty", John Stuart Mill argues that the majority are not justified in silencing the minority'*.

When quoting, you should always put the exact words in quotation marks. For example: *'John Stuart Mill claimed, "No one can be a great thinker who does not recognise, that as a thinker it is his first duty to follow his intellect to whatever conclusions it may lead"'*

Whether you paraphrase or use quotations, it is essential that you acknowledge your sources.

The IB Diploma Programme does not specify one way of doing this, but your school may have a preference. A standard way is to use footnotes or endnotes; another way is to give the reference in parentheses, with relevant page numbers if appropriate.

In your bibliography, you must set out any sources you have cited in a consistent and conventional method. For example:

T. McLeish, *The Poetry and Music of Science: Comparing Creativity in Science and Art*, Oxford University Press, 2019

For web-based sources, you should include the URL address and the date of access.

> **TOP TIP**
>
> Always write down your sources, including page numbers, as you do your research. They may be hard to find again if you leave it until later.

16.6 Summary

Key features of the TOK essay

What the essay is	What the essay is not
an enquiry into a knowledge question	a research essay like the extended essay
knowledge-specific	subject-specific
about knowledge and knowing	about subject-specific information
an analysis of the connections and links between areas of knowledge	a description of areas of knowledge

Assessment

Who assesses the essay?	externally assessed by an IB Diploma Programme examiner
What is the word limit?	1,600 words
How is the essay marked?	holistic/global impression marking
How much it is worth?	65% of the total marks for TOK
What is the maximum score?	10 marks
How many essay titles are there to choose from?	Answer one from a choice of six prescribed titles.
How is the essay submitted?	It is uploaded electronically.

16.7 Planning and writing a TOK essay – checklist

The following checklist sets out some of the ingredients that make up a good TOK essay. Aim to include these features in your essay.

Analysing knowledge questions

Understand command words and key concepts in the title.

Make analytical rather than descriptive points.

Unpack your knowledge question.

- Identify key terms.

Planning and writing your essay

Develop a thesis and construct an argument.

- Construct a clear thesis.

- Plan a coherent argument.

Structure your essay.

- Develop a clear sequence of ideas.

- Make a paragraph plan, approximately 12 paragraphs.

- Use paragraphs to take your argument forward.

Develop your analysis.

- Use specific concrete examples based on real-life situations.

- Provide, evaluate and weigh up evidence.

- Make connections using the knowledge framework.

- Identify the similarities and differences between areas of knowledge.

- Consider different perspectives and identify assumptions.

- Consider implications.

Write the introduction and conclusion.

- Define your terms, but avoid dictionary definitions.

- Ensure that your conclusion summarises and evaluates your arguments.

Other considerations.

- Use an appropriate writing style and clear language.

- Use pronouns carefully.

Avoid plagiarism.

- Make a clear distinction between your own ideas and other people's ideas.

- Cite your sources and include a bibliography.

TOP TIP

The final essay needs to be submitted double-spaced in 12-point font. The spaces between your lines enable the examiner to make comments and annotations. Use Times New Roman, Arial or another standard font.

Final checklist

Use these questions as a final checklist. This is a rough guide. Every essay title is unique, and there are many ways of answering a question. When planning your response to an essay title, you will be on the right track if you have considered some of these questions.

1   How is the knowledge question related to the knowledge framework and areas of knowledge?

2   In what ways have I used the knowledge framework to support my analysis of the question?

3   Have I explored different ways of looking at the question?

4   Have I weighed up knowledge claims, counter-claims and evidence?

5   Have I used suitable real-life examples to illustrate my points?

6   Have I identified other perspectives and assumptions?

7   Have I considered implications?

8   What is my thesis statement?

SKILLS SELF-ASSESSMENT CHECKLIST

Reflect on what you have learned in this chapter and indicate your confidence level between 1 and 5 (where 5 is the highest score and 1 is the lowest). If you score below 3, revisit that section. Come back to this list later in your course. Has your confidence grown?

	Confidence level	Revisited?
Do I understand what is required when I write a TOK essay?		
Am I aware of how my TOK essay will be assessed and marked?		
Do I know how to plan my essay?		
Do I know how to develop a thesis and construct an argument to support it?		
Am I aware of the different elements of analysis, such as identifying and evaluating specific examples, identifying assumptions, evaluating points and counterpoints and thinking through implications?		
Do I know what is expected of an introduction and conclusion?		
Have I made a clear distinction between my own ideas and those of others? Have I cited all my sources in a bibliography?		

> Acknowledgements

The authors would like to thank: Alison Evans, Micaela Inderst, Hollie Graham, and Jayne Sly at Cambridge University Press for their organisation, advice and support. They would also like to thank Margaret Haynes, Michelle Daley, Sara Dev-Sherman, and Caroline Mowatt for their tireless work on the text. Wendy would particularly like to thank Susan Jesudason for being a wonderful co-author; Carl, William and Rosie Heydorn and Judy and Geoff Worham and David and Mary Heydorn for their support and patience; Beryl Maggs and Martin Otero Knott for intellectual inspiration; Katy Ricks and Tim Jones for their encouragement. Susan would particularly like to thank Wendy Heydorn for her enthusiasm and easy collaboration; Beryl Potter for her support and understanding, especially when time was short; John Puddefoot for his continual support as well as his invaluable insights, suggestions and corrections; and last, but not least, Zachary Puddefoot for ensuring a healthy work-life balance was maintained throughout the project and agreeing to model for some of the photographs.

The authors and publishers acknowledge the following sources of copyright material and are grateful for the permissions granted. While every effort has been made, it has not always been possible to identify the sources of all the material used, or to trace all copyright holders. If any omissions are brought to our notice, we will be happy to include the appropriate acknowledgements on reprinting.

Thanks to the following for permission to reproduce images:

Cover image: Jekaterina Nikitina/Getty Images

Chapter 1 Plume Creative/GI; Fig. 1.0 Susan Jesudason; Fig. 1.3 fstop123/GI; Chapter 2 Weeraya Siankulpatanakij/GI; Fig. 2.1 Anthony Redpath/GI; Fig. 2.2 Fotosearch/GI; Chapter 3 Isabel Pavia/GI; Fig 3.2 Samir Jana/GI; Fig. 3.3 Francisco Andrade/GI; Fig. 3.4 Pavel Dobrovsk/GI; Chapter 4 H.Armstrong Roberts/GI; Fig. 4.1 used by permission of Esther Honig; Chapter 5 MARK GARLICK/ SCIENCE PHOTO LIBRARY/GI; Fig. 5.1 Rafael Henrique/LightRocket/GI; Fig. 5.2 Vladimir Gerdo/ GI; Fig. 5.3 Horacio Villalobos/GI; Chapter 6 Jlrueda/GI; Fig. 6.1 Hitoshi Yamada/GI; Fig. 6.2 Tony Korody/GI; Fig. 6.3 Ricardo Rubio/GI; Chapter 7 Querbeet/GI; Fig. 7.1 Tracey Nearmy/GI; Fig 7.2 Ulrich Baumgarten/GI; Fig. 7.3 RichVintage/GI; Fig. 7.4 Annie Greevenbosch/GI; Chapter 8 Neha Gupta/GI; Fig. 8.2 Nitin Vyas/GI; Fig. 8.3 Peter Byrne/Shutterstock; Fig 8.4 Duncan1890/GI; Chapter 9 Jon Philpott Photography/GI; Fig 9.1 Nazar_ab/GI; Fig 9.2 Tibor Bognar/Alamy Stock Photo; Fig. 9.3 John White Photos/GI; Fig 9.4 Pixelfusion3d/GI; Chapter 10 Alex Halada/GI; Fig 10.1 Central Press/GI; Fid. 10.2 Frederic J.brown/GI; Fig 10.3 ESB Professional/Shutterstock; Chapter 11 Alberto Manuel Urosa Toledano/GI; Fig 11.1 Chesnot/GI; Fig 11.2 Zzvet/Shutterstock; Fig 11.3 CYC/Shutterstock; Fig 11.4 Andreas Nilsson/Shutterstock; Chapter 12 Oxygen/GI; Fig 12.1 Isabelle Rozenbaum/GI; Fig 12.2 Mark Wilson/GI; Fig 12.3 Art Collection 2/Alamy Stock Photo; Fig 12.4 Anantha Murthy HS/GI; Chapter 13 Roger Harris/Science Photo Library/GI; Fig 13.1 Picture Post/GI; Fig 13.2 Tony Stone Images/GI; Fig 13.3 Aleksei Verhovski/Shutterstock; Fig 13.4 Garry DeLong/GI; Chapter 14 Orbon Alija/GI; Fig 14.1 Paul Kane/GI; Fig 14.2 David M.Albrecht/Shutterstock; Fig 14.3 Pius Utomi Ekpei/GI; Fig 14.4 Michael Rosskothen/Shutterstock; Fig 14.5 Jonathan Nackstrand/GI; Chapter 15 Omar Marques/GI; Fig 15.1 Susan Jesudason; Chapter 16 PeopleImages/GI; Fig 16.1 Jack Taylor/GI.

Key: GI = Getty Images

› Index